THE MURAKAMI PILGRIMAGE

A GUIDE TO THE REAL-LIFE PLACES OF HARUKI MURAKAMI'S FICTION

Words, photography and design by Ken Lawrence.

Copyright © 2016 Sailingstone Press LLC

All rights reserved. No part of this publication may be re-produced, distributed, or transmitted in any form or by any means, including photocopying, recording, or other electronic or mechanical methods, without the prior written permission of the publisher, except in the case of brief quotations embodied in critical reviews and certain other noncommercial uses permitted by copyright law.

ISBN-13: 978-0-9984278-3-6
ISBN-10: 0-9984278-3-7

Published by Sailingstone Press LLC

690 S Hwy 89, Suite 200
Jackson, WY 83001
Contact: admin@sailingstonepress.com

www.murakamipilgrimage.com

Disclaimer:

The author has made every effort to ensure the accuracy of the information within this book at the time of publication. The author and publisher do not assume and hereby disclaim any liability to any party for any loss, damage, or disruption caused by errors or omissions, whether such errors or omissions result from accident, negligence, or any other cause. You are responsible for your own choices, actions, and results.

This guide book features many real-life locations mentioned in the fictional works of Haruki Murakami. This book is unofficial and is not authorized, licensed or endorsed by the original books' author or publishers. This guide book is meant only to supplement and not to be a substitute for reading any of the works of the original author. It is strongly recommended that you purchase and read the original works of fiction before using this guide book.

TABLE OF CONTENTS

- INTRODUCTION 4
- HOW TO USE THIS GUIDE 6
- JAPAN: GENERAL INFO 8
- TOKYO OVERVIEW 10

NOVEL GUIDES

- HEAR THE WIND SING • PINBALL, 1973 GUIDE 12
- A WILD SHEEP CHASE • DANCE, DANCE, DANCE GUIDE 26
- HARD-BOILED WONDERLAND AND THE END OF THE WORLD GUIDE 62
- NORWEGIAN WOOD GUIDE 74
- SOUTH OF THE BORDER, WEST OF THE SUN GUIDE 94
- THE WIND-UP BIRD CHRONICLE GUIDE 108
- SPUTNIK SWEETHEART GUIDE 126
- KAFKA ON THE SHORE GUIDE 138
- AFTER DARK GUIDE 164
- 1Q84 GUIDE 174
- COLORLESS TSUKURU TAZAKI AND HIS YEARS OF PILGRIMAGE GUIDE ... 192

- COMBINED ITINERARY 206

LOCATION REFERENCE GUIDE

- JAPAN LOCATIONS 208
- TOKYO LOCATIONS 215
- LOCATIONS AROUND THE WORLD 224
- NOTES AND REFERENCES 228

Introduction

I was lucky enough to read my first Haruki Murakami novels while I was living in Japan as a student. I was studying in a small town where English language books were incredibly hard to come by, and these were the days before ebooks. There were only several other native English speakers living in the same town and we'd often exchange whatever books we were finished reading. One day somebody handed me a copy of *A Wild Sheep Chase*. I had never heard of the author and didn't know what the book was about, but I didn't have much to do that day and started reading later that afternoon. And the next thing I knew, hours had passed. I was completely hooked.

A couple days later I'd finished the book and was hungry for something else like it, so I asked around if anyone had another Murakami novel. Luckily, I didn't have to wait too long before getting my hands on *Kafka on the Shore*. Again, I had no idea what the book would be about and I didn't care. This time, however, I was shocked and surprised to discover that the book takes place in Kagawa Prefecture - the very place that I was living.

Reading *Kafka on the Shore* for the first time in Kagawa was a special experience. The prefecture is no doubt a pretty obscure place for most people who pick up the novel, Japanese natives included. Us Kagawa residents, on the other hand, could easily picture the scenes from the book in detail, as these were our surroundings from everyday life. After finishing the book I remember how interesting it was to take walks around Kagawa's capital, Takamatsu, as I speculated where certain scenes from the novel might've taken place.

In a short period of time I would go on to read everything by Murakami that I could get my hands on. This included nearly all of his translated works up through *After Dark*. Probably due to a combination of burnout and being a little underwhelmed by that latest novel, it would be another six or seven years before I would pick up a Murakami book again.

A few years after its release, I finally got around to reading the massive *1Q84* shortly after moving back to Japan. As I started reading, I quickly remembered why I got so hooked on Murakami novels all those years before. And just like when I read *Kafka on the Shore*, I experienced another strange coincidence. In the novel, one of the main characters lives in the Tokyo neighborhood of Koenji. This just happened to be a short walking distance from my apartment.

Whenever I got the chance I'd go to a park or a coffee shop in Koenji to read. As I wandered the streets of the neighborhood and pictured the scenes from *1Q84* taking place in my surroundings, I thought about how other Haruki Murakami fans might desire a similar experience. That's when I first came up with the idea to create this guide book. After eventually finishing *1Q84* I proceeded to re-read every single Murakami novel and short story over again. And finally, armed with my camera and countless pages of notes, I embarked on the "Murakami Pilgrimage" that you'll find outlined in this book.

INTRODUCTION

My travels took me to sheep pens in isolated northern Hokkaido, retro jazz bars in downtown Kobe and obscure shrines off of backroads in rural Kagawa, a place I'd not returned to for many years. A large majority of Murakami's fiction, of course, takes place in Tokyo. But even though I was based there, tracking down each location wasn't always easy.

While there are plenty of real-life locations clearly named in the books, a number of other places are left vague or as complete mysteries. Finding these places required a fair amount of detective work. Sometimes I had to dig deep into what I could find on the author's life to discover clues. Still, in other cases, I could do nothing but visit the neighborhoods, walk around and see what I could find.

As I wandered the streets of what was often an incredibly humid Tokyo, drenched in sweat and with my shoulder sore from the weight of my notebooks and camera equipment, I felt especially close with the protagonists of Murakami's books. Much of the author's work revolves around the idea of some kind of search. The protagonists, though maybe reluctantly at times, often find themselves with no choice but to go on a hunt or a quest to find something. The object of the search might sometimes be clearly defined, whether it be a tangible object, a person or a piece of information. In other instances, the characters may not know exactly what they're looking for, yet feel compelled to continue searching anyway until they find it.

In Murakami's universe, ordinary things that people encounter in everyday life, such as stones, staircases or elevators, have the potential to open up portals to other worlds. Therefore, when exploring Japan from the perspective of Murakami's characters, one can't help but get the sense that something magical or mysterious could happen at any moment. Putting yourself into this mindset makes your search that much more interesting, whether it's your first time in the country or you've lived here for years.

Murakami's novels mean different things to different people. Accordingly, your search for and encounters with the real-life places of the novels will have a special significance that will be unique to you alone. Though not very physically demanding, your "Murakami Pilgrimage" could be likened to Japan's own Shikoku temple pilgrimage or the Camino de Santiago, which are considered to be just as much journeys of the mind as they are of the body. I've tried my best to help to make sure your physical journey goes as smoothly as possible. Whatever else it is that you're hoping to get out of this journey, well, that's going to be up to you.

Whether you'll be basing your entire travels around the contents of this book or will simply be browsing through it from time to time, I hope that this guide in some way helps enrich your Japan travel experience as well as deepens your appreciation for some of your favorite novels.
Happy searching!

HOW TO USE THIS GUIDE

BOOK STRUCTURE & SPOILERS

When I was first planning out how to structure this guide I contacted a number of friends and acquaintances that I knew were familiar with Murakami's work. When asking for feedback I noticed they all had one thing in common: none of them had read every single one of the novels. Therefore, I decided to structure this book in such a way that both people who've read everything and those who've only read a couple of the novels can get something out of it.

The main section of this guide book is divided into separate chapters dedicated to a particular novel. Each chapter contains spoilers for the novel it pertains to but you won't find spoilers for anything else. You'll find headings with the name of the novel clearly written at the top so you'll know if you're looking in the wrong place.

The chapters are ordered chronologically according to the release date of the novels. The one exception is *Dance, Dance, Dance* which was published in between *Norwegian Wood* and *South of the Border, West of the Sun*. Instead I've paired it with its prequel *A Wild Sheep Chase* due to them sharing the same narrator and a number of locations in common. Needless to say, that section of the guidebook contains spoilers for both books so please finish both before proceeding. The very first chapter of this guide book also combines the locations from Murakami's first two novels, so again it's recommended that you complete both of those books ahead of time.

Be aware that **everything beyond p205 contains spoilers for *all* novels and short stories!** If you have not read absolutely everything by Murakami then proceed at your own risk. A the end of the book you will find the **Combined Itinerary Ideas** section which is intended for those who've read all the Murakami books and who want to make the most efficient use of their time in Tokyo. And from p208 you'll find the **Location Reference Guide**. This section is a comprehensive list of just about every geographical location mentioned in every piece of Haruki Murakami fiction to date. As far as I know, this is the only such compilation of data of its kind. It includes everything from where major scenes happened to the most obscure locations simply mentioned in passing in a short story. Looking through the list, you may discover some very interesting connections or coincidences that you hadn't considered before. And if you're travelling around Japan to some off-the-beaten path locations, it can be fun to look up if the place you're in has ever appeared in Murakami's fiction.

ITINERARIES

In each of the main chapters you'll find at least one day trip itinerary and sometimes two. Though I'd originally planned to just provide a list of locations for each novel in alphabetical order, when it was time for me to visit and photograph each place, I quickly realized the importance of planning and logistics. Tokyo is an incredibly massive city, and even as a resident I needed to figure out the best routes in order to avoid needless backtracking or paying for more train tickets than necessary. And when travelling to far off locations like Hokkaido or Kagawa, I had to plan even more carefully to get the most out of my limited time there. I've shared the routes and transportation methods that I took so that you can find each location as easily as possible. But if you want to do things your own way then go ahead and mix up the order as you please.

The locations found throughout Murakami's fiction range from some of Japan's most famous sightseeing and nightlife districts to quiet, featureless residential areas. Going out of your way to see a particular car dealership by a highway or a random apartment complex in the suburbs may not be your ideal way to spend your precious vacation time. Therefore, I've also included recommendations that are not in the novels but that can easily be visited along with the sights that are. Going out of your way to see some of the more mundane locations from the novels won't seem so bad when there's a fascinating shrine or great hiking trails to check out nearby. To make it clear which locations are mentioned in a novel and which are purely my own recommendations, I've color-coded all the headings of the itinerary sections. At the beginning of each chapter you'll see the icon to your right. And you can always simply ignore my recommendations by just focusing on the places highlighted in blue.

HOW TO USE THIS GUIDE

QR CODES

Though people still love physical paper books, there's no denying the convenience of modern cell phones and tablets, especially when it comes to navigating a new city. Therefore, I've decided to optimize the best of both worlds by including QR codes for each location mentioned in this guide. Open your smartphone's QR code reader app (which can easily be downloaded if you don't already have one) and aim the camera at the block of code. You will then be shown a link that, when opened, will automatically bring up the destination on your phone's map application.

With that said, I highly recommend having a pocket wifi unit with you during your travels throughout Japan. You can find wifi rental shops throughout Tokyo and if you're staying at a vacation rental apartment, free pocket wifi is pretty much a standard amenity these days.

- 1-1 Kasumigaokamachi, Shinjuku
- ¥500
- 9:00 - 17:00
- Every day

Most destinations throughout this guide book will feature an address and when applicable, other information such as admission fee, operating hours and schedule. Instead of inputting the address into your phone manually, simply scan the QR code.

MAPS

Throughout the book you will also find static maps in each chapter. These mainly appear at the end but in some cases you'll also find them in the middle. The maps will come in handy if you don't have an internet connection. And even if you do, they'll allow you to get a sense of where you are relative to the other itinerary destinations or major landmarks.

OTHER THINGS TO NOTE

Wards and Cities: Tokyo is made up of 23 main wards which in Japanese are suffixed with *-ku*, such as Shibuya-ku or Shinjuku-ku. Tokyo's western suburbs (a.k.a. the Tama district) on the other hand, are suffixed with *-shi*, which simply means "city." For some reason all the English language signs throughout Tokyo refer to wards as cities. For example, Shibuya City or Meguro City. This is confusing and not an accurate translation. Just as you will find in most Murakami novels, I will be referring to wards as wards and I will also be using the terms 'ward' and '*ku*' interchangeably throughout this guide.

Spelling: Japanese is a fairly easy language to spell out in the Roman alphabet because there aren't too many sounds that can't be produced in English. But one sound that causes some confusion is ん, which can only come at the end of a syllable. It's generally pronounced like an 'n' but before a 'b' sound it may sound more like an 'm.' This results in slightly varied English spellings of Japanese location names, such as Jimbocho/Jinbocho or Namba/Nanba. Throughout this guide book I will be using the letter 'n' to spell out this sound, even if it's written differently in some of the novels.

JAPAN
TRAVEL TIPS & GENERAL INFO

WHEN TO GO

Japan, as locals love to point out, is a country with four seasons. While the country is chilly for much of the year, the winters rarely ever get as cold as places like New York or London and heavy snowfall in the large cities is rare. However, the lack of insulation in most buildings means that being indoors often feels just as cold as being outside. You would also need to pack heavy warm clothes which is not ideal for a country with living spaces so much smaller than what you're probably used to.

The ideal times to visit Japan are spring and autumn. Japanese summers are notorious for being incredibly hot and humid, and the rainy season throughout June and July can really put a damper on your travel itinerary. The most popular time to visit Japan would be springtime when the cherry blossoms are in full bloom. Everyone else, though, will have the same idea and things will be especially expensive and crowded. Visiting in May, shortly after the flowers have fallen off the trees, is an excellent choice. You'll get to enjoy the pleasant weather without all the crowds and you'll also just miss the rainy season in June. September and October are also some of Japan's best months weather-wise.

LANGUAGE

Despite Japan having adopted so many things from Western (and especially American) culture like baseball, fast food and rockabilly haircuts, the country very much remains monolingual and monocultural. Though the foreign language ability of the average Japanese likely won't improve anytime soon, the tourism industry has been booming in recent years. More and more businesses are starting to take advantage of this which means there are more English language services available now than ever before.

Nowadays there are plenty of web sites in English which allow you to book accommodation, train tickets, restaurants or day tours. Restaurants in central Tokyo are also making more of an effort to create English translations of their menus. And with the ease of renting a pocket wifi in Japan, you can simply use a GPS app instead of asking a stranger who may not understand you.

Regardless, it would still be wise to learn some basic greetings or how to order food in a restaurant before you arrive. I'd recommend carrying around a phrasebook with you or downloading some Japanese language apps to your phone or tablet.

JAPAN: TRAVEL TIPS & GENERAL INFO

GETTING AROUND

Every location mentioned in this book is accessible via public transportation, although certain locations require a significant amount of walking to access. You may decide to rent a car during your trip which would be helpful for Shikoku and especially Hokkaido. While you won't find any driving directions in this guide book, most Japanese rental cars have built-in GPS systems.

About the JR Rail Pass: Many visitors decide to get a JR Rail Pass before arrival. This could potentially save you money if you're going to be riding the Shinkansen (bullet train) a lot. There are also many JR trains that run within the cities that you can ride for free with your pass. Many visitors are surprised, however, by just how many different train companies exist in Japan. In most urban areas there are a lot of other rail companies which have nothing to do with JR. That means you will not be able to use your rail pass in many situations. Each itinerary in this book provides the names of the stations and train lines so you'll know in advance whether or not you'll be able to use your pass.

Recommended route around Japan: Apart from Tokyo, this guide book provides itineraries for Hokkaido, Nagoya, Hyogo and Kagawa. If you'd like to visit all these places on your trip, the best way to do so would be:
Start your trip in Tokyo and then fly round-trip to Hokkaido. Back in Tokyo, take either a bus or train to Nagoya and then head to Kobe or stay in a nearby city such as Osaka or Kyoto. From Kobe you can take a cheap ferry to Takamatsu, the capital of Kagawa. Then head back to Tokyo or to Osaka's KIX airport for the return flight back home.

SAFETY & FRIENDLINESS

Pick up an ordinary book on Japan and you'll likely read the typical statements about what a polite, considerate and harmonious society it is. As a long-term resident of Japan, I'd say that this is true...some of the time. The reality is that Japan is a culture of many faces and in day-to-day interactions with Japanese, context is everything. The good news is that if you're visiting Japan as a short-term tourist, this fact will be obvious and the face most people will present to you is that of the polite and hospitable host. The Japanese care deeply about how the outside world perceives their country and will often try their best to make sure that tourists go home with a positive impression.

On the other hand, it's also likely that others won't be too happy about foreign-looking faces showing up in their neighborhood. But they'll usually just mutter something under their breath which you likely won't be able to understand anyway. So while Japan is not really as open to foreign visitors as the tourism industry would like for you to believe, this 'other face' often goes undetected by visitors due to its subtle nature. Most importantly, violent confrontation in Japan is so rare that you pretty much never need to fear for your physical safety. As a tourist, the worst you'll likely experience is being told "We're full" or "Sorry, members only" when you attempt to enter a restaurant or bar that clearly has vacant tables.

Japan has virtually no 'bad neighborhoods' so when booking accommodation you only really need to worry about convenience. All areas, for the most part, are equally safe. Even the seedy-looking red light districts are pretty safe to walk around in late at night. Theft is also incredibly rare and most people don't think twice about leaving their valuables at their table when getting up to use the restroom. You may want to be careful setting down your bag or purse inside of nightclubs, however, as these seem to be exceptions to the rule.

MAIN AREAS FEATURED IN THIS GUIDE

TOKYO OVERVIEW

> ⓘ **TOKYO**
>
> **Population**: *14 million*
>
> **Region**: *Kanto*
>
> **Area**: *2,188 km²*

Tokyo, Japan's capital and largest city, makes an appearance in every single Haruki Murakami novel. Tokyo is so massive, however, that it's easier to think of it as a collection of cities contained within one single district. Throughout this guide book you'll learn about neighborhoods such as Koenji, Akasaka, Ueno, Shibuya, Aoyama and more. Each areas has its own unique atmosphere and storied history. After following the itineraries in this book you'll get a very good overall feel for the city. How long you spend in Tokyo is up to you, but at least one week is recommended.

WHERE TO STAY

When travelling to such a big city, choosing where to stay can be overwhelming. You may have heard of neighborhoods such as Shinjuku, Shibuya, Harajuku and Roppongi. These are all centrally located and would all be ideal for getting to the main sites featured in Murakami's fiction. The most convenient station in all of Tokyo would have to be **Shinjuku**. Shinjuku Station is an attraction in itself and it directly connects to pretty much every other neighborhood mentioned in this guide book, with only a few exceptions. The JR Yamanote Line, the JR Chuo/Sobu line, the Odakyu line and a multitude of subway lines run through Shinjuku Station, meaning you can get just about anywhere with no transfer. Understand, however, that while Shinjuku has many hotels and vacation rental apartments, it's hard to find something very close to the main station. You should always check which station is actually closest to your accommodation before confirming your booking.

    Shibuya is also a convenient place to stay. The neighborhood itself appears frequently throughout Murakami's work and it's connected to the JR Yamanote Line and a number of subway lines. Another very convenient, yet often overlooked station to stay nearby would be **Yoyogi**. Yoyogi Station gives you access to the JR Yamanote Line, JR Sobu Line and the Oedo Line, which connects directly to Roppongi and Aoyama-Itchome.

    These aren't the only convenient places to stay and regardless of where you base yourself, you'll still be doing a lot of travelling around the city. Most of the locations in this guide book are in central Tokyo's western half. Some eastern neighborhoods do appear a couple of times, however. Basing yourself somewhere along the **western half of the JR Yamanote Line** or anywhere relatively central on the **JR Chuo/Sobu Line** would be ideal. As far as subway lines go, the **Marunouchi Line** is probably the one that comes up the most often in this book. The line runs through places like Shinjuku, Yotsuya, Ginza and Ochanomizu.

GETTING AROUND

As mentioned on p9, Tokyo and Japan's other major cities have many different **train** lines. There will often be times where you need to not only switch trains but switch rail companies altogether. This is entirely normal for Tokyo residents but visitors from other cities which have their metro systems all run by a single company are often surprised. While the multitude of train companies means that transportation around Tokyo is incredibly efficient and convenient, it also comes with a price. When switching train companies in the midst of the route you will have to pay for two tickets. And unfortunately, there are no universal train passes to help you save money. The JR rail pass will allow you to ride the JR trains for free but it won't be of any use when you need to use the subway or the Odakyu Line, for example.

When travelling around Tokyo I recommend buying an IC card such as **Suica** or **Pasmo**. Understand, however, that these will not save you any money - only time. You can charge your card with cash and then when switching train lines you simply place your card on the ticket gate's IC reader instead of having to buy an individual tickets. Also, even if you buy a Suica card at a JR station, it will still work at stations and on train lines run by other companies. You should even be able to use it in a number of other Japanese cities and they'll also work on local buses.

Taxis are absolutely everywhere in the city and with the exception of during a typhoon, you'll rarely have a hard time catching one. Japanese taxis, though, are some of the most expensive in the world and the rides often start at over ¥700. Therefore, I'd recommend keeping taxi use to a minimum. They are really only useful if you miss your last train of the night or absolutely hate walking.

Ridesharing services such as Uber or Lyft have been slow to take off in Japan. But the vacation rental apartment industry was the same way until it practically exploded overnight. With that in mind, it's likely only a matter of time until ridesharing services suddenly become huge.

Tokyo has a comprehensive **bus** system but the destination names displayed on the timetables and on the buses themselves are often only written in kanji. And a bus ride can typically take twice as long as the same train ride. Therefore, I will not be mentioning bus routes in this guide. If you happen to be near a convenient bus stop, though, you might as well hop on.

HOTELS VS. RENTAL APARTMENTS

The vacation rental apartment business has been booming in Japan lately, to the delight of repeat visitors who are tired of the standard Japanese 'business hotel' experience. Japanese 'business hotels' (used as often by travellers as businessmen) are basically mid-range budget hotels with tiny beds, tiny bathrooms and virtually no place to store your luggage. As an added bonus, you're often greeted with the fragrance of the previous guest's stale cigarette smoke. Furthermore, the staff at these hotels often speak zero to minimal English and if you're traveling with another person, the price of the room will often double even if you share the bed. Thankfully, the vacation rental apartment option solves most of these issues and you often get twice the amount of space of a typical Japanese hotel room for half the price.

With sites like Airbnb and HomeAway, you can be sure in advance that you'll have a fluent or native English speaker to communicate with. Every apartment and every host is different, however. In some cases you may be staying in a vacant room in someone's house while other times you'll have the entire apartment to yourself. In the case of the latter, you may not even need to meet the host in person at all, as it's common to just find the key in the lobby mailbox.

The vacation rental apartment system is still far from perfect, though. As the business mostly exists in a gray zone, it's not unheard of for your host to suddenly be forced out of his or her apartment before your arrival. Fortunately, the booking web sites themselves often intervene to assist you in these situations. As a general rule, you should only book apartments that have a lot of positive reviews and if you have any questions, make sure that you ask your potential host before confirming the booking. Most listings have strict cancellations policies and require you to pay upfront. Also, watch out for deceptive titles such as "Shinjuku - 5 Minutes From Station!" The listing may very well be 5 minutes away from the station, but more likely an inconvenient station at the edge of Shinjuku Ward and not the main Shinjuku Station you were probably imagining.

Even with the system's faults, staying at a vacation rental apartment is often the best choice. If you still prefer the hotel experience, there are an abundance of Japanese hotels listed on sites like Booking.com or Agoda. Even if the staff don't speak English you can at least contact the site's customer service for support should any major issue arise.

Hear The Wind Sing and Pinball, 1973 are Haruki Murakami's very first two novels. The unnamed protagonist who narrates the story is the same in both books and is also the main character of the sequels - A Wild Sheep Chase and Dance, Dance, Dance. For years it was impossible to buy an official English translation of either book, but today they're widely available and even packaged together. This section of the guide book features the locations of the two novels combined, so please read them both before proceeding to avoid any spoilers.

Hear the Wind Sing largely takes place in Hyogo Prefecture, where the author himself grew up. Although the name of the town where the story takes place is left unnamed, it's likely a small town near the wealthy city of Ashiya, which is itself a suburb of the port city of Kobe. The town is described as having an "ocean in front . . . with mountains to the rear and a giant port next door."[1]

An unnamed tiny town by the ocean could be any number of actual towns in Hyogo Prefecture. But there are at least a couple of places mentioned in the novel that we can find in real life. When the narrator first meets the Rat, they were drunk at 4 in the morning, driving around intoxicated when their car crashed into a stone pillar in a park with a monkey cage. The name of this park is "Ashiya-Uchide Park" and the monkey cage still remains - albeit without any monkeys. Just behind the park is the Uchide branch of the Ashiya Public Library. While only mentioned briefly in the novel, this is the library where the author himself spent a lot of time as a teenager. Considering the prevalence of libraries in Murakami's later works such as Kafka on the Shore, Hard-Boiled Wonderland and The Strange Library, this particular building clearly had a major impact on the author's life and career.

The "J's Bar" featured prominently in both Hear The Wind Sing and Pinball, 1973 does not actually exist, but the next best thing can be found in the central Sannomiya district of Kobe. In 1981, a film adaptation of Hear The Wind Sing was released in Japan. The J's Bar scenes were filmed in a bar called Half Time which is just a couple minute walk from Sannomiya station. The bar even features a pinball machine just like in the novels! The atmosphere is close enough to make you feel as if you were really in Murakami's world.

Half of Pinball 1973 takes place in Tokyo, where the narrator works at a translation service after having graduated from college. Not too many specific locations are mentioned here, but the sequel, A Wild Sheep Chase, reveals that he lives in Mitaka City during the events of the book. The golf course the narrator often visits with the twins is now a public park, meaning anyone can now relax on the grass and play backgammon while watching the sunset from the 8th hole.

HYOGO
Population: *5.6 million*
Region: *Kansai*
Capital: *Kobe*

FEATURED IN NOVEL

RECOMMENDED

HYOGO DAY TRIP ITINERARY ● 兵庫県

Hyogo Prefecture is part of the Kansai Region and is located just next to Osaka. Its capital and largest city, Kobe, is a bustling, multicultural city that's home to over 1.5 million people.

Despite its close proximity to Osaka and Kyoto, Kobe maintains its own unique charm. The city has a beautiful skyline consisting of tall skyscrapers against a backdrop of green, misty mountains. One of only a few cities to be open to foreign trade during Japan's period of isolation, Kobe features a unique array of architecture, from Western-style brick buildings to the traditional Chinese style of Chinatown.

Hear The Wind Sing, *Pinball, 1973*, and part of *A Wild Sheep Chase* are Murakami's only novels to be set in Hyogo Prefecture, but the region comes up in other works such as *Norwegian Wood* and *After The Quake*. It's often the place where a character is *from* rather than a destination. However, there's plenty to enjoy in Hyogo Prefecture, making it well worth a visit for a couple of days.

This day trip itinerary requires a combination of train and foot, but a taxi can also be used to get from place to place in Kobe. By the end of the day we'll have checked out some significant locations from Murakami's early novels as well as some of the prefecture's most interesting sightseeing spots. Let's begin in the very town where the author himself grew up: Ashiya.

ACCOMMODATION: For those staying in Kobe, basing yourself near Sannomiya or Kobe station would be ideal, but the outskirts are also fine considering the region's efficient transportation system. Kobe is also easily accessible by train from Osaka, especially from the city's Umeda district. When staying in Kansai, vacation rental apartments will give you the best value for money by far.

1 ASHIYA PUBLIC LIBRARY ● 芦屋市立図書

Looking at a map, you'll see that the library and the park with the monkey cage are closest to a station called Uchide, but that station is difficult and time consuming to access. The larger **Ashiya Station** is much easier to get to and the walk to the library isn't so far.

Bear in mind that there is more than one Ashiya Station - one for the Hanshin Line and another for the JR. Both are about a 10 to 15 minute walk from the library. However, getting off at the Hanshin station allows you to enjoy a great view of Ashiya's famous cascading river as you head toward your destination.

For those staying in Kobe, take the **Hanshin Line** from Kobe-Sannomiya over to Ashiya. If you're coming from Osaka, board a Hanshin train from either Osaka-Namba or Umeda stations. The journey from Umeda only takes 19 minutes. After exiting the station, take in the scenery as you walk north along the river. Eventually you'll get to a large east-west road where you want to make a right, heading east. Then keep walking straight for about 10 minutes. Shortly after you see a Royal Host family restaurant on the right and then a Gusto on the opposite side, you'll want to make a right, heading south. After a minute or so you should come across the library. If you have any doubts, scan the QR Code below or check the static map on p20.

> "It never changed: a river and a tennis court, a golf course . . . a handful of tidy restaurants and boutiques, an old library . . . a park with a monkey cage."[2]

◉ 15-9 Uchide-kozuchicho, Ashiya, Hyogo

② UCHIDE PARK ● 打出公園

Just around the corner from the library is the park with the monkey cage, otherwise known as Uchide Park. Despite no monkey living inside any more, the cage has been preserved all of these years. Other than that this is just a typical park, but it's still fun to picture the scene with the Rat's Fiat 600 as you walk around.

Now it's time to head over to Kobe. Instead of the Hanshin Line let's take the **JR** instead. Head back over to the main road and start walking back west. Walk on the right side of the street (the same side as the Gusto). Just after passing a small river take a right. There's a beautiful temple called Shouzen-ji which you should be able to spot on the way. Keep heading northwest until you eventually get to the **JR Station**.

③ MERIKEN PARK ● メリケンパーク

Take the JR train from Ashiya straight to **Kobe Station**. One ticket costs ¥220. From Kobe Station you can walk over to Meriken Park in about 15 minutes and on the way you'll pass **Harborland**, a shopping and entertainment area that's home to the Anpanman Museum. This might be worth a stop if you're travelling with young children.

Keep heading in the direction of the **Kobe Port Tower**, easily spottable from a distance. It costs ¥700 to ascend Japan. You can which is a good deal compared to other towers in a rotating coffee enjoy the view from multiple levels and there's even tower, there shop on one of the floors. Coming down from the Meriken Park are a number of art sculptures scattered throughout along with the **Kobe Maritime Museum**.

- 5-5 Hatobacho, Chuo-ku, Kobe
- ¥700
- 9:00 - 21:00
- Every day

4 CHINATOWN • 南京町

From Meriken Park it's only about an 8 minute walk north to Chinatown. This is one of only 3 prominent Chinatowns in Japan, the others being in Yokohama and Nagasaki. The Kobe Chinatown has been around since the 1800's when Kobe was one of the only ports to be allowed open for Chinese trade during Japan's period of isolation. Enjoy some street food or sit down in one of the district's many restaurants, whether you're craving Chinese food or Kobe beef. Next to Chinatown is a long shopping arcade with an abundance of great coffee shops. If you look closely you can find a little record store on one of the side streets, quite similar to the one where the "girl with the missing finger" works in *Hear The Wind Sing*.

A small record shop

THE GREAT HANSHIN EARTHQUAKE

In January of 1995, the city of Kobe was struck by a magnitude 6.9 earthquake which resulted in over 5,000 deaths. Hundreds of thousands of buildings were damaged and so were many highways. Incredibly, the city was able to recover within a couple of years and very little evidence that such a disaster took place can be found in the city today. One section of Meriken Park, however, has been preserved as a reminder of what happened. Murakami's short story collection "After The Quake" touches on the emotional toll which the incident took on people throughout the country.[3]

5 HALF TIME (J's BAR) ● ハーフタイム

Now let's head to Half Time, the closest thing in real life to J's Bar from the novels. From Chinatown, head east for ten to fifteen minutes until you reach the **Sannomiya** district, which you'll recognize from the large crowds and neon flashing lights. The bar opens at 7pm, but there are plenty of shopping options nearby if you have some time to kill. You can also easily walk to the famous **Ikuta Shrine**.

Once at the bar, it's easy to pretend like you're in Murakami's world as you soak up the intimate and retro feel. If you're into classic jazz, there's also plenty to discuss with the owner. The bar has its own pinball machine although it's not always in working order.

If you need to get back to Osaka, take either the JR line to Osaka Station from Sannomiya or the Hankyu line to Umeda from Kobe-Sannomiya station, both of which are nearby the bar.

📍 5-4-11 Kotonoocho, Chuo-ku, Kobe
🕐 19:00 - 24:00
📅 Closed Sun. and Holidays

🍴 KOBE BEEF

For meat lovers around the world, the name 'Kobe' is synonymous with high quality beef. But what makes Kobe beef so special? The meat is especially tender and is fattier than other types of beef. Furthermore, the inspection process is especially stringent, with only the highest quality cuts making their way onto the market. One of the reasons Kobe beef tastes so good is because the cows are treated especially well during their lifetimes, although certain claims that they're served beer and given regular massages may be nothing more than hearsay.

There are a lot of places around Kobe to try this local delicacy but it won't come cheap. You'll see many Kobe beef restaurants around the Chinatown area and there are also plenty of options in the Sannomiya district. Understand that many restaurants require reservations in advance.

AROUND TOWN

If you have some extra time before your visit to Half Time, you may want to take a train from Sannomiya to either Nada (JR) or Iwaya (Hanshin) stations where you can access both the **Kobe Earthquake Memorial Museum** and the **Hyogo Prefectural Museum of Art**. Both usually close at around 18:00, but it's best to check the schedule in advance before you go.

Another popular tourism destination in Kobe is **Mount Rokko**. At the top of the mountain you can find a botanical garden, museums and even a golf course. Many simply go for the fantastic view. To get there you need to use a combination of train, bus and cable car. Take a Hankyu train to Rokko Station which arrives in just 7 minutes. Then take bus number 16 to get to the cable car up the mountain.

HYOGO MAPS

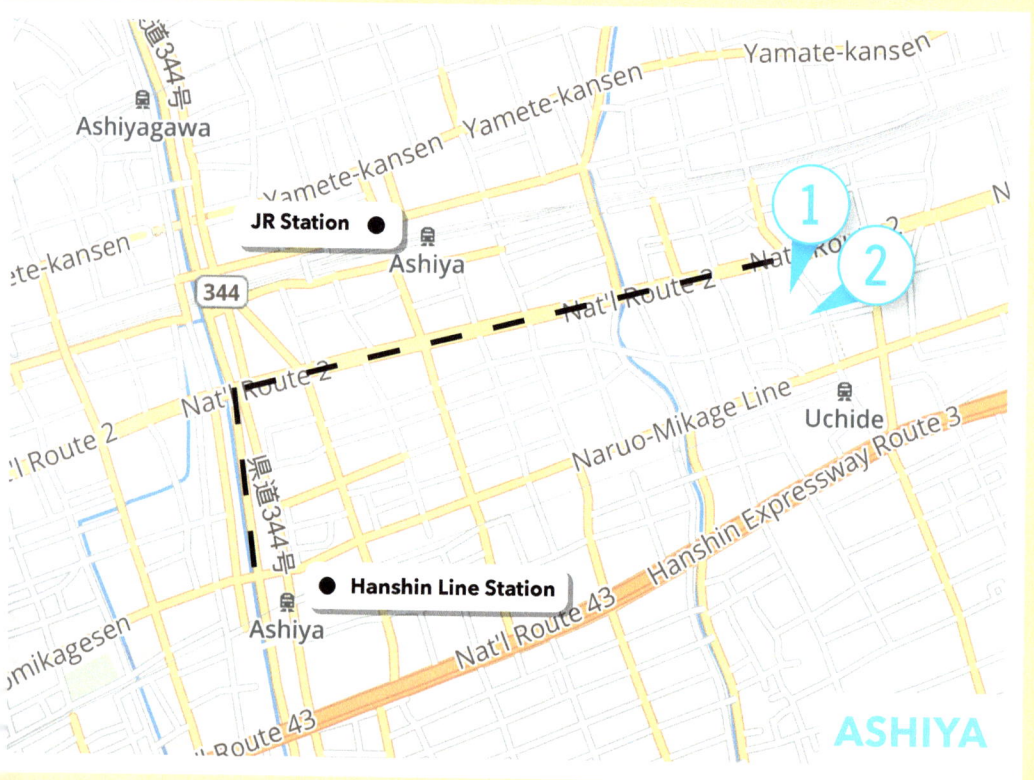

HEAR THE WIND SING ● PINBALL, 1973 GUIDE 21

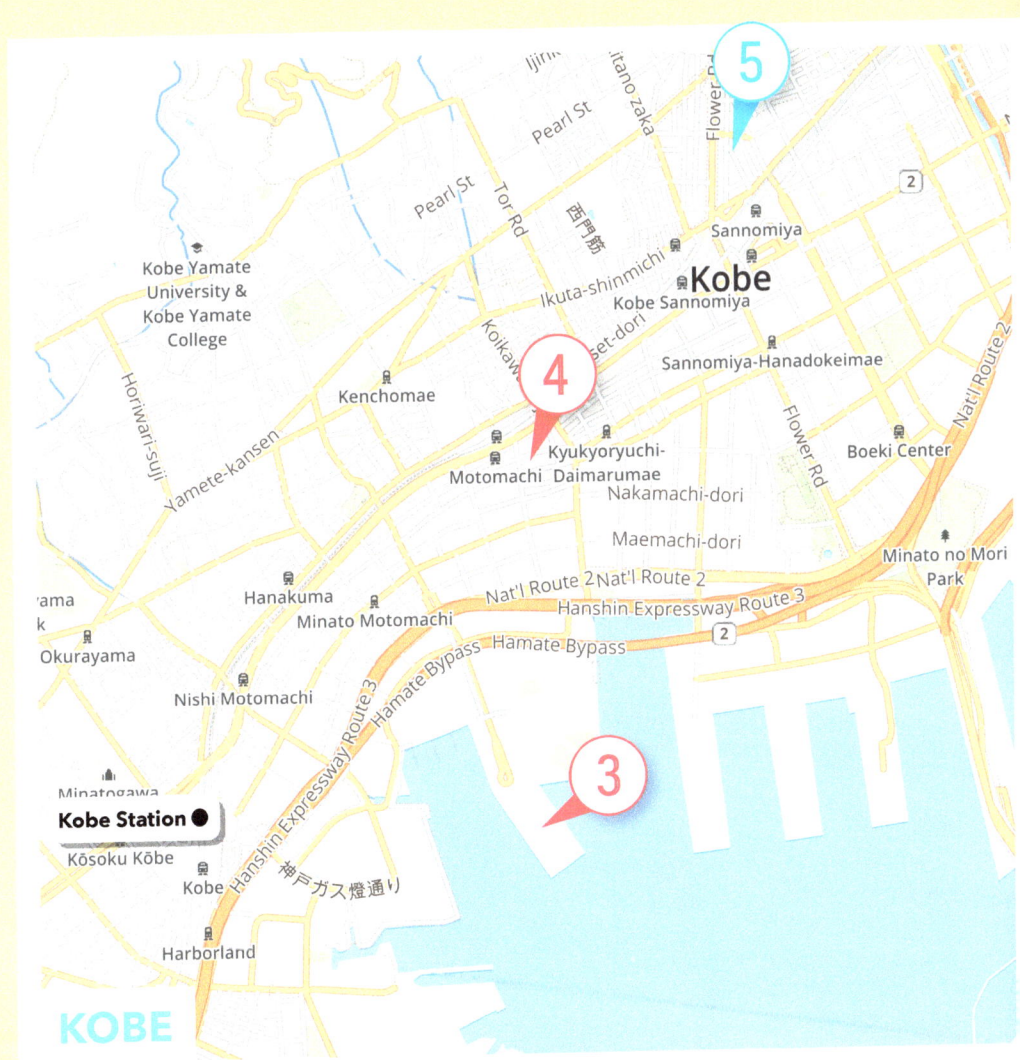

TOKYO LOCATIONS

In *Hear The Wind Sing*, no specific Tokyo locations are mentioned except for **Hibiya Park**, where the narrator talks about feeding pigeons with his wife in the epilogue at the very end of the book.
Hibiya Park, located in Chuo-ku, can be accessed by Hibiya or Kasumigaseki Stations and is definitely worth a stop if you're already in the area.

Hibiya Park

In contrast to its prequel, half of *Pinball, 1973* takes place in Tokyo. The narrator's office is in the Nanpeidai area of Shibuya and a few other locations are mentioned, but overall the descriptions of the city remain pretty vague. Without giving too much away for those who haven't read it, the sequel *A Wild Sheep Chase* finally reveals where our narrator lived with the twins during the events of *Pinball, 1973*. In the beginning of that book, the same narrator reminisces over his time spent living near the **International Christian University (ICU)** campus. This is enough information to figure out exactly where the **golf course** is that he visits many times with the twins.

Both the university and the (former) golf course are way out in the suburbs and if you're in central Tokyo, this excursion could take up much of your day. If you want to integrate this visit into a day tour of other locations in western Tokyo from various novels, have a look at p207 (contains spoilers).

📍 1-1-1 Higashi-cho, Koganei-shi

International Christian University Campus

HEAR THE WIND SING • PINBALL, 1973 GUIDE

The ICU and the old golf course are right next to each other and can be accessed from **Higashi-Koganei Station** on the JR Chuo Line. You can take a train directly from Shinjuku, heading west. From the station it's about a 20 minute walk south just to get to the entrance of the campus and then it also takes awhile to walk through it. You can cut off 10 minutes of walking time by transferring at Musashi-Sakai station (on the Chuo Line) to the Seibu-Tamagawa Line, then traveling one stop to **Shin-Koganei Station**.

At the campus, there's not a whole lot to do except walk around but at least the scenery is nice. From there you want to head to **Nogawa Park**. The was converted to a park from the old ICU golf course back in 1980. While technically a park, the area still very much resembles a golf course today. And since it's now open to the public, you won't have to sneak in by climbing over a chain link fence.

Accessing Nogawa Park is somewhat tricky because you can't simply walk straight through the campus to get there. Try heading west first until you get to the busy road and then head south from there. Eventually you'll come across the entrance on your left.

Once you make it, why not crack open a beer while enjoying the sunset from the eighth hole? (wherever that may have been)

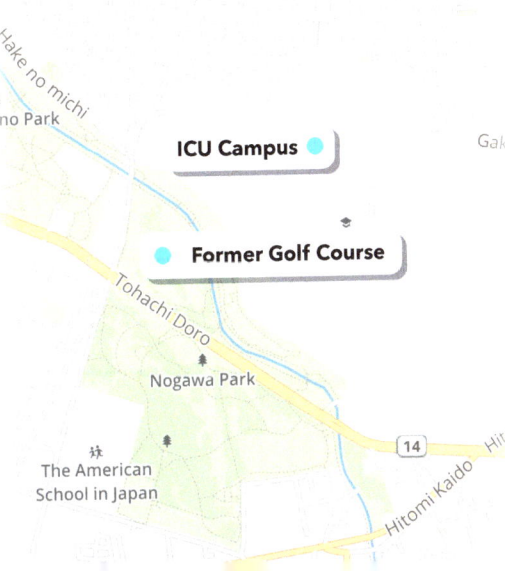

- 1-3-6-4, Osawa, Mitaka-shi
- FREE
- Every day

THE PINBALL WAREHOUSE

At the end of *Pinball, 1973*, the narrator finally gets the chance to play his beloved "Spaceship" pinball machine that he used to play at J's bar in Hyogo and later on at an arcade in Shinjuku. The machine belongs to a mysterious man who owns an entire warehouse full of rare and vintage pinball machines, many of which he finds at junkyards.

Before heading to the warehouse, the narrator meets the pinball-enthusiast Spanish lecturer somewhere in Shibuya-ku or Shinjuku-ku. From there their taxi heads north up **Meiji-dori** before turning onto **Waseda-dori**, heading west. They turn again onto **Mejiro Blvd.**, a street which would take them in a northwest direction. They drive for awhile and the narrator even has to ask if they're still in Tokyo.

It turns out that they still are.

There's no way to tell for sure but they likely end up in one of the northern neighborhoods bordering Saitama Prefecture such as Itabashi or Nerima Ward.

The present-day closest thing to a "small game center in Shinjuku"[4] where the narrator put "an endless stream of coins"[5] into the pinball machine would be a place called **Mikado**. This game center is located in Takadanobaba, which is technically part of Shinjuku Ward. There are only 3 or 4 machines, however, and none of them are as old as the Spaceship.

If you really want to relive the novel, the closest thing would be to play pinball at the machine at Half Time in Kobe, assuming it's in working order.

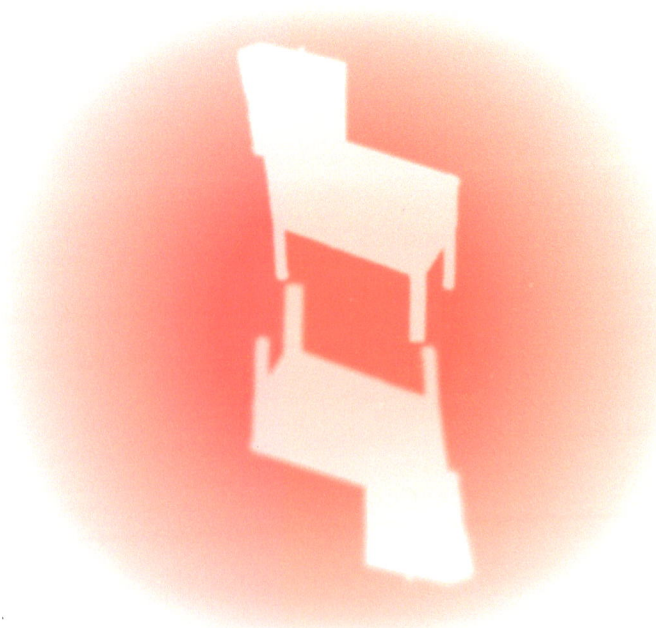

"Ever since I was a little boy, my father's told me about the white sheep that came to him in his dreams. So I always thought that's what life is like. An ongoing search."⁶

A WILD SHEEP CHASE

A *Wild Sheep Chase*, Haruki Murakami's third novel, takes us to Hokkaido, Japan's northernmost major island, through the eyes of the same protagonist from the first two books. This is the first novel where Murakami experiments with the surrealist and supernatural storytelling elements that he would become known for.

The main character and his girlfriend Kiki first arrive in Sapporo to start their hunt for the sheep with the star on its back. Very few landmarks, streets or station names are revealed in this section of the book. Even the location of the enigmatic Dolphin Hotel is left a mystery to the reader. It's possible, however, that its original inspiration is waiting to be discovered somewhere near Sapporo or Susukino Station.

The climax of *A Wild Sheep Chase* takes place in a fictional town called Junitaki-cho. It's highly likely that the basis for Junitaki is a town called Bifuka. There are a number of reasons why people believe this to be so: the name of Junitaki translates to "twelve waterfalls." Bifuka is also famous for waterfalls, but has 16 instead of 12. Junitaki is also described as being around 150 miles, or 240 kilometers from Sapporo. Bifuka is just about the same distance away. And of course, Bifuka is also home to many

羊をめぐる冒険

ダンス・ダンス・ダンス

sheep, somewhat of a rarity in Japan.

Bifuka will likely be the highlight of your trip to Hokkaido. True to the novel, though, it's not an easy place to get to. Making the journey to this isolated northern part of Hokkaido is only for the most dedicated of Haruki Murakami fans, but when you finally make it you won't be disappointed. In Bifuka you'll have the chance to stay at a place incredibly reminiscent of the house that the Sheep Professor built. Farm Inn Tonto, as it's called, has been attracting lots of media attention in recent years for its stark similarity to the setting of the novel.

In *Dance, Dance, Dance*, the same protagonist decides to make a return to the Dolphin Hotel, only to find that it's been completely rebuilt. Aside from his trips to Sapporo, most of the action takes place in Tokyo but also in Hawaii and Kanagawa Prefecture.

In Tokyo we can easily find the part of town where Yuki lives as well as the Akasaka Police Department where the narrator gets taken in for questioning. In the sequel he lives in Shibuya and he often visits neighboring districts like Harajuku and Aoyama. All of these locations will be covered in this section of the guide.

DANCE, DANCE, DANCE

HOKKAIDO ITINERARIES

ⓘ HOKKAIDO

Population: *5.5 million*

Area: *83,454 km²*

Capital: *Sapporo*

Most trips to Hokkaido will begin and end in Sapporo, the island's main transport hub. Not too many specific Sapporo locations are named in either novel so the locations relevant to the books can be visited within a day. To see the other attractions the city has to offer, though, an additional couple of days is recommended. Remember that you'll likely return to the city a second time before you leave Hokkaido, so you can always try to squeeze in the things you missed before departing the island.

Depending on your schedule and tolerance for long train rides, you may either decide to head straight for Bifuka (Junitaki-cho) from Sapporo or make a brief stop in Asahikawa. If you're travelling in summer, visiting the Biei/Furano area is recommended as well.

Hokkaido is the most difficult place in Japan to travel around without a car but it certainly can be done. All of the locations mentioned in this chapter can be reached by train or bus. As the towns in Hokkaido all seem to be a few hours apart, transport can be both time consuming and expensive compared to the Kanto region. Also be sure to take travel time into consideration when planning your trip.

☁ WEATHER

Hokkaido is the northernmost island of Japan and therefore can get extremely cold, with the average temperature in winter sinking below 0°C. Sapporo is host to a famous snow festival in February, but Bifuka and other locations may be difficult to access during the snowy season. Summers, on the other hand, are similar to the rest of Japan but without the humidity. While the novel itself takes place in autumn, coming during the warmer seasons is recommended.

📍 GETTING THERE

Both the quickest and cheapest way to reach Hokkaido is to fly. Budget flights from Tokyo to Sapporo's New Chitose Airport can go for under ¥10,000 one-way.

SAPPORO DAY TRIP ITINERARY ● 札幌

FEATURED IN NOVEL

RECOMMENDED

ACCOMMODATION

Sapporo has an abundance of both regular hotels and vacation rental apartments. Most of the cheaper hotels are in the Susukino/Nakajimakoen area, which is a very convenient place to stay. Staying nearby Sapporo Station or Odori Koen is also recommended. Overall, the city is not too big and you can easily get from one place to another by subway or on foot.

Sapporo is a charming modern city with plenty to do and see. Known for Sapporo Beer and the winter snow festival, the city is also where the protagonist and his girlfriend arrive to start their search for the mysterious white sheep.

This day trip itinerary can be carried out almost entirely on foot except for a quick subway ride at the end.

1 SAPPORO TV TOWER ● さっぽろテレビ塔

1-chome, Odorinishi, Chuo-ku
¥720
9:00 - 22:00
Every day

Let's start the day off at the Sapporo TV Tower which is perhaps the city's most famous landmark. Located at the eastern edge of Odori Koen, the observation deck offers excellent views of the city. The tower is an easy walk from either **Odori** or Bus Center Mae subway stations.

② ODORI PARK ● 大通公園

"At the five o'clock bell, I went out to sit on a park bench and eat corn with the pigeons."[7]

The TV Tower offers splendid views of Sapporo's most famous park and you'll know exactly where to find it once you exit the tower. Odori Park is not named in the novel, but given the abundance of both pigeons and food carts selling corn on the cob, it's safe to assume that this is where our protagonist takes a break while hunting for clues.

The long, narrow park stretches over 12 blocks and is home to the snow festival in the winter and lively beer gardens in the summer. There are even some places to hear live music.

③ FORMER GOVT. OFFICE ● 北海道庁旧本庁舎

About a ten minute walk from the park is the original Hokkaido government office, one of the city's most famous landmarks. Originally constructed in 1888, this red-bricked American-style building now welcomes visitors for free. Inside you can find various exhibits about the development of Hokkaido. On the way from Odori Park you'll also pass Sapporo's iconic **Clock Tower**.

◉ 6-chome, Kitasanjo-nishi, Chuo-ku

⏱ FREE

🕙 8:45 - 18:00

📅 Every day

4 HOKKAIDO UNIV. BOTANICAL GARDENS
北海道大学植物園

A short 6 minute walk from the former Hokkaido Government Office, the Botanical Gardens provide a brief respite from the concrete jungle of Sapporo. Walking through the gardens, one can forget for a moment that they're in the middle of one of Japan's largest cities. The gardens, which are managed by Hokkaido University, are home to thousands of different plant species. In addition to the greenery there's also a small Ainu museum if you're interested in learning more about the region's indigenous people.

Once finished, let's head over to Sapporo Station, about a ten minute walk northeast from the gardens.

- 8-chome, Kitasanjo-nishi, Chuo-ku
- ¥420
- 9:00 - 16:30
- Closed Mon.

THE AINU

The Ainu are an indigenous people native to Hokkaido and neighboring northern islands such as Sakhalin and the Kurils. Traditionally, the Ainu functioned as a hunter-gatherer society but they also grew vegetables. Their culture and religion placed a strong emphasis on man's relationship with animals and nature.

One of the Ainu's most significant rituals was the bear sacrifice. The Ainu believed that spirits and gods took on the form of animals when visiting this dimension. Families would raise bear cubs indoors, taking excellent care of them until the day would finally come to send the spirit back to its own world - by means of bow and arrow. The whole village would gather for the event, performing traditional songs and dance.

In *A Wild Sheep Chase*, it was an Ainu youth who guided the original group of settlers from Sapporo to what would become Junitaki-cho. Sadly, today the Ainu culture has mostly died out, but there are numerous Ainu museums spread through Hokkaido if you're interested in learning more.

⑤ SAPPORO STATION • 札幌駅

📍 JR East Tower 6F
⏱ ¥720
🕙 10:00 - 23:00
📅 Every day

Sapporo Station is not directly named in the novel, but when the protagonist takes the train from the airport and later from Hakodate in *Dance, Dance, Dance*, this is where he would've first arrived. At the station, the **JR Tower Observation Deck T38** is another great place to see panoramic views of the city.

The station's 10th floor is home to the Sapporo Ramen Republic, which offers different types of ramen from around Hokkaido. The station also has a movie theatre and some donut shops, both of which appear frequently in the second book.

⑤ THE DOLPHIN HOTEL

The Dolphin Hotel, of course, doesn't actually exist, but what if the inspiration for either the original or the newer incarnation existed somewhere in Sapporo today? Skip ahead to **p26** for more details. Sapporo Station is a good spot to start your 'Dolphin Chase,' or you could also have a look around the Susukino/Nakajimakoen area.

⑥ SUSUKINO • すすきの

Susukino is a good place to end your day with dinner and drinks. The area could be considered Sapporo's version of Shinjuku or Shibuya. Susukino is a bit seedy but also safe. Aside from the many adult-entertainment establishments in the area, there are also plenty of normal restaurants and bars. Also be sure to check out the neon lights of **Susukino Crossing**. Coming from Sapporo Station, just take the **Nanboku subway line** two stops south. Susukino could also potentially be the area where the protagonist stays in the book.

Susukino Crossing

SIDE TRIPS FROM SAPPORO

Moerenuma Park, known for its large pyramidal structures, was designed by famed sculptor Isamu Noguchi in 1982. It's excellent for families with children and art-lovers alike.

Take the 69 or 79 bus from Kanjo-Dori-Higashi Sta. on the Toho Line. Free admission.

Otaru is a port town famous for its canal, where you can see brick buildings preserved from the 1800's, a rare sight in Japan. The town is also known for its sweets and glass souvenirs.

Otaru can be reached from JR Sapporo station in 30-45 minutes.

Hitsujigaoka Observatory is most well-known for its statue of William S. Clark, an American who aided in the early development of Hokkaido. You can also look at some sheep in front of a backdrop of the Sapporo skyline. The observatory, however, is complicated to access, and you'll likely be spending less time there than the journey itself takes one way.

A Wild DOLPHIN Chase

In both *A Wild Sheep Chase* and its sequel *Dance, Dance, Dance*, the mysterious Dolphin Hotel is almost like one of the characters of the story. Drawn to the hotel by the strange psychic power of Kiki's ears, the couple check-in and just happen to encounter the Sheep Professor, the exact person they need to help them on their quest. The original hotel then got demolished and replaced by a large, modern hotel of the same name. The mystery behind the Dolphin Hotel only grows stronger in the sequel, as its second incarnation acts as some sort of switch panel between dimensions. The Sheep Man, whom we know from Junitaki at the end of *A Wild Sheep Chase*, has become a

Keio Plaza Hotel

Hotel Route-Inn Sapporo

resident of one of the hotel's secret floors. Though the description of such a place would scare most people away, many Murakami enthusiasts wonder if it's possible to find the inspiration for the Dolphin Hotel in real-life, present-day Sapporo.

Sapporo has a lot of hotels. Most big cities do, of course, but Sapporo's abundance of hotels becomes especially apparent when searching for one that doesn't actually exist. Neither *A Wild Sheep Chase* nor *Dance, Dance, Dance* provides us with a clear location of the hotel, but it would be safe to assume that it's fairly centrally located, as the narrator did not mention having to walk very far from the station to find it.

When describing the original hotel in *A Wild Sheep Chase*, the narrator mentions it being five stories tall and that it "might as well have been a giant matchbox stood on end."[8] Just outside of Sapporo Station, **Hotel Route-Inn** more or less fits this description. Though it's actually ten stories tall, the shape of the hotel very much resembles a vertical match box. And then there's something even more interesting on the next corner.

Just a few buildings down from the Route-Inn is the Kobayashi Skin Clinic which prominently features a logo of a dolphin on its window. Could this have been there all the way back in 1982 when the novel was first published? Not likely, but it's a strange coincidence nonetheless.

When the narrator and Kiki first arrive in Sapporo, they go see a movie before heading to the hotel. The narrator then says that the hotel is "located three blocks west and one block south of the movie theater we'd gone to."⁹ The name of the theater is not revealed but just outside of Sapporo Station is the Sapporo Cinema Frontier. And just three blocks west and one block south of the movie theater is the **Keio Plaza Hotel**. This is a luxurious hotel that's much closer to the modern hotel in *Dance, Dance, Dance* than it is to the original. The Keio Plaza has 22 floors, just several short of the 26 mentioned in the book. There is a hotel, however, that has exactly 26 stories - the **ANA Hotel Sapporo**.

The ANA Hotel is also located near the station and features a massive lobby just like in *Dance, Dance, Dance*. Other than that, however, its outward appearance does not come very close to the hotel's description in the book.

All three of these examples can be found right around Sapporo Station, but it's also likely that Murakami was picturing the **Susukino** area when writing about the hotel. In between Susukino and Nakajimakoen Stations there's a countless number of hotels - many resembling the original Dolphin, some resembling the newer one, and a lot more in between.

While, as we know, there is nothing called the 'Dolphin Hotel' anywhere in Sapporo, a restaurant called **Cafe Dolphin** does exist. Established in 1967, there is some possibility that Murakami visited this cafe, or at least walked by it, when doing research for the first book.

In any case, Cafe Dolphin happens to be a pretty good restaurant. It's located nearby Kitasanjo-Higashi Station, or about 20 minutes on foot from Sapporo Station. Serving a mix of Japanese and Western food, their lunch sets are delicious and can be enjoyed for around ¥1,000.

📍 4-1-1 Kita-14-jou Higashi, Sapporo

🕐 10:00 - 18:00

📅 Closed Sun.

ANA Hotel Sapporo

THE MURAKAMI PILGRIMAGE

SAPPORO MAP

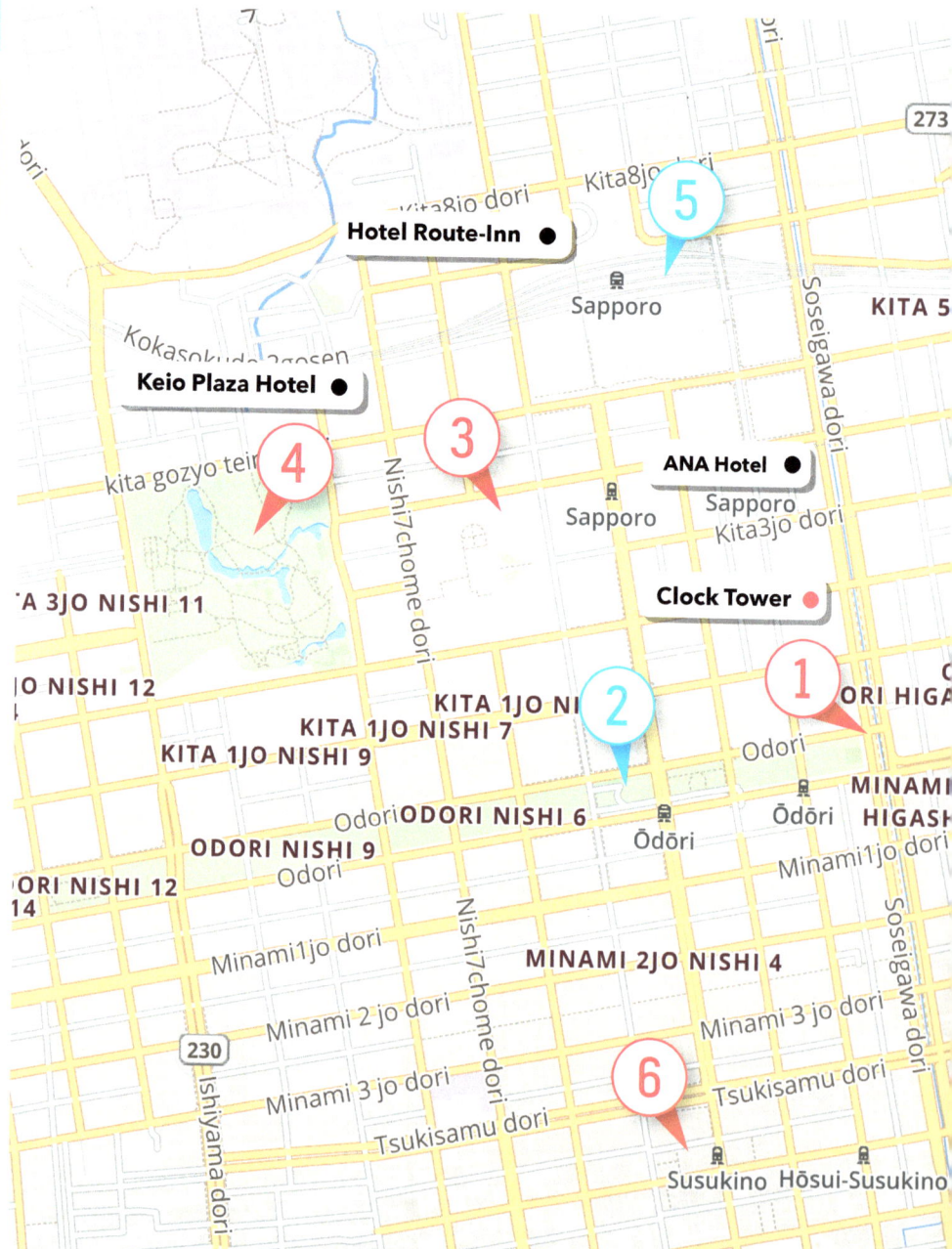

A WILD SHEEP CHASE • DANCE, DANCE, DANCE GUIDE 39

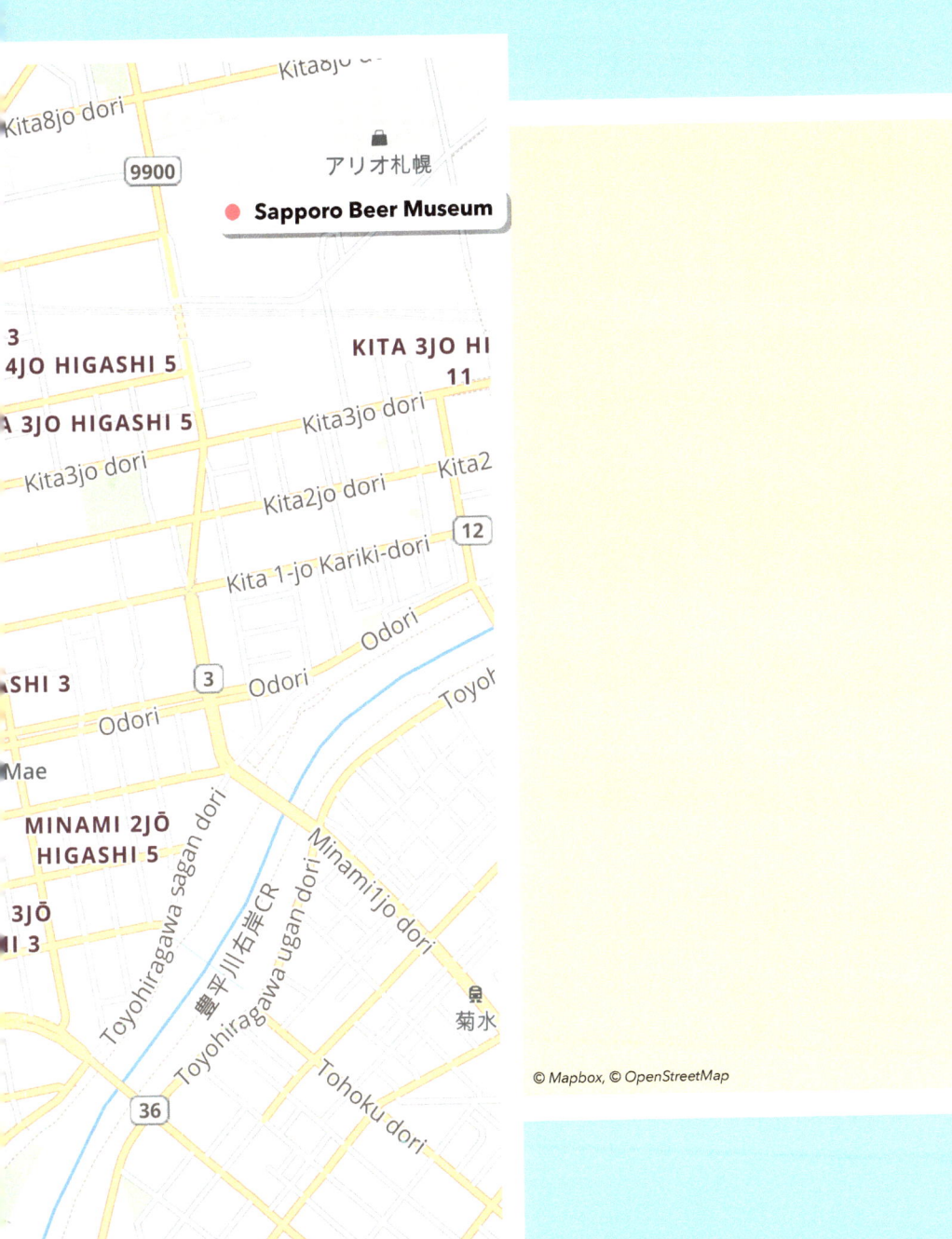

BIFUKA ITINERARY ● 美深

There are more than enough clues for us to conclude that the fictional Junitaki-cho in *A Wild Sheep Chase* is based on the real life town of Bifuka. Bifuka is known for its waterfalls and it's even the same distance (240 km) from Sapporo that Junitaki is in the book.

Today the town's population is estimated to be around five or six thousand, with roughly 100 people leaving the town annually. In the novel, the station attendant tells the narrator that while the official estimate is 7,000 people, he thinks it's actually closer to 5,000. Now, decades later, the town is still hanging in there, but not too much has changed. Locals are concerned about the declining population and the increase in vacant buildings.

Recently, as more and more people discover that Bifuka is the town featured in *A Wild Sheep Chase*, it may end up being Haruki Murakami fans themselves that help save this town.

The main destination of your Bifuka trip will be a visit to Farm Inn Tonto (pictured left), a house eerily similar to the one that the Sheep Professor built.

📍 GETTING THERE

If you're coming straight from Sapporo, you can take the 12:30 Ltd. Express Sarobetsu train which arrives in Bifuka at 15:35. A one-way ticket costs ¥7,650. If you're coming from Asahikawa, you can take the 12:31 JR Soya train which requires a half-hour wait at Nayoro Station. Then hop on the 14:36 train which arrives in Bifuka at 15:02 for a total cost of ¥2,050. Look at the next page for info on how to reach Farm Inn Tonto.

🏠 ACCOMMODATION

In this case, the main attraction is the accommodation itself (see next page). If Farm Inn Tonto is all booked up, the town of Bifuka still has a couple of inns, just like in the novel. Next to the station is Shirabashou, with rates of around ¥4,000 per night. There's also Guest House Bifuka, about a ten minute walk from the station, with the cheapest room going for ¥5,500. However, you may have difficulty managing the reservations if you don't speak Japanese.

BIFUKA STATION ● 美深駅

Bifuka Station contains a special room dedicated to the works of Haruki Murakami. The room also features photography of the local area, showing the locations around town which are especially reminiscent of scenes from *A Wild Sheep Chase*.

"The GUIDE TO THE TOWN, posted next to the deserted rotary, was so weathered you could barely make it out."[10]

Fortunately, the sign is in much better shape these days and contains information on nearby waterfalls and local hiking spots.

A WILD SHEEP CHASE • DANCE, DANCE, DANCE GUIDE   43

"To the left of the rotary were a half dozen old warehouses, from the days of shipping by rail."[11]

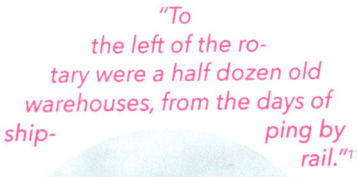

Somewhere in Bifuka, The Sheep Man awaits.

The town as viewed from the station.

FARM INN TONTO ● ファームイントント

It's pretty surreal just how closely Farm Inn Tonto resembles Murakami's descriptions in the novel. It's a strange yet exciting feeling to come across the very scenery you've pictured in your head so many times before. The only major difference is that the house is red and not white. Otherwise, everything from the birch trees to the sheep in the pasture to the mountains in the distance are just as they are in the story.

You may be wondering if Murakami himself came to stay at this house and used it as inspiration for the novel. But that would be impossible, as the inn wasn't even built until 1995.

Was the inn deliberately constructed to match the scene in the book? No, as the owners had not even read the book until other people pointed out the similarities. Now the owners are well-versed in Murakami's literature, and thanks to the incredible coincidence, Farm Inn Tonto warmly welcomes Murakami fans from around Japan and the rest of the world.

Farm Inn Tonto may be the most difficult location to access in this entire guide book, but it's also an incredibly rewarding experience once you finally make it. As you relax and look out at the same scenery that was likely captured in the Rat's photograph, you'll be glad you came.

The inn costs ¥7,000 a night which also includes meals. To make a reservation, visit their web site or make a call.

There are a mix of traditional Japanese tatami rooms and Western style rooms with beds. The dinners mainly consist of *"jingisukan,"* or sheep grilled on a metal hot plate. There are no restaurants within walking distance of the inn, so if you're a strict vegetarian you may have some difficulty. If you have a car, you can drive into town or you may want to consider bringing your own food from Sapporo or Asahikawa.

- 660 Niupu, Bifuka, Nakagawa
- ¥7000
- matsuyama-farm.com/contact
- tonttu@mb.infoweb.ne.jp
- 9:00 - 16:30
- (81)-0134-23-8201

Transportation

The inn is accessible by direct bus, a 30 minute drive from the station. The bus will only come if you've reserved it in advance, but the inn will kindly handle this for you once you've informed them of your arrival time. Look out for the gray vehicle which will come to the bus stop by the town map. The final bus departs at 15:50, so whether you're coming from Sapporo or Asahikawa you'll have plenty of time to make it. A single ride to the inn only costs ¥550.

Farm Inn Tonto

"Straight on across the pasture stood an old American-style two-story wood-frame house."[12]

The View of The Pasture

"It was unsettling seeing with my very own eyes a scene I had by now seen hundreds of times in a photograph."[13]

Around The Area

"Without exercise and without smoking, I had quickly gained six pounds. So I started to get up at six and jog a crescent halfway around the pasture."[14]

AROUND TOWN

Bifuka is nearly impossible to get around without a car, but if you don't have one, there's a chance one of the other guests staying at Farm Inn Tonto might be kind enough to offer you a ride. There are a few interesting spots nearby the inn to check out if you can. If time allows, staying in Bifuka for two nights would give you a full day to both enjoy the view of the pasture and also explore the surrounding area.

The **sheep pen** is managed by the same family that runs the inn, and you will likely get a tour of the pen from the owners' son. The pen is home to dozens of sheep and if you're lucky, you may even arrive there after a baby's just been born.

ⓘ These sheep are not the Suffolk sheep breed described in the novel, but Suffolk can be found in the nearby town of Shibetsu which is one of the towns Murakami visited while doing research for the book.

The **Rail Car Kingdom** (トロッコ王国), just by the sheep pen, is an old abandoned station called Niupu. Nowadays, visitors can ride in small rail cars across the old tracks and enjoy the scenery along the way. For around ¥1,500 a person you can take a car along the route which takes 40 minutes or so to complete. Officially, you're supposed to have a driver's license to participate, although the staff person may or may not ask to see it.

Some believe that it was actually this now abandoned station where the narrator and Kiki arrive in the novel and not the current Bifuka Station. As neither station has a bird fountain out front it's hard to tell for sure.

View from the rail car

As mentioned earlier, Bifuka, like Junitaki-cho, is famous for its **waterfalls**. Instead of the fictional town's 12, Bifuka has 16. If you take a drive throughout the area, you should be able to spot at least a couple.

BIFUKA MAP

A WILD SHEEP CHASE ● DANCE, DANCE, DANCE GUIDE 49

ASAHIKAWA ● 旭川

As the couple make their way from Sapporo to Junitaki (a.k.a. Bifuka), they transfer at Asahikawa Station. Little is written about the city in the novel, although the narrator describes seeing a "main street, modest department store, bus terminal, tourist information center" from the station platform. "A singularly dull town, if first impression were any indication,"[15] he concludes. Over 30 years later, this description is still pretty much accurate.

Nowadays, you can take a train directly from Sapporo to Bifuka, so would there be any reason to stop in Asahikawa at all? Yes and no. While Asahikawa plays a very minor role in *A Wild Sheep Chase*, it's interesting to note how often the city is referenced in other works such as *The Wind-Up Bird Chronicle* and *Norwegian Wood*. Asahikawa is also where the Dolphin Hotel receptionist, Yumiyoshi, from *Dance, Dance, Dance* grew up. As it comes up fairly often in Murakami's fiction, the city must have left some kind of impression on the author in one way or another.

Asahikawa is mainly known for one thing: the **Asahikawa Zoo**. While featuring all the exotic animals one would expect to see at a zoo, you can even find a dog and a cat here, which was referred to in the short story *New York Mining Disaster*. Other than the zoo, there's nothing much to do or see except a walk through **Tomikawa Park**. The city does, at least, have an abundance of hotels and restaurants.

BIEI & FURANO

Farm Tomita in Furano

On your way to or from Bifuka, you may want to pass through the popular sightseeing towns of Biei and Furano. This region is best enjoyed in the summer when the area's trademark flower beds and lavender fields are in full bloom. The top sites in this region are the Blue Pond, just outside of Biei, and Farm Tomita, just outside of Furano.

While the region is best explored by car, getting to the main sightseeing spots is still possible with public transportation. A train can be taken directly to Farm Tomita while there are buses which can take you to the pond. Furthermore, if you base yourself in Biei then the scenic Patchwork Road area can viewed on foot or bicycle if you don't mind the long journey. With that said, the transport system in this rural area is not nearly as efficient as in the cities, so without a car you may find yourself constantly worrying about the bus and train timetables.

There are plenty of places to stay in either area but vacation rental apartments have been slow to catch on and the inns and hotels are surprisingly pricey for such a rural area. Staying for a couple of nights in the region is plenty to experience the major sights. Whether you're coming from Sapporo or returning there, a transfer at Asahikawa station is usually necessary to get to either town.

Depending on the weather, the 'Blue Pond' may not always be blue

HOKKAIDO

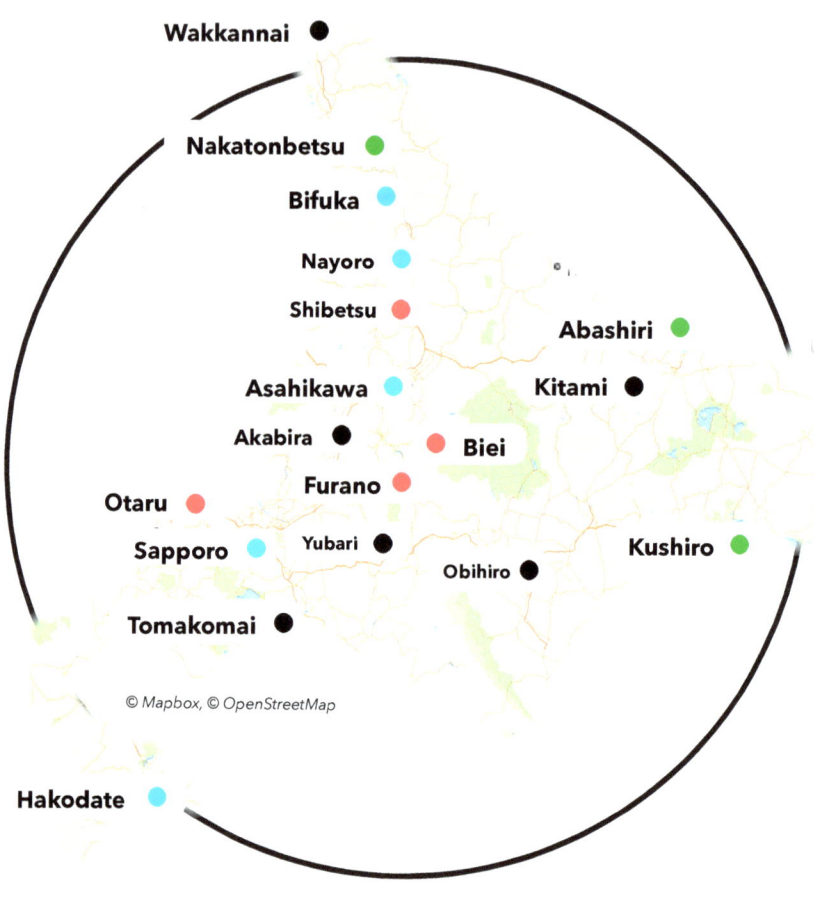

© Mapbox, © OpenStreetMap

- 🔵 : mentioned in novel
- 🔴 : recommended in this chapter
- 🟢 : mentioned in another Murakami work
  See p209 (contains spoilers)

TOKYO LOCATIONS

SHIBUYA

We don't know exactly where the narrator lives in *A Wild Sheep Chase*, but at some point before the events of the sequel he moves to Shibuya. His apartment is located somewhere by the Shuto Expressway which passes right outside his window. This expressway also happens to pass through Nanpeidai, the area of Shibuya where this same protagonist worked in one of the earlier prequels, *Pinball 1973*.

Shibuya at night

📍 12-18 Udagawacho
🕐 10:00 - 21:00
📅 Every day

Later on in the book the protagonist mentions running into the Akasaka police officer that interrogated him just outside of **Tokyu Hands**. This department store in Shibuya's Udagawacho district sells nearly everything, from souvenirs to bicycles to stationary. Tokyu Hands is a fun visit even just for window shopping.

At the end of *Dance, Dance, Dance*, the narrator and Gotanda meet in a **Shakey's Pizza**. Which chain they meet in is not clear but there happens to be one in Shibuya, a couple minute walk from Tokyu Hands. As the protagonist also lives in Shibuya, this is likely the same restaurant where Gotanda confesses to murdering Kiki.

📍 32-15 Udagawacho
🕐 11:00 - 23:00
📅 Every day

Shibuya appears in many other Murakami novels and comes up several more times throughout this guidebook, mainly in the section on *After Dark*. If you're looking for tips on shopping, nightlife and restaurants in the area, be sure to check out **shibuyaguide.com**.

HARAJUKU

Harajuku, despite being such a prominent neighborhood in Tokyo, rarely appears in Murakami's work. *Dance, Dance, Dance* is one of the few exceptions. While nothing dramatic occurs here, the protagonist makes a number of stops in the neighborhood over the course of the novel, such as when he relaxes among the greenery outside of **Meiji Shrine**. At one point he also walks down **Takeshita Street**, Harajuku's iconic street for shopping, fashion and youth culture. Tsuruoka, the tempura restaurant he visits in the book, is unfortunately no longer in business. Harajuku is also where the narrator starts his usual walking course which you can read about on the next page.

AZABU

Azabu is the posh, upper-class neighborhood where Gotanda lives in *Dance, Dance, Dance*. The area is also home to many foreign embassies, giving Azabu a particularly international feel. Azabu is most famous for the Tokyo Tower, which is mentioned in the novel as being clearly visible from Gotanda's apartment windows. Tokyo Tower, built in 1958, is currently overshadowed by the much taller Sky Tree, but at least nowadays you can enjoy the tower and its views of the city without all the crowds that there used to be.

4-2-8 Shibakoen
¥900
9:00 - 23:00
Everyday

THE "USUAL COURSE"

". . . I'd leave the theater and walk my usual course. From Harajuku to the Jingu Stadium, Aoyama Cemetery, Omotesando, past the Jintan Building, back to Shibuya."

A few times over the course of *Dance, Dance, Dance*, the protagonist walks the long route mentioned in the quote above, usually after seeing the film "Unrequited Love" in a Shibuya movie theater.

In an earlier description of the route he goes into more detail, mentioning the Nezu Museum and the Kinokuniya supermarket on Aoyama Boulevard, which he also visits several other times over the course of the novel. This helps paint a pretty clear picture of the exact route he takes.

The Nezu Museum, by the way, is definitely worth a visit, and you can read more about it on p99. (While part of the section on *South of the Border, West of the Sun*, you won't run into any spoilers if you stay on that page.)

If you've read everything by Haruki Murakami and have limited time in Tokyo, be sure to take a look at **p207**. As this route overlaps Sendagaya, Aoyama and Shibuya - all focal points of other Murakami novels - you could do an extended version of this route by taking your time in each area over the course of an entire day, or maybe even two. That page, of course, contains spoilers for other novels.

A WILD SHEEP CHASE • DANCE, DANCE, DANCE GUIDE 57

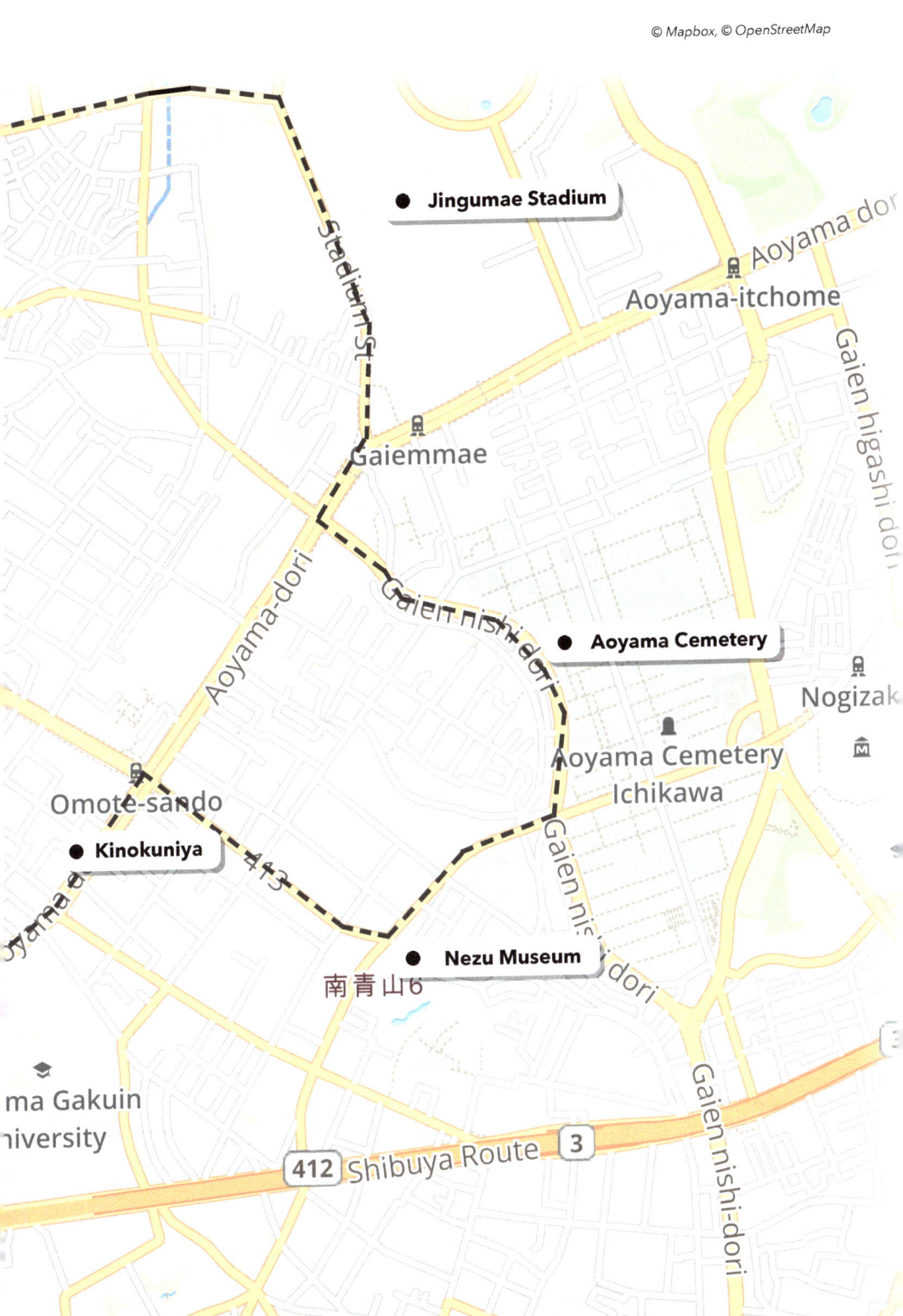

AKASAKA

Over the course of *Dance, Dance, Dance*, the large Minato-ku neighborhood of Akasaka appears many times. It's even where the mysterious company that rebuilt the Dolphin Hotel supposedly has its headquarters. Below are the other Akasaka locations mentioned throughout the novel.

Yuki and her mother live in a condo right by **Nogi Shrine**, a shrine dedicated to Nogi Maresuke, a Meiji Era general. Originally established in 1927, the shrine was rebuilt after the war in 1957. Yuki's condo is described as being built of brick, and several brick buildings can be spotted around the shrine area.

8-11-27 Akasaka
6:00 - 17:00
Every day

After his namecard was found inside the wallet of Mei, the murdered prostitute, the narrator gets taken to the Akasaka Police Station where he undergoes an exhausting interrogation. Nearby the police station is Toyokawa Inari, a Buddhist temple which venerates the fox, or *inari*, a common spirit in Japanese folklore. This 19th century temple has a fascinating history if you're interested in how temples managed to survive the Buddhist persecution of the Meiji Era.

1-4-7 Motoakasaka
6:00 - 20:00
Every day

A WILD SHEEP CHASE • DANCE, DANCE, DANCE GUIDE

Mei was murdered in a luxury Akasaka hotel. Could it have been the Akasaka Excel Hotel Tokyu (pictured left)? Another possible candidate is Hotel New Otani, also near Akasaka-Mitsuke Station.

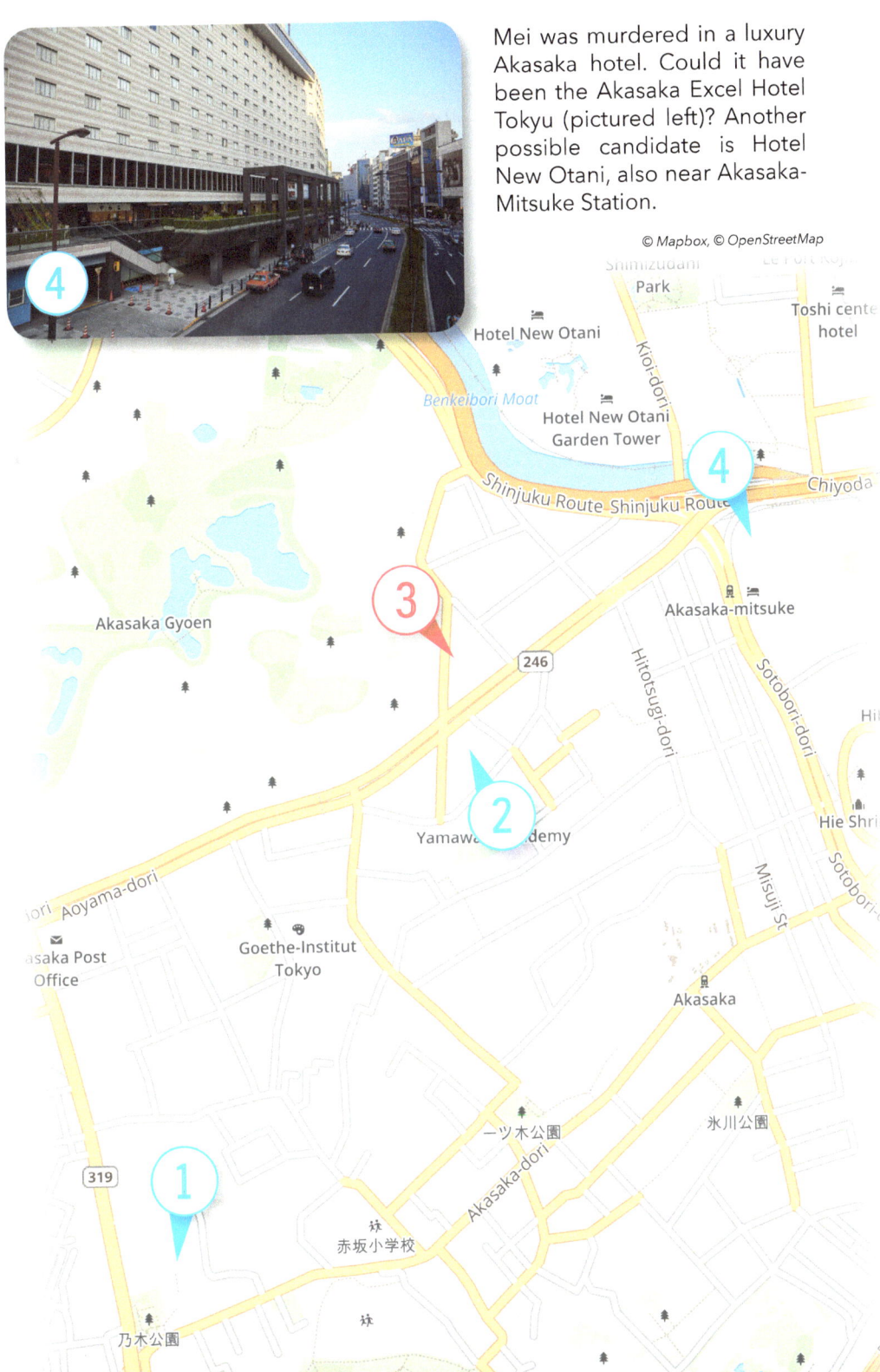

OTHER LOCATIONS

KANAGAWA

Throughout *Dance, Dance, Dance*, there are a number of scenes that take place in Kanagawa, a neighboring prefecture of Tokyo. Yuki and her mother live in the resort town of Hakone, which is famous for its hot springs and magnificent views of Mt. Fuji. Later on in the book, when the narrator visits Yuki and her grieving mother, he and Yuki take a boat ride around Lake Ashi and eat ice cream at the Fujiya Hotel.

Yuki's father lives in a villa in Tsujido, a part of Fujisawa City. On the way there, the pair stop for a walk near the beach across from Enoshima island, also a part of Fujisawa. Close by Kamakura, this scenic island is home to a botanical gardens and a shrine dedicated to Benzaiten, the goddess of music. If the weather is right, you can even spot Mr. Fuji from the beach.

Later on in the book the protagonist and Gotanda drive together from Tokyo to Yokohama, Kanagawa's biggest city and the second-largest in all of Japan. Yokohama is known for the Marine Tower and for having one of the oldest Chinatowns in Japan.

All of these destinations make for a nice day trip from Tokyo. The Odakyu rail company operates trains to both Hakone and Enoshima which depart from Shinjuku. There are a also number of JR trains which connect Yokohama to various parts of Tokyo.

View of Mt. Fuji from a Kanagawa beach

HYOGO

As we know, *A Wild Sheep Chase* is the third book in what's referred to as the "Rat trilogy." Its two prequels take place in an unnamed town in Hyogo Prefecture, often just referred to as "the town." In the third book the protagonist returns here for the first time in 4 years. Per the Rat's request, he goes to meet a few people which the Rat regretted never saying goodbye to before skipping town. This includes J, the Chinese bar owner as well as the Rat's ex-girlfriend from *Pinball, 1973*.

The previous chapter's itinerary goes into more detail on the Hyogo prefecture locations of this series, but "the town" is generally considered to be somewhere around the city of Ashiya. While J's Bar is fictional, a close representation exists in the bustling Sannomiya district of Kobe. In the early '80's a movie was made based off of *Hear The Wind Sing* and the bar Half Time is where they filmed the bar scenes. In the sequel, however, the location of J's bar has moved "to a quarter of a mile away."[17]

At one point in *Dance, Dance, Dance*, the narrator describes to Yuki in detail the ingredients of a smoked-salmon sandwich that he loves. Though omitted from the English translation, the Japanese original mentions a Kobe restaurant called Tor Road Delicatessen.[18] Also located in Sannomiya, this is one of the best spots in Kobe to get Western-style sandwiches.

• •

HAWAII

At the urging of both of Yuki's parents, the narrator and Yuki spend awhile in Hawaii during the events of *Dance, Dance, Dance*. Some of the locations mentioned include Waikiki, Makaha and Honolulu. It's in downtown Honolulu that the narrator spots someone who looks like Kiki and follows her into the strange room with the six skeletons.

HARD-BOILED WONDERLAND

世界の終りとハードボイルド・ワンダーランド

Hard-Boiled Wonderland and The End of The World is one of Murakami's most surrealistic and experimental novels and perhaps the only one that could be categorized as true 'science fiction.' Only half of the book takes place in the 'real' world, with each alternating chapter taking us to the walled town located deep within the protagonist's subconscious.

In Tokyo, a secret information war between the Calcutecs (of which the protagonist is a member) and the Semiotics is taking place, as an old scientist with an underground lab is behind a lot more than he first lets on. Furthermore, grotesque creatures known as the INKlings have an underground base beneath important Tokyo government buildings, and it's suspected that they may be in cahoots with the Semiotics.

Many of the notable scenes of the novel take place deep underground beneath Tokyo, but we're at least given descriptions of under which landmarks the characters are traversing. Much of the action happens below the Sendagaya area, in between Sendagaya and Aoyama-Itchome stations. Sendagaya is home to the Jingu baseball stadium and a famous ramen shop and it's even where the author himself used to run a jazz bar.

Our narrator lives in an unnamed part of Setagaya Ward, and all we really know about it is that it contains a library. Some other Tokyo scenes take place in Shinjuku station, where the narrator stores the unicorn skull in a locker, and Ginza, where he goes shopping toward the end of the book. The novel's finale takes us to Hibiya Park, where the protagonist decides to spend his last day alive drinking a couple of beers with his librarian girlfriend.

SENDAGAYA WALKING TOUR ITINERARY ● 千駄ヶ谷

Sendagaya is a fashionable yet calm and quiet neighborhood which is located in Shibuya and Shinjuku wards. The area is home to the Meiji Jingu Stadium and the Tokyo Metropolitan Gymnasium. It was the home of the original National Olympic Stadium, and, at the time of writing, a new stadium is currently being built on the same spot. With that in mind, finding your way around Sendagaya's Gaien Park area may be confusing leading up to the 2020 Olympics due to all the construction taking place.

For this walking tour we're going to be focusing on the area in between Aoyama-Itchome and Sendagaya stations. This is the main area through which the characters traverse underground in the story. And this is also where the author himself lived for awhile which is likely why so many small details about Sendagaya are written about in the book.

Depending on where you're staying in Tokyo, it may be more convenient for you to ride the JR Sobu Line to Sendagaya Station and carry out this itinerary in reverse. Also bear in mind that Sendagaya is just north of the Aoyama area heavily featured in *South of the Border, West of the Sun*, so if you've read that book you might want to visit both neighborhoods in a single day.

This itinerary can be carried out entirely on foot and should take no more than just a couple of hours.

1 AOYAMA-ITCHOME STATION ● 青山一丁目駅

Let's start off the day at Aoyama-Itchome station. This is where the narrator and the girl in pink emerge after their trek through the tunnels deep below Tokyo. There are a couple of different train lines running through this station, but the narrator is very specific about arriving at the Ginza line platform. Standing at the end of the platform, it's easy to picture just where the two characters emerged from, caked in grime and mud.

At the time of writing, the platform still looks exactly as described in the novel, but that may not be the case for much longer. A short time ago, a blind man tragically fell and died at this platform, prompting the call for Tokyo Metro to finally build protective barriers at Aoyama-Itchome as they have at other stations around the city.

Depending on where you're staying, you might not be coming via a Ginza line train. If you simply want to see the platform, try getting through the gate with an IC card (Pasmo or Suica) before telling the station staff that you made a mistake and want to get back out. It's almost like reliving the scene from the novel where the protagonist tries to explain that he lost his ticket!

2 MEIJI JINGU STADIUM ● 明治神宮野球場

○ 3-1 Kasumigaokamachi, Shinjuku
○ ¥1300-¥5000
○ From 18:00
○ Check schedule

"At Jingu Stadium, Yakult lost to Chunichi, 6-2. And no one the wiser that there was a huge hive of INKlings right under them."[19]

Jingu Stadium, home to the Yakult Swallows baseball team, is mentioned a couple different times in the novel, but the protagonist never actually visits. Instead, he walks under it while traversing through the INKling lair. It was in this very stadium, however, that the author decided he had what it took to become a novelist after witnessing a spectacular homerun. If you'd like to catch the Swallows play, games usually start in the evenings at 18:00.

3 HOPE-KEN ● ホープ軒

Now let's head over to **Gaienni-shi-dori** and make a right. On the left-side you'll spot the famous ramen restaurant 'Hope-ken.' This is a certain type of restaurant where the customers stand up as they eat, which is great if you're in a hurry, but not so great if you're tired from walking.

In the novel, the protagonist thinks about Hope-ken while walking underneath it: "I pictured the world above ground. We were directly under [. . .] those two landmark ramen shops – Hope-ken and Copain."[20] While Copain apparently no longer exists, Hope-ken can still be visited 24 hours a day. The ramen here is nothing too special but it's not bad either. The cheapest bowl can be ordered for ¥750 while the options with more toppings go for around ¥1000.

Hope-Ken on Gaiennishi Blvd.

- 2-33-9 Sendagaya, Shibuya-ku
- 24 Hours
- Every day

When you're done eating, turn left out of the restaurant and then make a left at the next intersection, walking straight for about 5 minutes.

SHINJUKU STATION

The protagonist leaves a Nike sports bag containing the unicorn skull in a locker in Shinjuku Station. Shinjuku, the world's busiest station, naturally occurs throughout much of Murakami's work, but the area is only mentioned a couple of times in *Hard-Boiled Wonderland and The End of The World*.

4 PETER CAT & BOOK HOUSE YUU

Peter Cat was the name of Murakami's jazz club which moved to Sendagaya from its original location in the western suburbs of Kokubunji. It was while running this jazz club in Sendagaya that Murakami first started his early novels. The club closed down way back in 1981, but the location, now just a generic restaurant, is still a pilgrimage spot for diehard fans.

Peter Cat was even once featured in the Japanese magazine called *Brutus*, and Murakami uses this scenario in his 1992 novel *South of the Border, West of the Sun*. In that book the main character runs a jazz bar in the neighboring Aoyama district, which you can read more about in that section of this guide book.

Just around the corner is the bookstore called 'Yuu,' a small store that Murakami and his wife would often visit while living in the area. Today a small shrine to Murakami can be found in the back, and you can even see one of the original lanterns used by the old Peter Cat.

Former Peter Cat
1-7-12 Sendagaya

Book House Yuu
1-21-4 Sendagaya

THE IMAGINARY BEINGS

In *Hard-Boiled Wonderland and The End of The World*, several different mythological creatures appear throughout the story. In the 'real life' portions of the book, we're introduced to the INKlings, an acronym for "Infra-Nocturnal Kappa." In Japanese folklore, kappa are green, amphibious creatures who can be found in large bodies of water. They're generally depicted as turtle-like creatures that walk on two legs like humans. Their main defining characteristic is the bowl-shaped area on their head which is full of water, the main source of a kappa's strength and life force.

In some legends, the kappa are portrayed as benevolent water gods that may like to play tricks on humans from time to time, but are otherwise harmless. Other folktales, however, portray them as flesh-hungry killers that won't hesitate to pull unsuspecting humans down into deep water - much like the INKlings of the novel. Interestingly, the original Japanese version of the novel does not use the word 'kappa' but instead refers to these creatures as *yamikuro* - roughly translating to something like "dark beings." While *yamikuro* is Murakami's made-up word, most readers in Japan would immediately associate these underground-dwelling creatures with kappa, similar to how Westerners would picture a vampire when reading of a sharp-toothed, blood-sucking humanoid.

Fans of Haruki Murakami may be interested in picking up the 1927 novella *Kappa* by legendary Japanese author Ryunosuke Akutagawa. The walking and talking kappa in this story are a lot more friendly and human-like than the INKlings, as the work is generally considered to be a satire on Japanese society at the time. But the story does share similarities with *Hard-Boiled Wonderland* and other Murakami novels in the sense that it deals with the concept of alternate realities and portals from one world to another.[21] This is a common theme throughout much of Murakami's work.

OF MURAKAMI'S
WONDERLAND

The Spanish language version of *Kappa* includes a foreword by surrealist Argentine short-story writer Jorge Luis Borges - an author directly referenced in *Hard-Boiled Wonderland*. When the protagonist and his librarian girlfriend are looking for clues on the mysterious unicorn skull that's sitting in his apartment, they consult Borges and Margarita Guerrero's *The Book of Imaginary Beings*, a compilation of folktales surrounding mythical creatures from around the world. The description of the Chinese Unicorn, or *kilin*, documented in Borges' book is very similar to the appearance of the unicorns in the walled town.

Elsewhere in *The Book of Imaginary Beings* is a section called "The Kami" about a Japanese legend surrounding a giant fish or eel-like creature. This creature lives underground and causes earthquakes throughout the country whenever it shakes.[22] This legend is not directly mentioned in the novel but the INKlings do worship a giant fish with no eyes, even going as far as building a massive underground sanctuary for it that they won't even dare enter themselves. When the protagonist and the girl in pink traverse through this giant sanctuary, they experience a tremor before being attacked by a massive horde of leeches. In Murakami's short story *Super-Frog Saves Tokyo*, it is a giant worm living beneath Shinjuku that causes violent earthquakes whenever it gets angry.[3]

Oddly missing from Borges' book is any mention of the kappa, although his contribution to *Kappa*'s Spanish edition came out two years after *The Book of Imaginary Beings*' publication.

If you happen to find a copy of the Japanese version of *The Book of Imaginary Beings*, you'll notice a drawing of a big Cheshire Cat on the cover. The Cheshire Cat happens to be the symbol Murakami chose for his jazz bar, Peter Cat. As detailed on p67, the now-defunct Peter Cat was located in Sendagaya - directly above a massive kappa lair.

SETAGAYA

The novel's protagonist lives in an apartment somewhere in Setagaya Ward but we're not told where. Considering how Setagaya is one of the largest and most populous wards in Tokyo, it's hard to guess exactly where he lived. Interestingly, the main character of *The Wind-Up Bird Chronicle* also lives near an unnamed Setagaya station.

Sangenjaya, Setagaya Ward

⑤ GAIEN PARK ● 明治神宮外苑

> "I'd go to the barber, get a shave, stroll over to Gaien Park, lie down and gaze up at the blue."[23]

Gaien Park consists of the entire group of stadiums, sports facilities and smaller parks in the Sendagaya area. But when most people think of the term 'Gaien Park' they think of the area around the **Meiji Picture Gallery**. This picture gallery documents the life of Emperor Meiji, who ruled Japan from 1867 - 1912 - a time of radical change for the formerly isolationist nation. Nearby the gallery you can find a large fountain and a grassy area where you can lie down and wait for the end of the world.

📍 1-1 Kasumigaokamachi, Shinjuku
💰 ¥500
🕘 9:00 - 17:00
📅 Every day

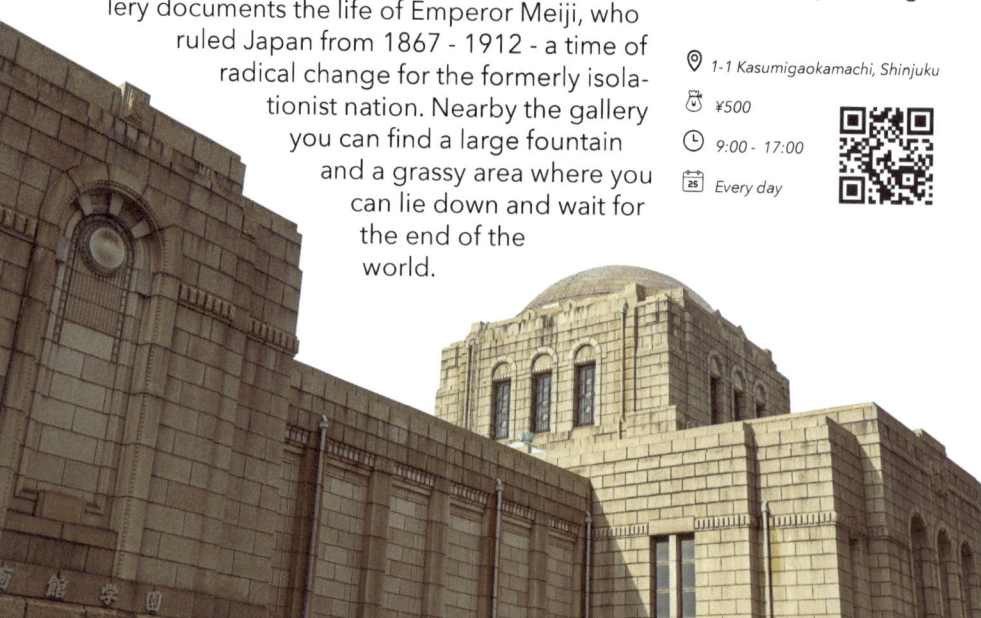

SENDAGAYA MAP

GINZA

On his "last day," the narrator decides to go to Ginza to do some shopping. He buys some new clothes, visits a beer hall and then goes over to the Sony Building, a multi-storied Sony showroom which displays both the current products on sale and some of the company's latest prototypes. Ginza, which tends to be popular with an older crowd, is known for its high-end shopping and eating options and department stores like Wako and Mitsukoshi.

HIBIYA PARK

At the end of the book, Hibiya Park is where the protagonist and his librarian girlfriend have their final date. On a Monday morning they lay on the grass and drink beer together, talking about divorce and *The Brothers Karamazov*. Hibiya Park, located in Chuo-ku, can be accessed by Hibiya or Kasumigaseki Stations and is worth a stop if you're already in the area.

NORWEGIAN WOOD

ノルウェイの森

Even 30 years after it was written, *Norwegian Wood* still remains Haruki Murakami's most famous novel. Say the author's name to a random person in Japan and in most cases, "Norway no Mori" is the first thing they'll say back to you. This is the book that launched Murakami's career into the mainstream and it's easy to see why. Though the story takes place in the time of the wild student demonstrations of the late 1960's, a time almost unimaginable in today's Japan, the book deals with subjects like friendship, death and young love - concepts which are universal across borders and eras. The novel has had a significant impact on many, and even today the sites and neighborhoods that appear throughout the story attract a number of visitors.

When examining the settings of Murakami's fiction, *Norwegian Wood* is unique in the sense that its characters live and play in certain Tokyo neighborhoods that hardly get any attention in the author's other works. If you read all of Murakami's books, you'll notice that the eastern half of Tokyo rarely gets mentioned, with *Norwegian Wood* being a unique exception. This section of the guide book features two day tours, taking you to neighborhoods like Jinbocho and Ueno that you won't find mentioned in any of the other chapters.

However, some of Tokyo's western neighborhoods also play a significant role in the story too, so prepare to cover a lot of ground as you put yourself into Watanabe's shoes.

PART 1: WATANABE AND NAOKO WALKING TOUR

"She turned right at Iidabashi, came out at the moat, crossed the intersection at Jinbocho, climbed the hill at Ochanomizu and came out at Hongo. From there she followed the tram tracks to Komagome."[25]

Watanabe and Naoko take many walks together each Sunday in the beginning of the novel, but only their first walk together is outlined in detail. After their chance meeting on the Chuo Line, Naoko suggests they get out at Yotsuya, located roughly in the center of Tokyo. Hopefully you've brought some comfortable shoes with you because that simple quote above is the outline for a grueling 4 plus hour walking journey! Fortunately, the course takes us through some of the most interesting neighborhoods of eastern Tokyo, with plenty of landmarks to appreciate on the long trip to Komagome.

THE MURAKAMI PILGRIMAGE

NORWEGIAN WOOD GUIDE

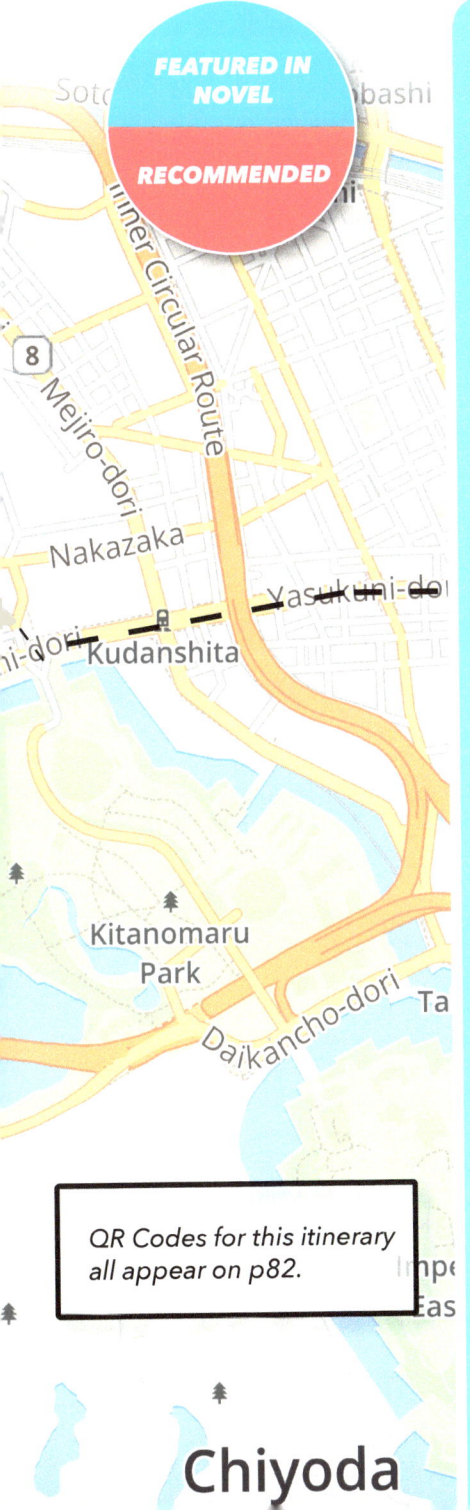

QR Codes for this itinerary all appear on p82.

Yotsuya Station is accessible via the JR Chuo Line, the JR Sobu Line and the Marunouchi and Namboku subway lines. Come out of the Akasaka exit, or any exit that has you facing north. Next you want to head toward the river, eventually passing **Ichigaya Station**. Enjoy the scenery as you take a peaceful stroll in the shade for the next 20 minutes or so. If you get tired, there are some nice views of Tokyo's business districts to enjoy from the benches. Keep walking straight and eventually you will find yourself in the business district of **Iidabashi**.

Once in Iidabashi, make a right on **Waseda Dori**. Looking at the map, this turn doesn't make much sense, as we've just been heading northeast but now we'll be going southeast. But remember, in the novel this is an aimless walk with no clear direction in mind. And given the crazy geography of Tokyo, single streets can take all sorts of twists and turns without it being obvious at first. Walking straight down Waseda Dori for about 10 minutes, we'll eventually find ourselves in the **Kudanshita** district.

Arriving in Kudanshita, on your right you should see a big shrine gate (or *torii*) which is the entrance to the highly controversial **Yasukuni Shrine**. This is where Japan's war dead are enshrined, including a number of Class A war criminals, and a war of words erupts every year between Japan and its neighbors whenever politicians visit. Visit the shrine if you wish, or keep moving forward to where you'll come across the moat mentioned in the story.

① KITANOMARU PARK ● 北の丸公園

Walk across the moat and you'll find yourself in Kitanomaru Park, part of the Imperial Palace's outer garden. You'll soon see the **Nippon Budokan**, a world famous venue for martial arts and live music events. Next you'll find a big, green park. Kitanomaru also has two museums: the **Science Museum** and the **National Museum of Modern Art**. When finished, come back out from the same entrance and make a right, heading **east down Yasukuni-dori** toward Jinbocho.

© Mapbox, © OpenStreetMap

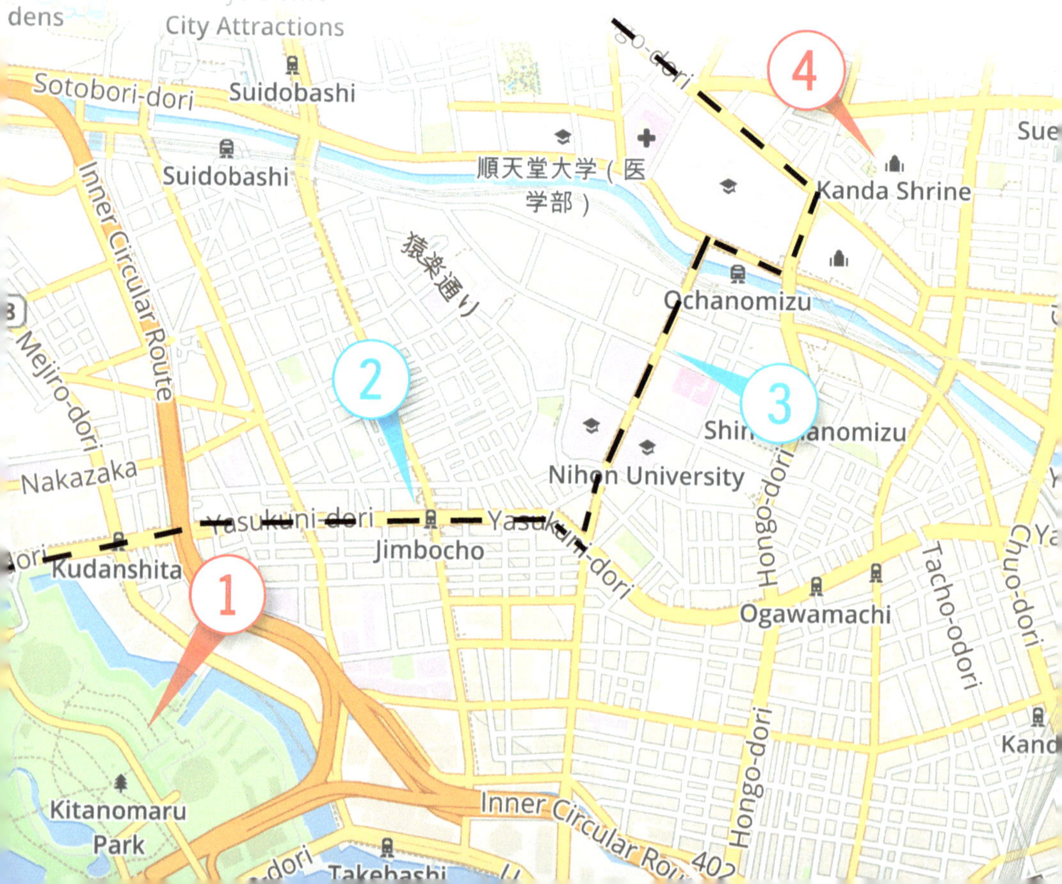

② JINBOCHO ● 神保町

Jinbocho is a district synonymous with used books. There are dozens of book shops throughout the area, many of them specializing in niche topics. Unfortunately, very few shops carry any English-language books, but there is an excellent antiquarian called **Subun-so** that's an exception. Established in 1941, they sell old and rare foreign language books that you'd even have a hard time tracking down in the West.

For a neighborhood dedicated to books, one would think Jinbocho would show up a lot more in Murakami's work, but *Norwegian Wood* and *Sputnik Sweetheart* are the only cases where it's mentioned, and only briefly in each.

③ OCHANOMIZU ● 御茶ノ水

Next let's head over to Ochanomizu. As Jinbocho is to books, Ochanomizu is to musical instruments. You won't be able to miss all the music shops as you pass Meiji University and head toward Ochanomizu Station. Ochanomizu is also the location of the hospital where Watanabe and Midori visit her father later in the book.

Next, **walk past the station** and go to the other side of the river, then **make a right**. Keep heading straight and after several minutes you'll find yourself at an intersection just outside of the Akihabara electronics district. Now **make a left, followed by another quick left onto Hongo-dori**. This is the street that Watanabe and Naoko take all the way to Komagome - still around an hour walk from this point. But there are a couple of interesting detours you may want to check out if you have the energy.

④ KANDA SHRINE ● 神田明神

Kanda Shrine was originally built in the year 730 near Otemachi but was moved to this spot in the year 1616. The shrine was once frequented by shogun Tokugawa Ieyasu in the Edo Period, but today the shrine is popular with many gaming and electronics enthusiasts from the nearby *otaku* mecca, Akihabara. They even sell talismans to protect your electronic goods from harm!

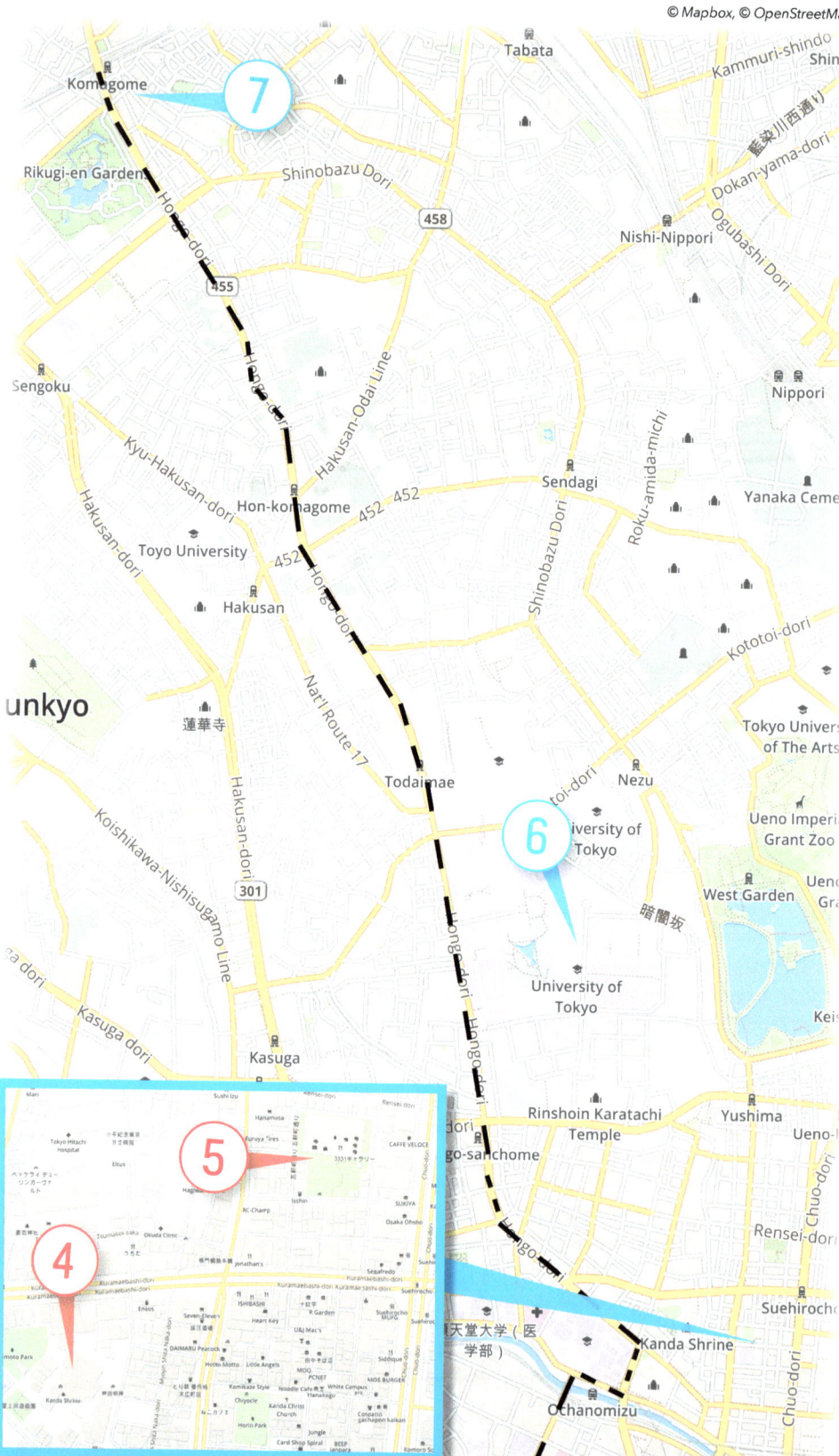

5 3331 ARTS CHIYODA

3331 Arts Chiyoda is a former junior high school that's been converted into an art space. The 2nd floor contains many free contemporary art galleries situated in old classrooms. Not only is the art itself worth a look but the unique atmosphere makes this place really special. There are occasionally temporary exhibitions on the first floor which require a ticket, but the other floors are accessible for no charge. The build-

ing is about 7 or 8 minutes on foot from Kanda Shrine.

Leaving 3331, find your way back to Hongo-dori and keep heading in the direction of Komagome.

6 TOKYO UNIVERSITY ● 東京大学

Back on the main road, another 15 minutes or so of walking will take you right past the campus of Tokyo University. Watanabe does not mention walking through the campus in the book, but this is the school that his friend Nagasawa attends. While not so well-known internationally, Tokyo University is considered to be the most prestigious school in all of Japan. It also has a nice campus which you can easily stroll through on your way to Komagome. The campus even has a little forest and a scenic pond.

THE MURAKAMI PILGRIMAGE

Kitanomaru Park
📍 2-3 Kitanomarukoen, Chiyoda-ku

Subun-so
📍 33-Kanda Ogawamachi, Chiyoda-ku
🕐 10:00 - 18:00
📅 Closed Sun.

Kanda Shrine
📍 2-16-2 Sotokanda, Chiyoda-ku

Arts 3331 Chiyoda
📍 6-11-14 Sotokanda, Chiyoda-ku
💰 FREE
🕐 10:00 - 21:00
📅 Every day

Tokyo University
📍 7-3-1 Hongo, Bunkyo-ku

Rikugien
📍 6-16 Honkomagome, Bunkyo-ku
💰 ¥300
🕐 9:00 - 17:00
📅 Every day

© Mapbox, © OpenStreetMap

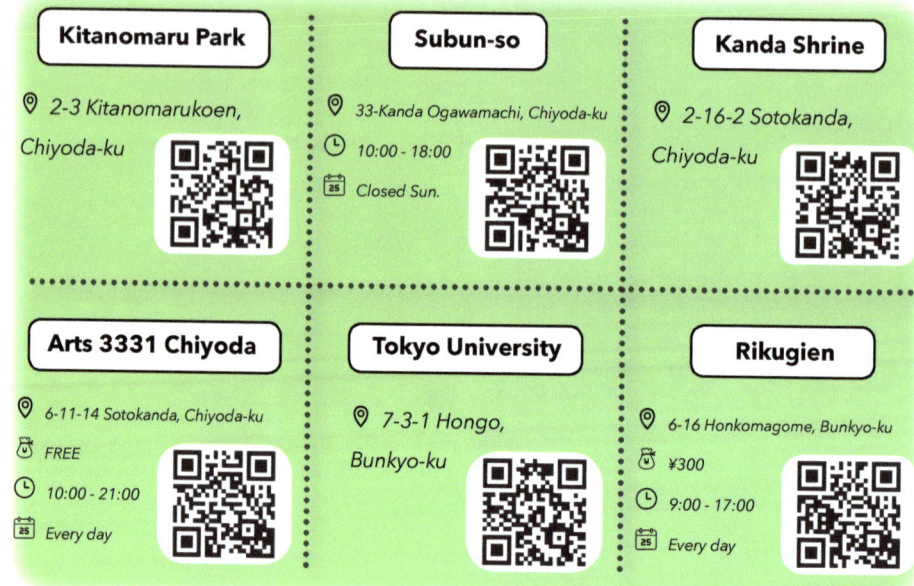

⑦ KOMAGOME ● 駒込

After about 30 minutes on foot straight down Hongo-dori you'll finally reach the Komagome neighborhood. If you managed to make it this far, congratulations! If not, don't worry - Komagome is an easy stop to make during the second itinerary of this chapter. In any case, the neighborhood is worth a visit for its **Rikugien Gardens**, named after the six forms of traditional *waka* poetry. Constructed in 1702, the garden itself is said to represent common scenic images of classical poetry, but it can certainly be appreciated by anybody.

In the novel, after Watanabe and Naoko finally make it to Komagome, they stop in a soba noodle restaurant. This restaurant is not named in the English translation but in the original Japanese version it's revealed to be **Komatsuan**.[27] This soba restaurant is just next to the entrance of Rikugien in the direction of the station. Be aware in advance that Komatsuan is especially pricey for a noodle shop. While a cheap soba chain sells bowls of noodles for three of four hundred yen, the cheapest dish here goes for around ¥1,000, with sets costing ¥3,000 or more. So is the soba here worth the price? No, not quite, but it's still delicious and the quiet atmosphere of the restaurant is a relaxing way to celebrate your completion of this incredibly long walk. Komagome Station is on the JR Yamanote Line, making it an easy journey back to central Tokyo.

Rikugien Gardens

A bowl of soba at Komatsuan

PART 2: TOKYO DAY TRIP ITINERARY ● 東京

This day tour itinerary will take us from the western suburb of Kichijoji all the way to the northeastern neighborhood of Ueno. However, if you're staying in the eastern part of Tokyo it's entirely possible to carry out this tour in reverse order.

After Kichijoji, where Watanabe lives later in the book, we'll head over to Shinjuku, the location of his part-time job and where he often goes on drunken adventures with Midori. Then we'll visit Waseda University, the inspiration for the unnamed university in the novel. From there it's an easy walk to the dorm where Watanabe lives with Stormtrooper in the first half of the book. After a brief stop in Otsuka via streetcar, we'll end the day in Ueno.

This itinerary involves using multiple train lines but there will be a couple of opportunities to use your JR rail pass. Also be aware that if you weren't able to make it all the way to Komagome at the end of Watanabe and Naoko's walking tour, you can easily fit that in between Otsuka and Ueno stations by simply getting off at Komagome Station on the JR Yamanote Line.

If you're short on time, you may want to skip Kichijoji for now and save it for a day when you're exploring the locations of *Sputnik Sweetheart* or *Pinball, 1973*.

NORWEGIAN WOOD GUIDE

1 KICHIJOJI ● 吉祥寺

In the second half of the novel, Watanabe moves to a standalone house somewhere in a quiet residential part of Kichijoji. Kichijoji is most famous for the beautiful **Inokashira Park**, which is a must-see for anyone visiting the western Tokyo area. If you walk through the park and come out on the opposite side, you'll see houses very reminiscent of the one Watanabe describes in his letters to Naoko.

Kichijoji is popular for used clothing stores, record shops and laid-back coffee shops. These days it's considered one of the most desirable places to live in Tokyo. A train ride from Shinjuku takes about 11 minutes and it's also directly accessible from Shibuya. Kichijoji is also a prominent neighborhood in *Sputnik Sweetheart (p130)*. Once you're finished, take the **JR Chuo or Sobu line** train to Shinjuku.

> "Originally a gardener's shack or some other kind of cottage, it stood [. . .] separated from the main house by a large stretch of neglected garden."[28]

2 DUG ● ダグ

Arriving at Shinjuku, come out of the **JR East Exit** and head over to Yasukuni-dori where you can find Dug, one of Watanabe and Midori's favorite hangouts. Just as described in the novel, it's underground and behind Kinokuniya. But this current incarnation of the bar, first established in the 1960's, was originally an add-on to a larger main bar that got shut down. Dug no longer hosts live performances but a few live albums, such as Mal Waldron's *Meditations* (1972), were recorded at the original. Aside from the great music, Midori liked the place because "They don't make you feel embarrassed to be drinking in the afternoon."[29] Also around the area are record shops similar to the one where Watanabe works in the novel.

- 3-15-12 Shinjuku
- ¥550 cover
- 12:00 - 2:00am
- Everyday

3 WASEDA UNIVERSITY ● 早稲田大学

From Shinjuku, hop on a JR Yamanote Line train and ride just two stops to **Takadanobaba**. This station is a 20 minute walk from our destination, but if you want to shorten the distance you can transfer to the Tozai Line and ride one stop to Waseda Station. Just keep in mind that this is not a JR Line so you'd essentially be paying for two tickets.

From Takadanobaba, all you have to do is simply walk east down Waseda-dori until you arrive at Waseda University. From the Waseda subway station it's just a 6 or 7 minute walk in the northwest direction.

The name of Watanabe's university is not given to us in the novel but it's very likely based off of Waseda University, as this is the university Murakami himself attended in his youth. Watanabe mentions that the entrance exam for his university didn't require much study, but Waseda, in contrast, is considered to be the most prestigious of Japan's private schools. Perhaps Murakami wanted to make his protagonist seem more relatable by having him attend an average-level school. Aside from Haruki Murakami, Waseda alumni include numerous prime ministers and heads of major corporations. Today the university is attended by around 50,000 students.

In the *Norwegian Wood* Watanabe majors in drama, just as the author himself did at Waseda. On campus you can find the **Tsubouchi Memorial Theatre Museum**, which is likely a place that Murakami and his classmates visited numerous times as students. The museum has free admission and many of the exhibits are translated into English, so it's worth a stop even if you're not particularly interested in drama. Around campus you can also find the library where Watanabe often spends time in the novel. Just outside of campus, there are many local cafes and restaurants reminiscent of the place where Watanabe and Midori first meet.

The Tsubouchi Memorial Theatre Museum

- 1-6-1 Nishiwaseda, Shinjuku-ku
- FREE
- 10:00 - 17/19:00
- Every day

Engravings of sheep

④ WAKEIJUKU ● 和敬塾

Wakeijuku is the all-male student dormitory where Watanabe first lives in the novel and where Murakami himself also lived as a student. The descriptions of the dorm in the novel fit the actual setting perfectly. One of the first things you'll notice is the statue of the dorm's founder right next to the flagpole where the flag-raising ceremony takes place every morning at 6am in the book.

The dorm is about a 10 minute walk north of the university. After passing the river, you'll know you're close once you start walking up a steep hill. After arriving on the compound, you may notice that the resident students you happen to pass by will greet you in Japanese. This is a unique phenomenon in central Tokyo, where ignoring strangers is somewhat of an art form. Greetings are actually considered to be part of Wakeijuku's "Three Rules," the others being following the local orders and participating in the dorm's events.

📍 1-21-2 Mejirodai, Bunkyo-ku

④ TODEN ARAKAWA LINE ● 都電荒川線

This is technically a means of transportation rather than its own destination, but due to its prominence in the novel and its uniqueness in modern-day Tokyo, this could be one of the highlights of your day. The Toden Arakawa streetcar is what Watanabe takes from Waseda to Otsuka when visiting Midori. The Waseda tram station is in a different location from the Waseda subway station, but all you have to do is walk back down the hill from Wakeijuku and you'll find it to your right on the main street, Shin-Mejiro Dori. A single ticket costs ¥170 and you want to stay on for several stops before getting off at Otsuka-Ekimae station.

Streetcars used to be much more common throughout Tokyo, but this line is one of only two left in the entire city, the other being the Tokyu Setagaya Line. This is a special transportation experience that even many lifelong Tokyo residents have never tried.

⑤ OTSUKA ● 大塚

Otsuka is the neighborhood where Midori first lives in the novel, just above the Kobayashi Bookshop. While conveniently located on the Yamanote Line, there's really not too much going on here, just as described in the book. Nevertheless, it's worth walking around for a little awhile to get a feel for the place, imagining the street where Midori's bookshop may have been. There are also plenty of restaurants around the station if you want some food or coffee.

When finished, head back to the main station and board the **JR Yamanote Line**. Ride the train in the direction of **Ueno** and get off there, or get off at Komagome first (p83) if you didn't get the chance already.

KOBE

Kobe, the bustling port city and capital of Hyogo Prefecture in Japan's Kansai region, is the town where Watanabe, Naoko and their late friend Kizuki grew up. It's also where Haruki Murakami himself was raised. Hyogo is the location of Murakami's very first two books and if you check out the first chapter of this guide book you'll find a short itinerary for it. Hyogo is also visited briefly by the protagonist in *A Wild Sheep Chase*. Watanabe does not make a visit to Kobe over the course of *Norwegian Wood* but Naoko mentions returning briefly to her parents' house before her admission to Ami Hostel. Despite Kobe often being a place from which Murakami's characters escape, the city has its own charm and is worth at least a day trip if you find yourself in Kansai.

• •

KYOTO

Kyoto Prefecture is the location of Naoko and Reiko's mental hospital, Ami Hostel. We're not given the name of its exact location but we know that it's somewhere in the mountains about an hour north of the city. Watanabe makes the trip from Tokyo to Kyoto several times throughout the novel. Kyoto City, of course, is one of Japan's most popular tourist destinations and a definite must-visit if you're travelling to the country. It's interesting to note, however, that *Norwegian Wood* is one of the few novels in which the city appears at all. And even then, Watanabe only passes through it to get to the mountains. Kyoto City has so much to see that describing all the sights could take up a book of its own. Luckily it's not too far from Kobe if you're aiming to see all the sites mentioned in this book.

6 UENO ● 上野

Ueno somehow plays a prominent role in *Norwegian Wood* despite it not appearing much at all. The neighborhood is first mentioned by Midori's ailing father at the hospital in Ochanomizu when he and Watanabe are alone together.

He mumbles something incomprehensible about a ticket, Midori and Ueno Station. When Watanabe tells this to Midori, she recalls running away to Fukushima Prefecture via Ueno Station when she was younger. It was her father who came to get her, and the train rides back were some of the few times they'd ever had a heart-to-heart conversation.

At the very end of the book, Watanabe accompanies Reiko to Ueno Station before her journey onward to Asahikawa, Hokkaido. The novel finally ends with Watanabe calling Midori from the station, referring to it as "this place that was no place."[30] But actually, Ueno is one of Tokyo's most interesting neighborhoods with plenty to do and see.

UENO PARK

Right next to the station is **Ueno Park**, one of Tokyo's most prominent public parks along with Yoyogi, Hibiya and Inokashira. This massive park used to be the site of a temple built to protect Tokyo from dark spirits. After the temple's destruction during the Boshin War, a Meiji Era civil war, the space was converted into a public park in 1873.

The park area is also home to a number of famous Tokyo museums. These include the **National Science Museum**, the **Tokyo Metropolitan Art Museum**, the **Tokyo National Museum** and the **National Museum for Western Art**. Most museums close at 17:00 or 17:30 but are open a few hours later on Friday or Saturday evenings. The admission prices are reasonable and most can be accessed for under ¥1,000. The most well-known museum in the area is probably the Tokyo National Museum, the oldest museum in Japan which houses traditional Japanese and international art throughout multiple buildings.

Tokyo National Museum

Ueno Park is also famous for **Ueno Zoo**, the oldest zoo in Japan known for its panda bears. In addition, the park is home to a number of temples and shrines, like Kaneiji Temple, Toshogu Shrine, Bentendo Temple, and Kiyomizu Kannon Temple. Most of these were all part of the main Kaneiji Temple before it got destroyed in the war.

The golden Toshogu Shrine

AROUND THE AREA

Nearby the station's Park Exit you can find the entrance to **Ameyokocho** (アメ横), one of Japan's most famous outdoor markets. The site was originally the place to buy black market goods after World War II, but today the area is a basic market where you can buy things like clothes, food and spices.

Also nearby the station is another Tokyo landmark, Shinobazu Pond. Kaneiji, the temple which occupied what is now Ueno Park, was modeled after Kyoto's Enryakuji Temple which faced Lake Biwa. Therefore, a little island was constructed in the middle of this body of water to model Eryakuji's view of the lake. Today the area around the water is a popular gathering spot for locals.

THE MURAKAMI PILGRIMAGE

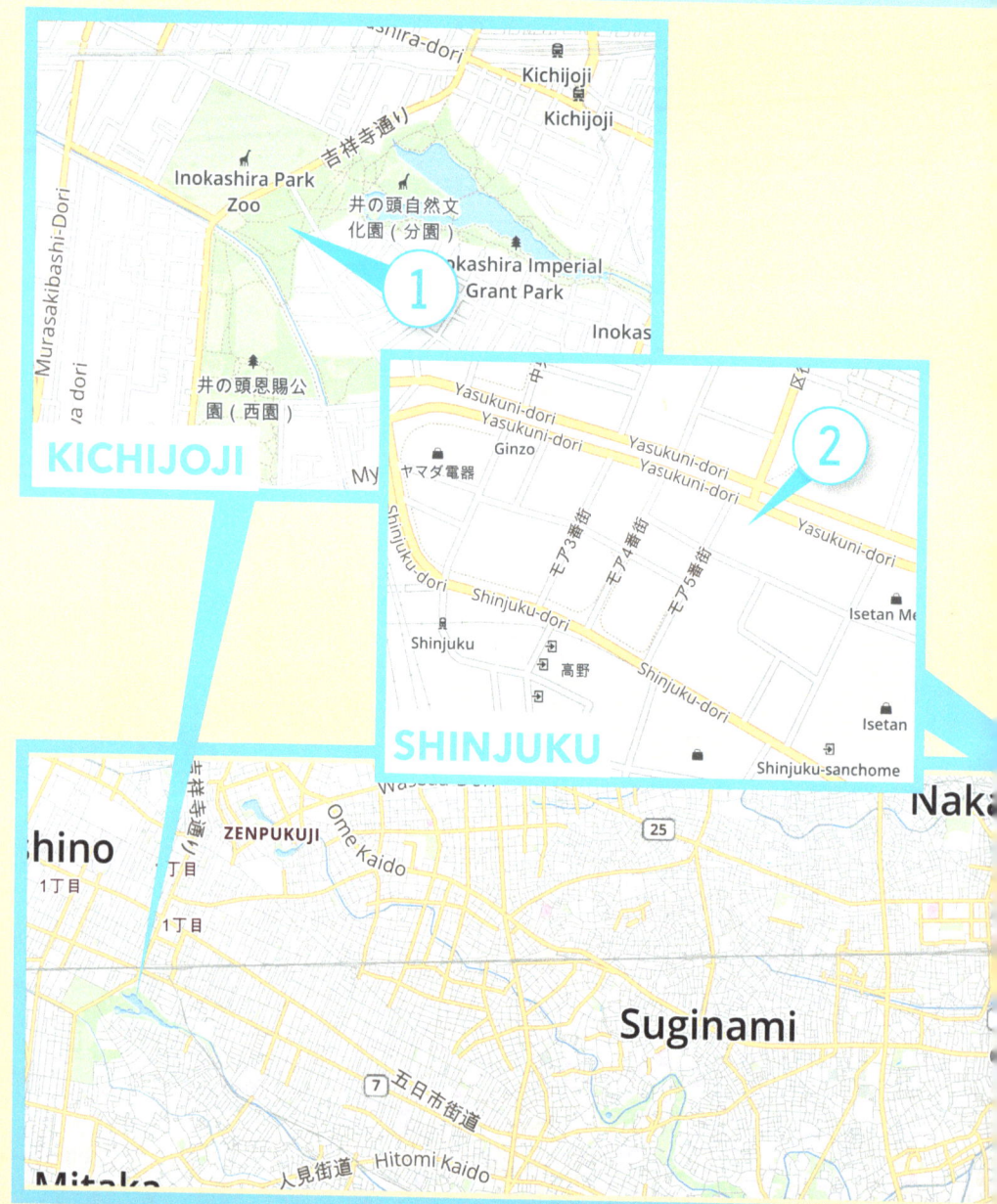

NORWEGIAN WOOD TOKYO DAY TRIP: PART 2 MAPS

NORWEGIAN WOOD GUIDE 93

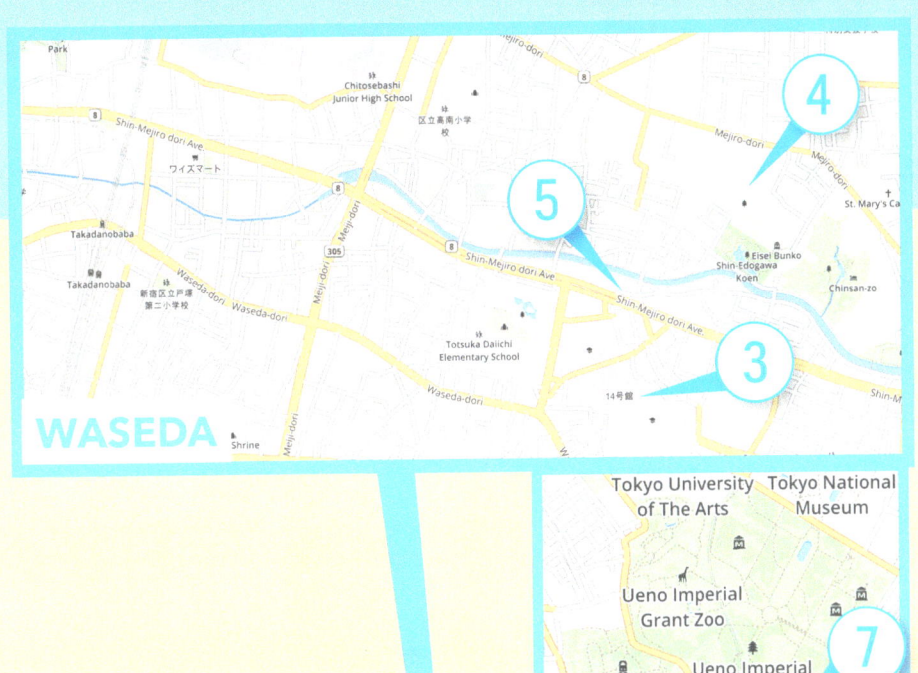

WASEDA

UENO

SOUTH OF THE BORDER, WEST OF THE SUN

South of the Border, West of the Sun almost entirely takes place in the chic neighborhood of Aoyama. It's where the protagonist Hajime lives, runs his two jazz bars and goes on lunch dates with his childhood friend Shimamoto. Luckily, Aoyama happens to be one of the most interesting areas of Tokyo and there's plenty to do and see when tracking down the locations of South of the Border, West of the Sun.

While Aoyama is the main focus of the story, other parts of the novel take place in Hajime and Shimamoto's hometown, which is not revealed to the reader. Hyogo Prefecture is a likely possibility considering it's the author's hometown and it's where a number of his other protagonists have grown up.

The mountain town of Hakone in Kanagawa Prefecture is the location of Hajime's cottage and where his final meeting with Shimamoto takes place. Also within Kanagawa is Fujisawa, the

town nearby Enoshima and Kamakura where Shimamoto moved to with her family and lived until going to university.

An important scene of the novel also takes us to Ishikawa, a prefecture on the island's western coast facing the Sea of Japan. Aside from these few other scenes, however, almost all of the action takes place in both the Shibuya and Minato Ward sections of Aoyama.

South of the Border, West of the Sun is one of just a few Murakami novels to be centered around one main neighborhood. Exploring the scenes of this novel will be a great opportunity to focus on a single area and soak up the local atmosphere. You may have also noticed that Aoyama gets mentioned often in other Murakami novels and short stories, such as *Dance, Dance, Dance* and *Kino* and you'll get the chance to see some of those locations as well.

AOYAMA DAY TOUR ITINERARY ● 青山

FEATURED IN NOVEL

RECOMMENDED

Aoyama is synonymous throughout Japan with high-end fashion, architecture, art, music and delicious food. The neighborhood caters to more of an adult crowd than neighboring Shibuya or Harajuku, but there are enough interesting things going on in the area to appeal to people of all ages.

You could easily spend an entire day hanging out in Aoyama, either by yourself or with friends and family. To see everything mentioned in this itinerary, you might want to start around noon, especially if you're interested in sticking around to hear some live jazz at night.

Bear in mind that this itinerary will involved a fair amount of backtracking. Aoyama's museums and jazz venues are all in the same area but there are a few hours in between when the museums close and when the music starts. Luckily, there are plenty of excellent restaurants and coffee shops in the area which you can learn more about by visiting **www.shibuyaguide.com**.

Overall, the Aoyama district is a pretty big one, taking up a sizable chunk of both Shibuya and Minato Wards. The only Tokyo station with Aoyama in the name is Aoyama-Itchome, but this is actually the one part of Aoyama we'll be ignoring for this day trip. The parts of the neighborhood covered in this guide are accessible from Omotesando, Gaienmae and Shibuya stations. To follow this day tour in order, let's first start at Shibuya Station and come out the East Exit.

1 MIYAMASUZAKA STREET ● 宮益坂

Miyamasuzaka is a short sloped street which connects Dogenzaka and Aoyama Boulevards on the east side of Shibuya Station. This is where Hajime first spots Shimamoto in Tokyo before he follows her uphill into an Aoyama coffee shop. Miyamasuzaka is a lively street full of restaurants and it's also the easiest way to get from JR Shibuya Station to Aoyama. Coming out of the station, do not come out the Hachiko Exit but the **East Exit** of the station's South Gate. Walk uphill and you'll soon find yourself on Aoyama Boulevard.

2 AOYAMA BOULEVARD ● 青山通り

Kinokuniya Supermarket

Aoyama Boulevard is mentioned frequently throughout Murakami's fiction, but nowhere as prominently as in *South of the Border, West of the Sun*. The **Kinokuniya supermarket**, visited by many of Murakami's protagonists can be found here. Just a bit further down the road is **Natural House** which also gets a brief mention in the book. The street is also home to a number of other famous landmarks, such as Aoyama Gakuin University, Aoyama Spiral, the Aoyama Building and United Nations University, which hosts a farmers market every weekend. Shortly before the UNU is one of Taro Okamoto's famous sculptures right outside the now defunct National Children's Castle.

"Children's Tree" by Taro Okamoto

3 ART IN AOYAMA

Aoyama is one of Tokyo's best neighborhoods for art lovers. It has a wide variety of galleries and museums for people of all tastes to appreciate. Walking in the direction away from Shibuya Station, you'll come across the building known as **Spiral** on the right hand side of Aoyama Boulevard, roughly opposite the Kinokuniya supermarket. Spiral regularly hosts free art exhibitions by well-known Japanese contemporary artists. The building itself, named after the large spiral ramp found in the back, was designed by famous Japanese architect Maki Fumihiko. Spiral is also home to the stores Spiral Market and Spiral Records and it even contains a live music venue known as Cay.

📍 5-6-23 Minamiaoyama, Minato-ku
💰 FREE
🕙 10:00 - 20:00
📅 Every day

Next let's head over to the **Taro Okamoto Memorial Museum**, not to be confused with the standalone Okamoto statue in front of the UNU. Taro Okamoto was a famous Japanese artist known for his colorful and abstract sculptures and paintings. He was a contemporary of Pablo Picasso and other members of the Surrealist movement. This museum is located where the man himself lived and worked. The interior consists of two stories and though small, contains enough content, such as the artist's former workspace, to warrant the ¥620 admission price. The second floor regularly hosts exhibitions of up-and-coming local artists to keep things fresh. Outside, you can enjoy some of Okamoto's quirky sculptures as you sip coffee in the garden. While pricey, the gift shop is also excellent.

To get to the museum from Spiral, backtrack slightly by turning left when you walk out of the building, and then make another left at the next intersection. After that, walk straight for 5 minutes and you'll find the museum nearby Blue Note.

📍  6-1-19, Minamiaoyama, Minato-ku
💰 ¥620
🕙 10:00 - 18:00
📅 Closed Tues.

SOUTH OF THE BORDER, WEST OF THE SUN GUIDE

The **Nezu Museum**, just north of the Taro Okamoto Memorial Museum, is home to an impressive collection of traditional Japanese artwork. The items once belonged to former Tobu Railway Company president Nezu Kaichiro and were made available for public display upon his death in 1940. Aside from the collection inside, the Nezu Museum is also known for its architecture, designed by Kengo Kuma in 2009, and its magnificent garden in the back. The garden, which covers a space of over 17,000 square meters, was designed in a traditional Japanese style but contains sculptures and relics from other Asian countries like China. The Nezu Museum is one of the most popular art museums in Tokyo for good reason.

If you still have some time left over, Aoyama is also home to the **Watarium** on Gaien-Nishi Dori.

- 6-5-1, Minamiaoyama, Minato-ku
- ¥1100
- 10:00 - 17:00
- Closed Mon.

AOYAMA ARCHITECTURE

A) United Nations University

B) Ikubundo Building

C) Spiral

D) Ao Building

E) Prada Aoyama

F) The Jewels of Aoyama

The Aoyama and Omotesando areas are known for being home to some of Tokyo's most stunning architecture. See the map on p106 to get a better idea of where these buildings can be found.

G) Nezu Museum

H) SunnyHills

I) Coach

J) Hugo Boss Omotesando

K) Tod's Building

L) Omotesando Hills

④ OMOTESANDO STREET ● 表参道

Omotesando (written as 'Omote Sando' in the book) is one of Tokyo's most famous streets. It's known for its upscale shopping establishments, cutting-edge architecture and fancy restaurants. Omotesando makes numerous appearances throughout Murakami's work. In *South of the Border, West of the Sun*, it's where Hajime and Shimamoto often get together for coffee. Omotesando intersects with Aoyama Boulevard, and if you keep walking all the way down it you will eventually find yourself in Harajuku. While the street is visited by many for its luxury fashion boutiques, you can still appreciate the architecture even if you're not in the mood to shop.

⑤ AOYAMA CEMETERY ● 青山霊園

In the novel, Hajime lives with his family in a four bedroom condo with a view of Aoyama Cemetery from the window. He often looks out at the cemetery to contemplate the events occurring in his life, and even does so in the book's final scene. The cemetery, or *reien* in Japanese, is a special place in Tokyo - not only for the prominent historical figures buried there, but because it's one of the few places to find peace and tranquility in the center of such a crowded city.

Aoyama Cemetery is known for being the first public cemetery in Japan. It houses the graves of shogun Yoshinobu Tokugawa, novelist Yukio Mishima and even the famous dog Hachiko. The cemetery also features a 'foreign section' dedicated to experts from Europe and the US who came to aid in Japan's development during the Meiji Era.

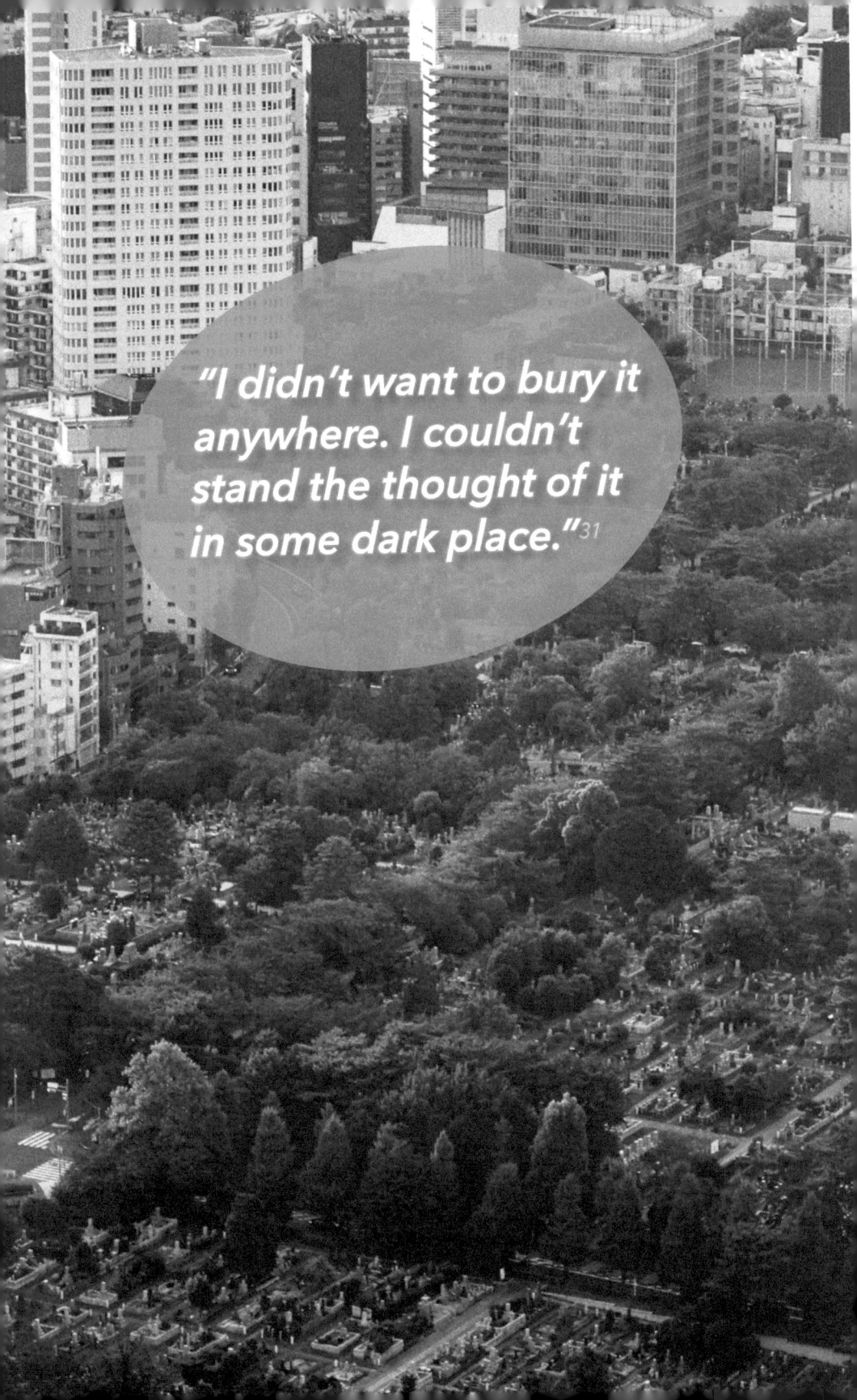
"I didn't want to bury it anywhere. I couldn't stand the thought of it in some dark place."[31]

6 BODY & SOUL

In the novel, Hajime runs two different jazz clubs, the first of which is described as "an upscale jazz bar in the basement of a brand-new building in Aoyama."[32] He then opens another bar called the Robin's Nest that features regular performances by a live jazz trio. While no venue with that name in Aoyama actually exists, the club Body & Soul shares some similarities with both of Hajime's fictional clubs. Body & Soul is located in the basement of a building nearby the Taro Okamoto Museum and it's been around since 1974, well before the novel takes place.

Of course, the main inspiration for Hajime's clubs must've come from Murakami's own experiences running the jazz club called Peter Cat, first located in Kokubunji and later in Sendagaya. In fact, Peter Cat was even featured in a 1980 edition of the magazine *Brutus*, while Hajime's bar gets mentioned by the same magazine in the novel. (To learn more about Peter Cat and its Sendagaya location, check out p67.) In addition to the memories of his own club, it's also possible that, given the venue's location, Murakami took some inspiration from Body & Soul when writing the novel.

Body & Soul typically opens from 7 with the music starting at 8, or an hour earlier on weekends. The club doesn't get the biggest international names but it's one of the best places in Tokyo to listen to seasoned local veterans. The venue happens to be very close to the much more well-known Blue Note, but Body & Soul provides a more intimate atmosphere for a more reasonable price. Entrance typically costs ¥3,800 per person, or more on special nights.

- 6-13-9, Minamiaoyama, Minato-ku
- From ¥3800
- 18:00, 19:00
- Closed Mon.

ISHIKAWA

Ishikawa is a rural prefecture which faces the Sea of Japan. After Shimamoto requests that Hajime take her to a river in a valley that flows into the sea, Hajime recalls visiting such a river in Ishikawa. The two head off there with Haijme still unsure of Shimamoto's motives. On a cold day, the pair walk along the river and this is where Shimamoto chooses to release her dead baby's ashes. The two don't spend much time in Ishikawa and in the novel we're not given much of a feel for the place, but the prefecture is best known for its stunning scenery, preserved samurai districts and traditional villages. This may be an ideal destination for those looking to experience "old Japan" away from the crowds.

• •

HAKONE

Hakone is the scenic resort town in Kanagawa Prefecture where Hajime and his family keep their summer cottage. And of course, this is where Hajime and Shimamoto finally spend the night together before she disappears from his life forever. Hakone is known for its hot springs and for being one of the best places to view Mt. Fuji. The town is accessible via a direct Odakyu train from Shinjuku, with the fastest train getting there in 85 minutes for around ¥2,000. Once in town you can get around by local train and cable car up the mountains. The main activities in the area are hiking, looking at the views around the lake and relaxing in an onsen.

THE MURAKAMI PILGRIMAGE

AOYAMA MAP

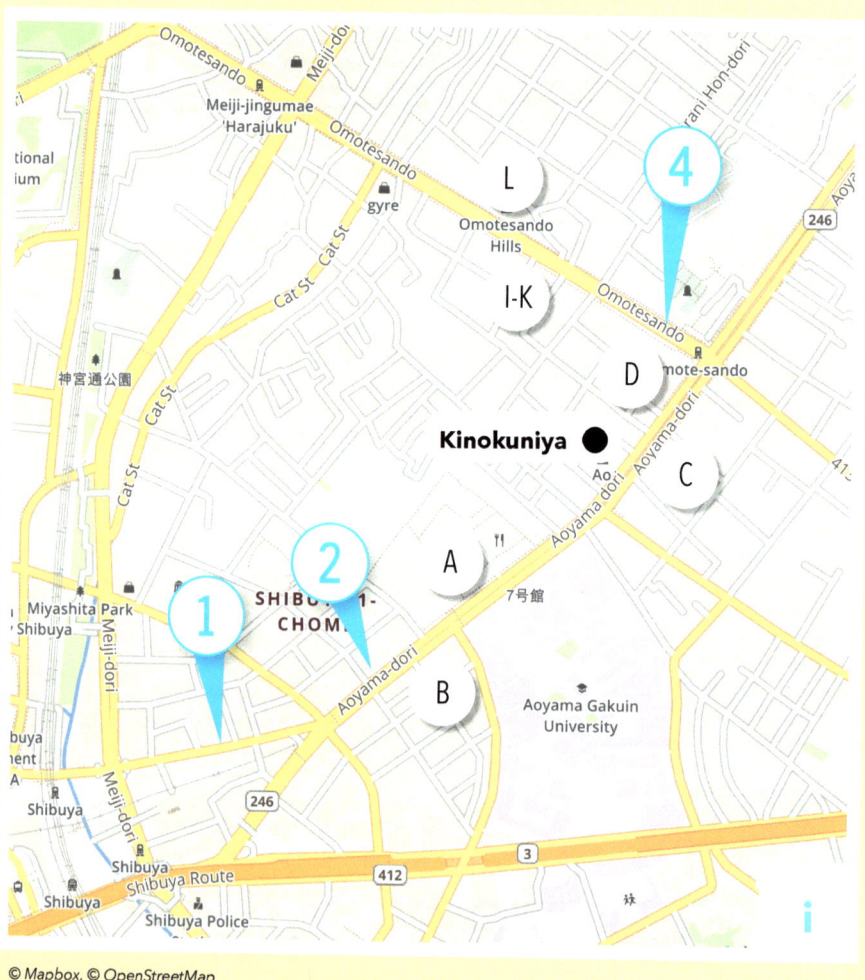

SOUTH OF THE BORDER, WEST OF THE SUN GUIDE

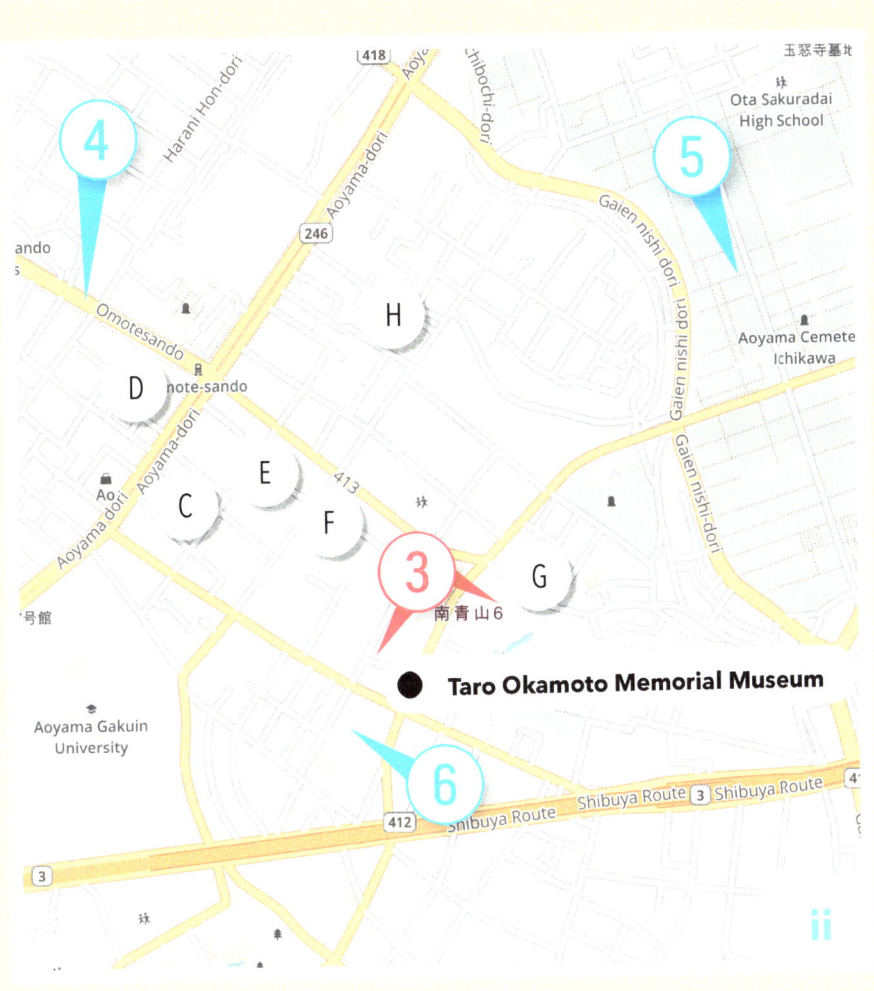

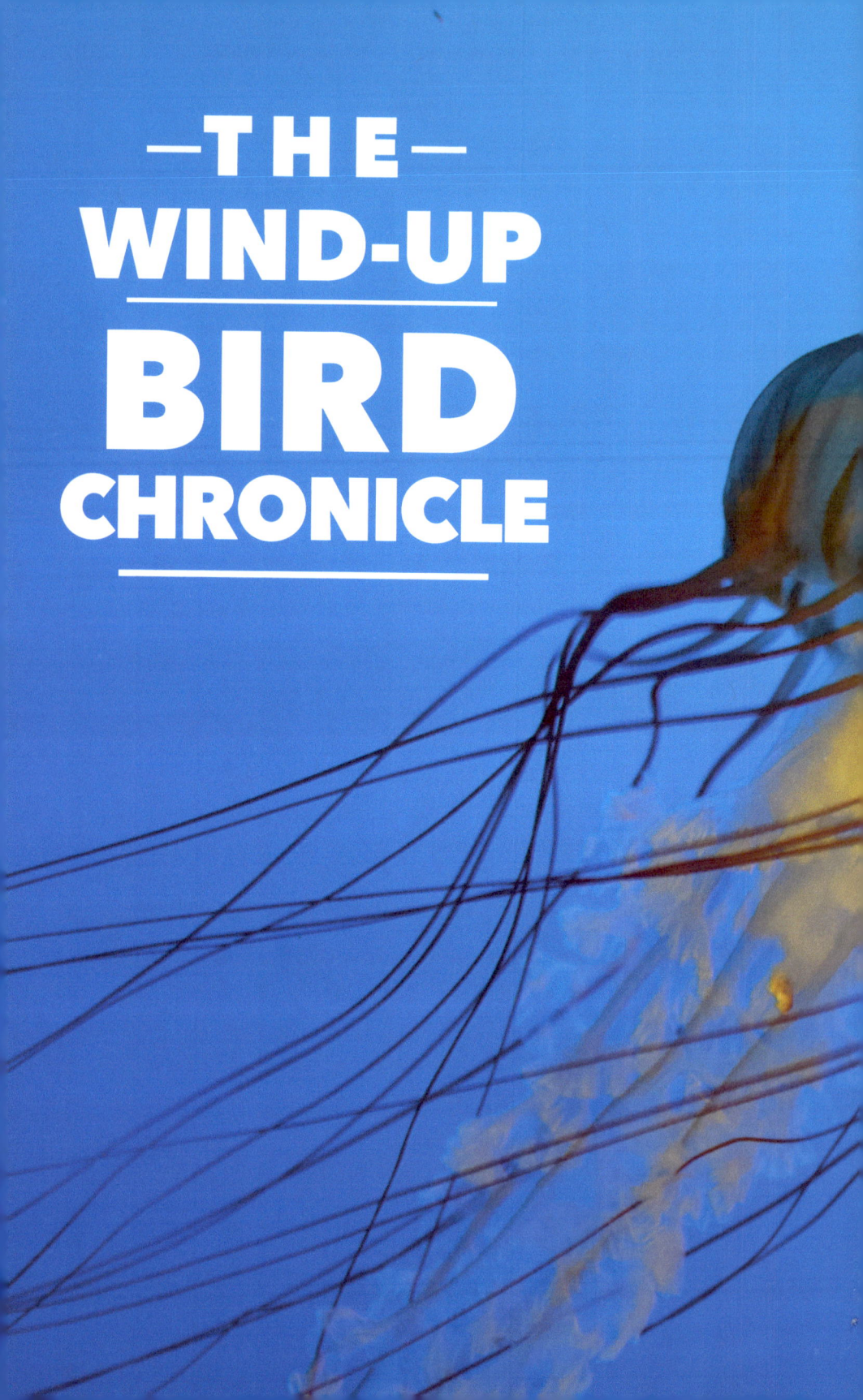

> "The real world is in a much darker and deeper place than this, and most of it is occupied by jellyfish and things. We just happen to forget all that."[33]

The Wind-Up Bird Chronicle is considered by many to be Haruki Murakami's masterpiece. Originally published in the mid 1990's, the novel is set in 1984 Tokyo (and possibly in the same universe as 1Q84). The story is told from the point of view of protagonist Toru Okada, who goes from searching for his missing cat to searching for his missing wife. Over the course of the book he has many strange experiences, such as entering another dimension via a portal at the bottom of a well and then doing an unusual job for a woman he meets in Shinjuku.

Toru's adventures take place entirely in Tokyo, although the lengthy monologues of Lieutenant Mamiya bring us to wartime Manchuria, Mongolia and the Soviet Union. Though a pretty common theme throughout Murakami's work, wartime Manchuria and Siberia play especially large roles in this novel.

Toru Okada and his wife live in a house in Setagaya Ward. We know that "The house was pretty far from the nearest station on the Odakyu Line,"[34] but this station is never named. Some likely candidates would be the neighborhoods of Umegaoka, Gotokuji or Kyodo. Considering how Gotokuji Temple is the birthplace of the beckoning cat figurine and that the novel begins with a cat gone missing, this would be the best area to visit when seeking out the place that Toru, Kumiko and May Kasahara call home.

Many of Tokyo's prominent neighborhoods make appearances throughout the novel, especially Shinjuku. No visit to Tokyo would be complete without a walk around Shinjuku, the area where Toru goes to stare at people's faces after the strange mark appears on his cheek. For days he sits outside the station and people watches. Eventually he moves on to "a small, tiled plaza outside a glass high-rise,"[35] which is where he first meets Nutmeg.

If you like people watching, Shinjuku is one of the best places to do it. Another great place to people watch is Ginza, the part of town where Toru and May go to survey male balding patterns. This eastern Tokyo neighborhood is famous for its high-end shopping and restaurants. Even if those things don't appeal to you, there are plenty of coffee shops where you can look down at the crowds and try conducting a survey of your own.

The swank Akasaka neighborhood in Minato Ward, also featured prominently in many other Murakami novels, again makes an appearance in *The Wind-Up Bird Chronicle*. This is where Nutmeg and Cinnamon have their office under the name of one of their mysterious shell companies, and it's also where Kumiko's brother Noboru Wataya has his own office. Fortunately, there are some interesting sites around the area, such as Hie Shrine, which make the trip to Akasaka worth the visit.

Other Tokyo neighborhoods which make minor appearances in the novel include Shinagawa, where Toru meets Malta Kano at the hotel lounge, and Ueno, where Toru and Kumiko went on their first date. Toru and his wife also mention having previously lived in Koenji, a fact that should be of special interest to those who've read both this book and *1Q84*.

Exploring the scenes of *The Wind-Up Bird Chronicle*, one of Murakami's most well-loved books, also takes us to some of Tokyo's most well-loved neighborhoods. Just don't expect to be coming across any mysterious abandoned wells that easily!

TOKYO DAY TRIP ITINERARY ● 東京

The Shinjuku skyline as seen from Roppongi

FEATURED IN NOVEL

RECOMMENDED

This day tour will take us from the east to the far west of what most consider to be "central Tokyo." There are four main neighborhoods you'll get to explore: Ginza, Akasaka, Shinjuku and Setagaya Ward. Bear in mind that it's entirely possible to see the sites in the reverse order if that's more convenient for you. If you're going to be starting later in the afternoon then beginning in Setagaya Ward instead of Ginza would be ideal, as the temple there closes at 18:00.

By the end of the day you'll have seen most of the significant locations from the novel, which can be accomplished with three separate train rides. You'll be boarding the red-colored Marunouchi Subway line twice and an Odakyu train once. None of these, unfortunately, are compatible with a JR rail pass.

If you're trying to squeeze in some shopping as you visit the sites from the novel, you should also factor this in to how you pace your day. Ginza is known for its high-end stores while Shinjuku has a little something for everyone.

As far as restaurants and nightlife go, Shinjuku and Setagaya are going to be kinder to those on a budget than Ginza or Akasaka.

① GINZA ● 銀座

"For the next three hours, we sat by the subway entrance by the Wako Building, counting the bald-headed men who passed by."[36]

Ginza first rose to prominence in the late 1800's during the Meiji Era, when, after a devastating fire, the government decided to rebuild the area in the Western style that was becoming popular at the time. Traditional Japanese construction was replaced with brick buildings and the area was promoted as an upscale shopping mecca. This reputation still persists today, and Ginza remains famous for its luxurious clothing and jewelry shops.

In *The Wind-Up Bird Chronicle*, Toru and his 15-year-old neighbor May Kasahara work part-time in Ginza, surveying the baldness of the men they see walk by for a wig company. They divide everyone into three categories according to level of baldness - A, B and C. They base their operations in front of the Wako Building, one of Ginza's iconic department stores. Ginza is also where both Toru's uncle and the ill-fated Kojiro Miyawaki ran their restaurants.

Other Ginza landmarks include the Sony Building, a multi storied Sony showroom, the Mitsukoshi department store and the Kabukiza Theatre. Despite being one of the more famous Tokyo neighborhoods, there's really not a whole lot to do in Ginza other than shopping and a stroll down Chuo Dori. And of course, Ginza is perfect for people watching.

Now let's board a **Marunouchi Line** train and head West to **Tameike-Sanno**.

2 HIE SHRINE ● 日枝神社

In the novel, Akasaka is where Cinnamon, Nutmeg and even Noboru Wataya have their office. Akasaka is a classy entertainment district in Minato Ward, full of nice hotels and restaurants. One of its famous landmarks in Hie Shrine, that, while not mentioned in the book, is certainly worth a visit if you're in the area. Coming from **Tameike-Sanno Station** on the Marunouchi Line, you can walk there in just about 4 minutes.

Hie Shrine derives its name from Mount Hie in Shiga Prefecture (north of Kyoto) and is said to enshrine the guardian deity of that mountain - one of many such shrines throughout Japan. This particular shrine was a favorite of the Shogun Ieyasu Tokugawa and he considered its deity a protector of the capital.

The shrine's current incarnation was built in 1659 after the previous shrine got burnt down in a fire. More recently, other parts of the shrine had to be constructed after the firebombing of World War II.

One of the highlights of the shrine is its dozens of red *torii* gates, reminiscent of Kyoto's Fushimi Inari Shrine. Every year in June, the shrine is host to the popular Sanno Matsuri, one of Tokyo's premier festivals.

2-10-5 Nagatacho, Minato
FREE
5:00 - 18:00
Every day

3 AROUND AKASAKA ● 赤坂

Akasaka 2-chome

In the 'newspaper clipping' segment of the novel, a reporter who is attempting to learn more about the mysterious new owners of the Miyawaki residence trace the purchase to a company called "Akasaka Research" - highly likely a shell company owned by Nutmeg Akasaka. The location is described as being in the **Akasaka 2-chome** district, which happens to be across the street from Hie Shrine. All we know about this office is that it's located in a small condo building, which is fairly easy to picture as you walk around 2-chome's narrow streets.

We're given a more adequate description of Nutmeg and Cinnamon's main office, Akasaka Fashion Design, and the narrator mentions at one point that it's located near **Akasaka-Mitsuke** station. There happens to be a building nearby the station in the 4-chome district that fits the description in the novel well. **Dear City Akasaka** is at the top of a sloped street with many bars and restaurants, just as Toru describes, and there's even a travel agency located on the first floor. The only difference being that the entrance of Dear City is more elaborate than described in the book.

Overall, Akasaka covers a large area and this part of the neighborhood mostly comes alive at night. Regardless of when you visit, however, this is a good place to grab some food or coffee. Now let's get back on the **Marunouchi Subway** line, this time from Akasaka-Mitsuke station, and ride three stops to **Shinjuku Gyoen Mae** station.

📍 4-2-3, Akasaka, Minato-ku

4 SHINJUKU GYOEN ● 新宿御苑

Shinjuku Gyoen, also known as 'Imperial Garden,' was built in 1772 and remains one of Tokyo's largest and most popular parks to this day. Like many other landmarks in Tokyo, much of it was destroyed during the second world war and the current incarnation of the garden was reconstructed in the 1950's.

Shinjuku Gyoen is mentioned only a couple of times in *The Wind-Up Bird Chronicle*. It's where Toru and Kumiko went on one of their early dates and it's where Toru first asked her whether or not she was single. Creta Kano also mentions going to Gyoen to sit and cry as she tried to cope with her stint as a prostitute after her attempted suicide. Other than that, Gyoen does not play a significant role in the plot of the novel but it's one of Shinjuku's most interesting spots and is surely worth a visit if you're in the area.

- 11 Naitomachi, Shinjuku
- ¥200
- 9:00 - 18:30
- Closed Mon.

Gyoen charges a ¥200 entrance fee and closes at 16:30. The park is especially popular in spring, as it's one of the best places in Tokyo to see cherry blossoms. Gyoen is massive with a circumference of 3.5 kilometers, so be sure to come out at the correct exit, the 'Shinjuku Gate.' When finished, head over to the main Shinjuku Station.

5 SHINJUKU STA. WEST EXIT ● 新宿駅西口

Toru Okada says that when he first decided to people watch, he "spent two full hours sitting on the low brick wall that ran along the edge of the raised flower bed outside Shinjuku Station."[37] Outside of the west exit there are a number of low brick barriers but it's unclear exactly where Toru takes a seat to watch the people going by. There are adequate places outside of the east exit to sit, but considering Toru used the Odakyu Line to commute, it's more likely he came out the West Exit. Apparently there used to be an old bus terminal outside of this exit so it's likely the area's undergone some transformations since the '90's when the book was written. Though today there aren't many places outside this exit to sit and people watch, the elevated walkway offers some good views of the area and the masses of commuters down below.

After giving up on the low brick wall, Toru then moves on to the **skyscraper district**, also on the west side of the station. Here he finds a plaza outside of a tall building which is much less crowded. Shinjuku contains many of Tokyo's famous skyscrapers, most of which can be accessed by walking to the underground part of Shinjuku station and then following a passageway with signs indicating where the skyscrapers are. Of course, the area can be reached above ground but the geography and layout of the roads can be confusing.

Outside the West Exit

Toru mentions the building having an observation deck, which means that the iconic Metropolitan Government Building (Tocho), Shinjuku Center Building or the NS Building are all potential candidates. It was while sitting in this district that Toru first meets Nutmeg who couldn't help but notice the strange mark on his face.

When finished in Shinjuku, head back over to the West exit and into the **Odakyu Line** area. Go down to the platforms number 8 and 9, which are underground, and board a local train headed west to **Gotokuji Station** (¥190).

SHINJUKU SKYSCRAPERS

Tokyo is such a massive, sprawling city that its skyline lacks a single distinctive shape, especially when compared to places like Manhattan or Hong Kong. When people think of the 'Tokyo Skyline,' they're usually picturing Shinjuku. The neighborhood is home to some of Tokyo's most impressive and imposing tall structures which can be fascinating to observe from either close up or at a distance.

The most iconic of these tall structures would have to be the Tocho, or Tokyo Metropolitan Government Building (pictured below), the base of Tokyo's prefectural government. Designed by Kenzo Tange in 1990, the famous structure splits into two towers at the 33rd floor. Another easily recognizable Tokyo building is the Mode Gakuen Cocoon Tower, completed in 2008. As its name suggests, this building is shaped like a cocoon and adds a unique flavor to Shinjuku's largely rectangular skyline.

The Shinjuku Park Tower is another landmark easily recognizable from a distance, as it's actually comprised of three different towers, the tallest standing 52 stories tall. This complex houses the Park Hyatt Tokyo which many know thanks to its role in Sophia Coppola's film *Lost in Translation*.

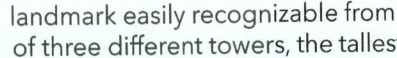

This only scratches the surface of impressive structures in Shinjuku. During your time in the area, a walk around the skyscraper district is a must for those with an interest in architecture. And, as mentioned in the novel, the area has a number of places to sit and relax. Who knows - you might even get approached by a stranger in a pink dress and sunglasses.

6 SETAGAYA WARD ● 世田谷区

"The Alley" refurbished?

We know that Toru lives somewhere in Setagaya Ward nearby an Odakyu Line station, but we don't know exactly where. "The house [...] was in a quiet residential neighborhood, and it had its own small yard,"[38] Toru explains. Setagaya is one of the largest wards in Tokyo and it also has the highest population, making guessing Toru's exact location difficult. We know that he lives near a library and a pool, both of which can be found near **Umegaoka** and **Kyodo** stations. However, let's visit the **Gotokuji** neighborhood, situated right in between the other two. Gotokuji is home to a famous temple that could be considered somewhat relevant to the novel, even if it doesn't make an appearance in the story.

7 GOTOKUJI ● 豪徳寺

Gotokuji is a quiet residential neighborhood and home to the famous temple of the same name. The station area has a number of restaurants and cafes around if you want to stop and eat first, as the main temple is at least a 10 minute walk (or longer if you get lost.) On both sides of the station you can spot laundromats - one of Toru's most frequently visited locations in the novel.

Gotokuji Temple, the main attraction in the area, is considered to be the birthplace of the 'maneki neko,' or beckoning cat. You may have noticed these cute cat figurines before in the windows of Japanese or even Chinese restaurants. They're considered to be good luck charms, especially popular among merchants.

Legend has it that during the Edo period, a feudal lord from Shiga Prefecture and his group of samurai warriors were passing by a run-down temple when visiting Tokyo. They noticed a cat which seemed to be beckoning them to follow it to the temple grounds. The monk of the temple then allowed them

Despite its large size, the temple is not very easy to find. There aren't many signs along the way to point you in the right direction and your phone's GPS system may get you somewhere close to the temple but not to the correct entrance. There are a number of different entrances but most of them seem to be closed. The main one is actually on the south side, facing the opposite direction from the station. Check the address that's linked in the QR code below to help you find it.

to rest there just before a large thunderstorm suddenly raged throughout the city. The lord, named Naotaka, felt grateful for his chance encounter with both the cat and the monk and decided he would fund the refurbishment and expansion of the temple. The original maneki neko figurine is said to be modeled after the temple's cat.

This is not the only maneki neko folktale, however. Other places such as Imado Shrine in Taito Ward also claim to be the origin of the beckoning cat, but Gotokuji is probably the most well-known.

It's unknown whether or not Murakami had this temple in mind when choosing a location for the home of Toru and Kumiko. But considering how *The Wind-Up Bird Chronicle* begins with the story of a missing cat, Gotokuji seems like the natural area to imagine the scenes of the novel. Another interesting connection is that Toru's neighborhood is mentioned as being in the 2-chome area of an unnamed district of Setagaya Ward. Gotokuji Temple, it turns out, is located in the 2-chome section of Gotokuji, Setagaya.

- 2-24-7 Gotokuji, Setagaya-ku
- FREE
- 6:00 - 18:00
- Everyday

TOKYO DAY TRIP MAP

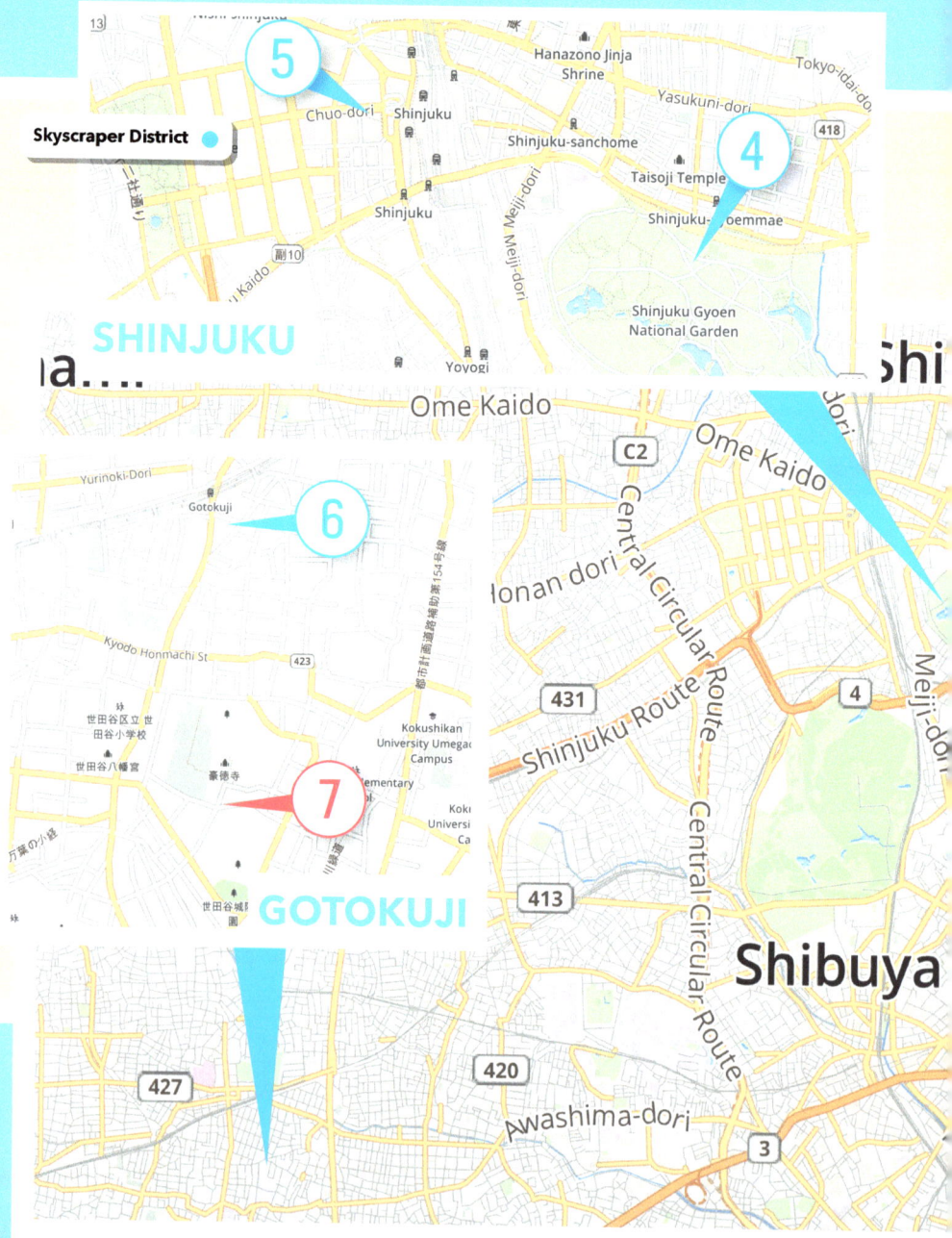

THE WIND-UP BIRD CHRONICLE GUIDE

UENO

Ueno Zoo is where Toru and Kumiko went on their first date. None of the characters visit Ueno again at the time the story takes place, but the zoo and its jellyfish are referenced several times throughout the novel. Ueno Zoo is Japan's oldest zoo and can be found inside of Ueno Park, surrounded by many of Japan's most famous museums. The Ueno area is also known for its Ameyokocho traditional market. If you've read *Norwegian Wood* you can find out more details about the Ueno area on p90.

SHINAGAWA

Toru first meets Malta Kano in person in a tearoom in the Pacific Hotel near Shinagawa Station. He visits the same spot again later in the book to speak with both Malta and Noboru Wataya. The Pacific Hotel was closed in 2010 but the Keikyu Ex Inn Shinagawa currently operates in the same building. Many people pass through Shinagawa when riding the Shinkansen, so you may want to make a brief stop in the area before boarding your train. Nearby you can also find the Nikon Museum and the Hara Museum of Contemporary Art.

SPUTNIK SWEET HEART

スプートニク
の恋人

"We're both looking at the same moon, in the same world. We're connected to reality by the same line. All I have to do is quietly draw it towards me."39

Benzaiten Shrine, Inokashira Park

Sputnik Sweetheart, narrated by the elementary school teacher simply known as K, revolves around a young woman named Sumire and her infatuation with her older boss Miu. Business obligations take the pair to Europe and they eventually decide to relax for awhile on a small, unnamed Greek island. After Sumire suddenly disappears into thin air, our narrator gets a call from a concerned Miu. He agrees to take a spontaneous trip to Greece to track down his friend Sumire, with whom he's madly in love.

This is one of the few Murakami novels where most of the significant points of the plot take place abroad. Aside from the small Greek island that the main characters visit, we also learn about a previous experience Miu had in a Swiss town that caused her hair to turn white. As this guide book only covers locations within Japan, we're not left with so many places to visit from this novel. There are, however, a few Tokyo locations mentioned in the book that make for an interesting day trip.

In the beginning of the novel Sumire is living in the fashionable neighborhood of Kichijoji which is known for its thrift stores and Inokashira Park. Partway through the book she ends up moving to another popular neighborhood, Yoyogi-Uehara, just next to Yoyogi Park.

The narrator lives in the less hip neighborhood of Kunitachi, which is about 20 or 30 minutes west of Shinjuku on the JR Chuo line. This is a suburban area where many universities are located. It's not a place most people living in other parts of Tokyo would normally visit, but the area does have a unique charm of its own. At the end of the novel, K goes to help his student Carrot, who's also the son of his girlfriend, in nearby Tachikawa. For fans of the book, this is a good opportunity to explore some western Tokyo neighborhoods that most visitors to Tokyo don't bother to go and see.

WEST TOKYO DAY TRIP ITINERARY

When most people think of Tokyo, they picture the crowded, urban neighborhoods within what makes up the city's 23 wards. But Tokyo is even much bigger than that. To the west of the urban center is the "Tama district" which consists of an additional 26 cities. It is within the Tama district that most of the Japan portion of *Sputnik Sweetheart* takes place.

There generally isn't much reason to visit the Tama district as a tourist or even as a resident living in central Tokyo. Most of the towns in this area are sleepy residential districts with few attractions. While perhaps not the most exciting region to explore, visiting the Western suburbs gives one a glimpse of another one of Tokyo's many faces. By the end of this day tour you'll get a better sense of just how massive and varied Tokyo really is. Even the author himself lived here for a time, which is why the western suburbs often appear in his work.

For this day trip we will solely be using the JR Chuo/Sobu line, which can easily be accessed from Shinjuku or Tokyo Station.

ⓘ

The JR Chuo/Sobu Line is an incredibly long train line which goes from east to west, traversing all of Tokyo. It's one of the main lines connecting the central 23 wards with the western suburbs, or Tama area. Discussing this train line can get confusing because it's actually made up of a couple of different lines which run along the same route. The Sobu Line is the green-colored local line that stops at every station in central Tokyo and goes all the way east to Chiba. The red-colored Chuo Main Line will take you from Tokyo Station all the way west to the mountain town of Takao. All of the destinations on this itinerary can be accessed by the red-colored Chuo Main Line, although Kichijoji is also accessible via both the red and green lines.

1 KICHIJOJI ● 吉祥寺

Kichijoji, about a 15 minute train ride west of Shinjuku, often tops polls and surveys of Tokyoites' most desirable neighborhoods to live in. This Musashino City neighborhood has a little bit of everything - an abundance of restaurants, shopping and nightlife, all while maintaining a more laid back vibe than that of central Tokyo. Kichijoji is also widely visited for Inokashira Park, widely considered to be one of the nicest parks in the region.

In *Sputnik Sweetheart*, Sumire lives in a one-room apartment nearby the park before eventually moving to Yoyogi-Uehara. In Kichijoji, she spends much of her time sitting on a park bench reading her favorite books, sometimes going into a nearby cafe when it rains. Without a phone of her own, the park's public telephone booth is what she uses to call K, typically at all sorts of weird hours of the night. The book was written in the late '90's but today Inokashira Park is still exactly as described in the novel. Despite phone booths becoming a much less common sight in the 21st century, you can still visit Inokashira to make a call should the need arise.

"I had to trudge out in the pitch dark all the way over here clutching this telephone card I got as a present at my cousin's wedding. With a photo on it of the happy couple holding hands. Can you imagine how depressing that is?"[40]

K and Sumire often sit at her favorite bench in the park to talk about life. Benches, you may have noticed, are a rare sight in Tokyo overall, but Inokashira Park has plenty.

📍 1-18-31 Kodenyama, Musashino-shi

Inokashira Park is the focus of a famous Japanese urban legend which states that any couple who rides a rowing boat together in the pond is doomed to break up. This is supposedly due to the jealous goddess Benzaiten, the main deity of the shrine within the park (pictured p128). Nevertheless, it's still common to see couples riding boats together around the park.

Kichijoji is a popular place to shop, especially for used clothing. Fashionable thrift stores line the narrow street leading up to the park. There's also plenty to shop for in the nearby shopping arcade, as well as the area right around the station.

When you're done exploring Kichijoji, head back to the **JR Chuo Line** and continue travelling west.

ⓘ Inokashira Park is also home to the **Ghibli Museum**, located on the Mitaka side of the park. An advance ticket for a specific day and time is required for entry. Tickets can be purchased at Lawson convenience stores or from designated vendors abroad.

② KOKUBUNJI ● 国分寺

Kokubunji, just two stops west of Kichijoji via the JR Chuo Commuter Rapid Train (or 5 stops on a slower train), is not mentioned in *Sputnik Sweetheart* but it may be of special interest for Murakami fans. The neighborhood is where the author once lived and ran his original jazz bar, Peter Cat. Kokubunji is also where Naoko first lives in *Norwegian Wood*. In the short story チーズ・ケーキのような形をした僕の貧乏, which has yet to be translated into English, the author recalls a time when he was flat broke, living on a strange triangular piece of land shaped like a cheesecake. Surrounded by train tracks on all three sides, he and his wife were bombarded daily by the sound of the trains, eventually gaining some relief thanks to a transport worker strike.[41] This triangle can be found just next to Nishi-Kokubunji Station.

Kokubunji is famous for the To-nogayato garden, a scenic traditional Japanese garden established in the early 1900's. Sugatami Pond is another scenic spot for bird watching.

Sugatami Pond

GREECE

Sputnik Sweetheart is one of the only novels by Haruki Murakami in which most of the significant events of the story take place outside of Japan. Sumire and Miu travel to a tiny unnamed island that's a short ferry ride from the island of Rhodes, near the Turkish border. Sumire eventually disappears and K travels to the island on short notice to look for her. If you've read the short story compilation *Blind Willow, Sleeping Woman*, you'll notice similarities between the novel and the story *Man-Eating Cats*. In that story, a Japanese couple, both of whom are cheating on their spouses, escape Japan and end up on a small Greek island. This story also touches on the subject of a sudden disappearance.[42]

3 KUNITACHI ● 国立

University Boulevard

Kunitachi is where the narrator K lives in the novel. Sumire even uses the local Kunitachi area code, 0425, as the combination for her suitcase. The suburb is known for its many universities and University Boulevard, the main street outside the station, is where you'll want to visit. The long boulevard is lined with lush greenery on each side and there are many cozy cafes to choose from. In the novel, K and Sumire have their favorite coffee shop somewhere near the station, possibly near the bar where K stops in for a Canadian Club on the rocks. Aside from a stroll down the main street, there's not a whole lot to do in Kunitachi, but it's a refreshing change of scenery from the concrete jungle of central Tokyo.

If you're coming straight from Kichijoji, the ride costs ¥220 and could take between 17 and 24 minutes depending on which train you board.

K's Apartment?

4 TACHIKAWA ● 立川

Tachikawa is where, at the end of the novel, K is called upon to meet with the supermarket security guard after his student Carrot (who's also the son of his girlfriend) gets caught shoplifting. Tachikawa is just one stop west of Kunitachi but the atmosphere is much more lively. It feels more like its own city than merely a suburb of Tokyo. There's not much here in the way of sightseeing, but there are plenty of places to dine before making your return to the city.

CENTRAL TOKYO LOCATIONS

SHINJUKU

K visits Shinjuku a couple of time throughout the course of the novel. During one trip he does some book shopping at the famous Kinokuniya book store which can be found outside the station's JR East Exit. Afterwards he goes to a movie and then out for some beer.

HARAJUKU

Miu has her small office in an apartment building somewhere near Meiji Shrine. In the first half of the novel, Sumire commutes from Kichijoji to Harajuku, where she writes letters and checks messages throughout the day. Meiji Shrine, nearby Yoyogi Park, is a must-see for all Tokyo visitors.

YOYOGI-UEHARA

Sumire eventually leaves her tiny one-bedroom apartment in Kichijoji and moves to the fashionable Yoyogi-Uehara neighborhood. This neighborhood is a good place to enjoy a nice meal followed by a drink at an intimate local bar.

AKASAKA

Sumire and Miu first meet in Akasaka at wedding in a fancy hotel, of which there are many in the district. Sumire also has another office here aside from the one in Harajuku. Akasaka is featured prominently in several other Murakami novels such as *Dance, Dance, Dance* and *The Wind-Up Bird Chronicle*.

These locations only play minor roles in the story but they are all more convenient to access than Tokyo's outer suburbs. If you want to make a little mini tour of these places, you could take the following route :

1. Starting in Shinjuku, ride the JR Yamanote Line to Harajuku.
2. After exploring Harajuku, board the Chiyoda line from Meiji-Jingumae Sta.
3. Ride to Yoyogi-Uehara and when finished board the Chiyoda Line again.
4. Take the train directly to Akasaka.

WEST TOKYO MAPS

SPUTNIK SWEETHEART GUIDE

KAFKA ON THE SHORE
海辺のカフカ

Murakami's 2002 novel *Kafka on the Shore* takes us from Tokyo to the island of Shikoku as we follow the journeys of 15-year-old runaway Kafka Tamura and the odd couple of Nakata and Hoshino.

Shikoku is the smallest of Japan's four main islands and it's also the least developed. The island now has three large bridges linking it to Honshu, but until only a couple of decades ago Shikoku was only accessible by boat or plane. To this day, Shikoku still lacks a bullet train route, but this is part of what gives the island its charm. In recent years, more and more foreign travelers have been taking an interest in Shikoku, hoping to catch a glimpse of "old Japan."

The island of Shikoku consists of 4 prefectures but a large majority of the novel takes place in Kagawa, the smallest prefecture not just of Shikoku but of the entire country. Within Kagawa, much of the action takes place in the prefectural capital of Takamatsu. However, not too many specific neighborhoods or landmarks are mentioned aside from the station and the bridge.

One part of the novel seems to reveal an exact address - when Colonel Sanders tells Hoshino and Nakata to visit the apartment in "Takamatsu Park Heights 3-chome."[43] But alas, no such neighborhood called Park Heights really exists. Part of the fun of your visit will be wandering around the city and imagining buildings that could have been Sakura's apartment or Hoshino and Nakata's private getaway.

One of the most important settings of the story, the Komura Memorial Library, is fictional, but the inspiration for it does exist in the city of Sakaide, about 15 minutes from Takamatsu by train. Sakaide is also home to what was likely the inspiration for the shrine with the entrance stone - a shrine with a fascinating backstory of its own, and well worth a visit for both Murakami fans and Japanese ghost story enthusiasts.

Unlike most of Murakami's other novels, only a few locations in Tokyo play any significant role in the story. The neighborhood of Nogata in Nakano-ku, where both Kafka and Nakata are from, can easily be accessed from the Shinjuku area.

"When you step into a labyrinth outside you, at the same time you're stepping into the labyrinth inside. Most definitely a risky business."[44]

KAGAWA DAY TRIP ITINERARIES

KAGAWA
Population: *1 million*
Region: *Shikoku*
Capital: *Takamatsu*

PART 1: TAKAMATSU DAY TOUR ITINERARY ● 高松

ACCOMMODATION

Like Kafka did, basing yourself in a business hotel by Takamatsu Station would be ideal. This also gives you easy access to the port. Somewhere nearby Sakaide or Marugame Stations would also be convenient, but as decent rental apartments are still hard to come by in the area, Takamatsu hotels are likely your best bet.

GETTING THERE

Most major airports in Japan have flights to Takamatsu and some budget carriers can get you there from Tokyo for under ¥10,000. Coming from Kansai, you can take a Jumbo Ferry from Kobe for around ¥2,000 and arrive in Takamatsu in about 4 hours. Shikoku is not linked to the shinkansen. Okayama, the closest station linked to the bullet train, is about 1 hour away from Takamatsu. You may also want to consider a bus ride, just as Kafka did in the novel.

Takamatsu, a city of approximately half a million people, can easily be traversed on foot. If you're not the walking type, the city also has a number of bus and train lines. The Kotoden Line, accessible from just next to the castle, can take you to the central shopping district and to Ritsurin Koen. The trains from the main station, on the other hand, mainly connect to neighboring cities. Over the course of this day trip we'll even get to experience a ferry ride across the inland sea.

Let's start the day off at the main station where Kafka first arrives after his long bus ride from Tokyo. By the end of the day we'll have visited the main areas mentioned in the novel as well as the city's best sightseeing attractions.

FEATURED IN NOVEL

RECOMMENDED

TAKAMATSU STA. & UDON SHOP

"At the station I pop into the first little diner that catches my eye, and eat my fill of udon."[45]

Takamatsu Station is mentioned many times throughout the novel and during your time in Kagawa you will be using it often. After Kafka first arrives at the station's bus terminal he tries 'Sanuki udon' for the first time. Murakami does not reveal the name of the restaurant, but there are a couple of udon restaurants outside the station and **Ajishou** is likely the one that Kafka visits.

The self-serve style of this particular restaurant is not ideal for beginners, as you need to assemble the ingredients by yourself. There's another udon restaurant down the road you may want to try instead and you can use the reference below to help you place your order.

- 5-15 Nishinomarucho
- 5:00 - 15:00
- Closed Sat.

🍴 SANUKI UDON

If there's one thing Kagawa Prefecture is known for, it's udon noodles. The locals take enormous pride in their local delicacy, or 'Sanuki udon' as they call it.

But what makes Sanuki udon special? The noodles are characterized by their square shape and chewy texture, made from a special variety of local wheat. During your visit you can't miss the opportunity to try some local udon at least a couple of times, if not once a day!

Be aware that the language barrier can make ordering a simple bowl of noodles a challenge. At most restaurants you need to go up with your tray and verbalize your order.

Here's a brief guide to some of the most common udon varieties you'll encounter:

- かけうどん (*kake udon*): the most basic type of udon with no special toppings
- ぶっかけうどん (*bukkake udon*): cold udon served with fish stock broth
- 釜玉うどん (*kamatama udon*): a local Kagawa favorite, served with raw egg on top of the noodles.
- 温玉うどん (*ontama udon*): similar to *kamatama* but with a soft-boiled egg instead of raw.
- 肉うどん (*niku udon*): warm noodles topped with beef
- カレーうどん (*karee udon*): udon served in curry rather than traditional broth
- ざるうどん (*zaru udon*): cold noodles served on a bamboo mat along with a separate bowl of dipping sauce
- きつねうどん (*kitsune udon*): udon noodles topped with sweet-tasting fried tofu

② TAKAMATSU CASTLE ● 高松穂

Takamatsu Castle, originally constructed in 1590, is just across from the main station area and well worth a visit. Much of the castle was destroyed during the Meiji Era but the park, moat and garden which still remain are all in great condition. You can also climb up one of the former castle walls to enjoy the view. On a nice day you could easily spend 30 - 40 minutes here and the ¥200 entrance fee is very reasonable.

- 2-1 Tamamocho, Takamatsu
- ¥200
- Early am - eve. (varies by month)
- Every day

ⓘ For ¥500 you can ride a boat around the moat for 30 minutes

3 OGIJIMA ● 男木島

Ogijima lighthouse

View from the boat

Ogijima is a small island easily accessible from Takamatsu by **ferry**. It takes around 40 minutes one way to get there, and spending 2 - 3 hours on the island should be plenty. Megijima, only 20 minutes away on the same ferry, is another option you may want to consider, but that island is much larger and will demand more of your time. Ogijima's size makes it perfect for an afternoon excursion and the island's landmarks are all entirely accessible on foot. Though Ogijima is not mentioned in the novel, it should be of special interest to Murakami fans due to it being known as a 'cat island.' But understand that how many you see around town will depend on the season and the weather.

To get to Ogijima, head north from the castle toward the water until you arrive at the **floating piers**. There are a number of ticket gates, but look out for these "男木島" characters. The ferry schedule changes depending on the season so it's best to do an online search for the 'Ogijima ferry timetable' in advance so you can plan your day accordingly.

Every 3 years, Ogijima hosts part of the Triennielle Art Festival along with neighboring islands in the Seto Inland Sea. There are still some permanent installations on display even if you visit during the off-season, but there are certain restaurants and cafes that will only be open when the festival is going on.

After checking out the art, head over to the lighthouse which takes about 30 minutes on foot. You'll also find a beach but swimming is discouraged. From just behind the lighthouse area you have access to some great hiking trails that offer fantastic views of the seto inland sea. Just be sure to make it back to the port in time for the return ferry.

④ RITSURIN KOEN ● 栗林公園

- 1-20-16, Ritsurincho
- ¥410
- Early am - evening
- Every day

Ritsurin Koen is the most popular sightseeing spot in Takamatsu and is an absolute must for any visitors to the region. The gardens were constructed during the early Edo period and even feature a tea room which is still used for tea ceremonies to this day.

From the main station area it's a straight 30 minute walk. Or, just hop on a **Kotoden Kotohira Line** train at Takamatsu-chikko station (next to the castle) to get there in three stops. The gardens close as late as 21:00 during summer or as early as 17:00 in winter. Anticipate spending at least an hour in the gardens, if not more, and with so much to see, you may even be tempted to visit Ritsurin Koen more than once during your stay.

TOKUSHIMA

Tokushima City, the capital of Kagawa's neighboring prefecture of the same name, is where Nakata and Hoshino first arrive in Shikoku from Kobe after crossing the Naruto Bridge.

"What a wonderful bridge. Nakata's never seen such a huge one before."[46]

Although no exact locations are mentioned, try to follow in Hoshino's footsteps by wandering around the city and visiting a sushi restaurant for "dinner and beer." Tokushima is also where Nakata undergoes his first long sleep marathon. The city is most famous for its massive Awa-Odori traditional dance festival held every year in August.

5 TAKAMATSU SHOPPING ARCADE

If you still have energy leftover, take a stroll through Takamatsu's sprawling shopping arcade and have some dinner or an evening coffee. Coming from Ritsurin Koen, it's possible to walk through the arcade to get all the way back to the station area. Within the shopping arcade you can find all sorts of clothing stores, book shops, restaurants and coffee houses.

In the novel, this is where Hoshino goes shopping for some clothes but has a difficult time finding his trademark aloha shirt. And it's also where he stumbles upon the old-fashioned coffee shop that's run by the classical music-loving former government minister. If you search carefully, you might just find something like it.

Shikoku's 88 Temple Pilgrimage

During your time in Shikoku, you'll likely come across people dressed all in white, walking through the countryside from temple to temple. These are pilgrims participating in Shikoku's 88 temple pilgrimage, inspired by Kagawa native and the founder of Shingon Buddhism, Kobo Daishi. Also known as Kukai, Kobo Daishi is said to have established or renovated these temples as part of a public works project in the early 9th century.

While some people today use modern transportation methods to complete the route, others still prefer to traverse Shikoku on foot, which can take an entire month or two to complete.

KOCHI

Kochi is Shikoku's largest prefecture. In *Kafka on the Shore*, of course, it's where Kafka goes to stay in the cabin in the woods. We know that this location is 2.5 hours from Takamatsu by car, but given Kochi's size and abundance of mountains, the cabin could be just about anywhere. While searching for the cabin and special library in the forest may be futile, Kochi Prefecture is worth a visit if you have the time. The capital, Kochi city, features an impressive coastline and has amazing sushi.

• •

YAMANASHI

Yamanashi Prefecture is where Nakata lived as a child during World War II. Before we're even introduced to adult Nakata of Nakano Ward, we learn of Nakata's childhood incident via U.S. government classified documents. It was in the Yamanashi mountains that Nakata passed out, entered a coma and woke up a completely different person.

Yamanashi is a few hours west of Tokyo and the prefecture is perhaps best known for being one of the jurisdictions to host Mount Fuji. The area is also famous for its lakes and skiing in winter.

TAKAMATSU MAPS

© Mapbox, © OpenStreetMap

KAFKA ON THE SHORE GUIDE

PART 2: SAKAIDE DAY TOUR ITINERARY ● 坂出

The entrance to the Kamada Museum

As mentioned, neither the Komura Memorial Library nor the shrine with the entrance stone are actual places, but the inspiration for both can be found in the nearby city of Sakaide. In fact, the character Kafka mentions that the train ride to the unnamed town with the library takes about 20 minutes from Takamatsu, which is about how long it really takes to get to Sakaide.

The shrine with the entrance stone, on the other hand, is described as being in central Takamatsu in the novel, but its real-life inspiration, Takaya Shrine, is in a much less convenient location.

This is going to be a long day and unless you have a rental car, be prepared for a lot of walking.

To start your journey, head to Takamatsu Station and board a JR train bound for Okayama, Kotohira or Kanonji. These will all stop at **Sakaide Station**.

The JR Marine Liner will take you there in 14 minutes and costs ¥970, while the JR Dosan Line Rapid Sunport arrives in 18 minutes for ¥450. Just avoid the local Yosan Line which takes over half an hour.

Our first destination, the Kamada Museum, is only a several minute walk from Sakaide Station and after the visit we'll be boarding a local train.

The Seto-Ohashi bridge as seen from Sakaide

① KAMADA MUSEUM ● 鎌田共済会郷土博物

The Kamada Museum no longer contains books but the premise of the museum is similar to that of the fictional Komura Memorial Library. Although the building was originally opened as a library in 1918, it was eventually converted into a museum. It was started by Katsutaro Kamada, a wealthy businessman who founded the Kamada Soy Sauce company and who was also a member of the House of Peers.

The museum displays calligraphy, information on Kagawa's history, and just like the Komura Library, poems. Unfortunately, only a small percentage of the information has been translated into English so it's not exactly the most riveting experience for non-native Japanese speakers. Perhaps more interesting than the main building itself is the garden area just next door.

In the novel, Kafka describes the area around the library as having a gravel path, manicured bushes and trees, and a small pond - all of which can be found in the garden next to the museum, known as "Kofuen." Furthermore, the library is described as a traditional Japanese house, and the building in the garden, called the "Suishoukaku," fits the description of the Komura Library even better than the Kamada Museum. The Suishoukaku, in fact, was used as a second residence by the Kamada family and there's even a smaller building next to it which one could imagine as the guest room where Kafka sleeps.

It seems likely that Murakami used the fundamental idea of the main Kamada Museum as the basis for the Komura Library, but took visual inspiration from the old house in the garden instead.

⌖ 1-1-24, Honmachi, Sakaide
⧖ FREE
🕘 9:30 - 16:30
📅 Closed Mon. and public holidays

② TAKAYA SHRINE ● 高屋神社

Takaya Shrine is one of the most off-the-beaten-path locations mentioned in this guide book and if you haven't rented a car, expect to walk for one hour each way. But the long journey makes it all the more satisfying when you finally get to glimpse the actual entrance stone. In the story, of course, the shrine with the entrance stone is located in the city of Takamatsu, but this quiet shrine on the outskirts of Sakaide is very likely the real inspiration for it (see p154).

From Sakaide Station, board a Takamatsu-bound local train and get off after only two stops at **Kamogawa Station** (鴨川). Coming out of the station's single exit, walk straight for about 10 minutes. Eventually, you'll see a hospital on your left, after which you want to turn left onto the main road. From this point on you have about 50 minutes of walking until you reach the shrine.

Keep walking down the main road along the river. A half hour or so later, make a right and then a left and you'll now be walking down the smaller parallel road in the same direction. Eventually, you'll get to another relatively large road (180) where you want to make a right. From here, just walk straight for 5 or 6 minutes until you see the shrine gate.

Takaya Shrine shares a space with a temple called Kanonji, which you can find on the left. The area with the stone is located up the staircase to the right.

Some minor differences aside, this stone generally fits the description of the one Murakami describes. The shrine, like the one in the novel, is surrounded by many trees and there are even hiking trails just beyond it.

 878 Takayacho, Sakaide

③ KANDANI SHRINE ● 神谷神社

On the way back to the station you many want to check out another famous local shrine called Kandani (alternatively pronounced "Kamidani"). Kandani Shrine is designated as a national treasure and the inner shrine structure is considered to be the oldest in all of Japan, built way back in the 13th century.

The shrine is only a slight detour on the way back and there's also a bathroom and rest area in the back should you need it.

📍 *5502 Kandanicho, Sakaide*

SAKAIDE UDON SHOPS

Non-Japanese Haruki Murakami fans may or may not be aware that the author has put out a lot more work than what's been translated into English. Most of these books are non-fiction travel memoirs. In the memoir *Sanuki: Chou Deep Udon Kikou* (讃岐・超ディープうどん紀行), Murakami writes of his travels through Kagawa and mentions five different udon restaurants, two of them being in Sakaide.[47]

In fact, the two noodle shops in Sakaide, Gamou (蒲生) and Yamashita (山下), are both located near Kamogawa Station, but in the opposite direction of the shrine. Gamou is about a 15 minute walk east of the station while Yamashita is another five minutes beyond that. Both places close in the afternoon so if you're interested you may want to get your fill before making the long trek to Takaya.

Gamou

📍 *420-3 Kamocho, Sakaide, Kagawa*
🕐 *8:30 - 14:00*
📅 *Closed Sun.*

Yamashita

📍 *147-1 Kamocho, Sakaide, Kagawa*
🕐 *8:00 - 15:00*
📅 *Closed Mon.*

EMPEROR SUTOKU AND THE BLOOD SHRINE

Emperor Sutoku, who ruled Japan from 1123 to 1142, was forced to abdicate the throne at the request of his father, Emperor Toba. Despite being a competent emperor, it was suspected that Sutoku was not actually Toba's biological son - one of the likely reasons behind their rivalry. It's speculated that Sutoku's real father was another former emperor named Shirakawa, who was actually Toba's own grandfather! Shirakawa himself had abdicated the throne voluntarily after the death of his wife, but he still held considerable influence over the imperial court for the remainder of his life. It was Shirakawa that pressured Toba to hand over power to Sutoku in 1123.

After Shirakawa passed away, Toba insisted that his 3-year-old son and Sutoku's half-brother, Narihito, take over the throne instead of Sutoku's own son. But when Narihito died at a young age, Sutoku was shocked again when Toba chose another younger sibling, Go-Shirakawa, to rule. Shortly afterward, Toba passed away and Sutoku took the opportunity to stage an uprising against Go-Shirakawa, known as the Hogen Insurrection. Sutoku's uprising failed, however, and he was banished to Sanuki Province (present-day Kagawa) for the remainder of his life. Sutoku would then shave his head and become a Buddhist monk.

The imperial court of Go-Shirakawa suspected that Sutoku had been placing curses on them from a distance (in fact, Narihito's mother believed that her son died as a result of Sutoku's curse). In the story called "Shiramine" which is part of the 1776 classic *Tales of Moonlight and Rain*, the ghost of Sutoku describes his deep longing for Kyoto and how he'd been sending over manuscripts in hopes that some small part of him could remain there.[48] But Go-Shirakawa and his court rejected all of Sutoku's letters out of fear of a curse, thus angering Sutoku even more.

When Sutoku finally died 8 years after his arrival in Sanuki, Go-Shirakawa would not even allow for a special funeral to take place. Sutoku's caretakers were stuck waiting with the casket for weeks, unsure of what to do with the body. Legend has it that when the coffin was finally being taken for cremation, a large thunderstorm began, forcing the caretakers to run for cover. Having left the coffin on some stones outside, they were shocked upon their return to find the stones soaked in blood. One of these stones, the likely inspiration for *Kafka on the Shore*'s entrance stone, is currently enshrined in Takaya Shrine today.

Even after Sutoku's death, all sorts of unfortunate events surrounded Go-Shirakawa and his successors, most of which were blamed on the former emperor's vengeful spirit. In hopes of calming the angry ghost, a mausoleum was constructed at the mountain of Shiramine in Sakaide and Sutoku was finally enshrined as a god, or *kami*, at Shiramine Shrine in Kyoto during the Meiji Era.

It's worth pointing out that Ueda Akinari's classic book *Tales of Moonlight and Rain* is mentioned a couple of times in *Kafka on the Shore*. At one point in the library, Oshima tells Kafka about the story "The Chrysanthemum Pledge" and Colonel Sanders even quotes a line from the book to Hoshino on their way to the shrine. The book, known as *Ugetsu Monogatari* in Japanese, contains nine classic ghost stories. "Shiramine," which feature's a conversation between Sutoku's ghost and a monk named Saigyou, is the very first story to appear. While the "Shiramine" short story itself is not mentioned anywhere in *Kafka on the Shore*, the multiple references to *Tales of Moonlight and Rain* provides us with a big hint that Murakami took inspiration from Emperor Sutoku's story when writing the book. Furthermore, Murakami also mentions visiting Sakaide in one of his non-fiction travel memoirs.

Takaya Shrine is nicknamed "*chi-no-miya*," or the "blood shrine," which is also likely inspiration for the scene where Kafka wakes up in the shrine covered in blood. Blood is a recurring theme and important symbol throughout the novel. Fortunately, one can visit Takaya Shrine today in peace and walk out unscathed.

SAKAIDE MAPS

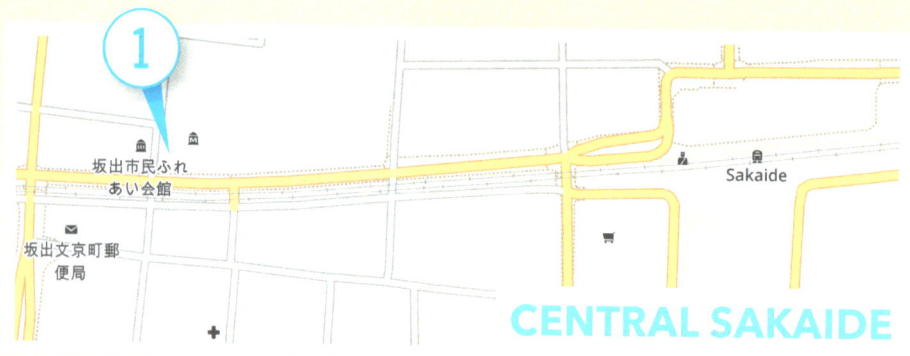

CENTRAL SAKAIDE

SAKAIDE AREA

© Mapbox, © OpenStreetMap

KAFKA ON THE SHORE GUIDE

SIGHTSEEING AROUND KAGAWA

KOMPIRA-SAN • こんぴらさん

Konpira-san, located in the town of Kotohira, is a famous shrine situated above 1,000 steps. The shrine was built in dedication to sailors and is still visited today by tourists and pilgrims from around Japan. If you want a real challenge, there's an even higher shrine another 500 steps past the main hall.

ZENTSUJI • 善通寺

Zentsuji is the hometown of Kukai, one of Japan's most important historical and religious figures. Kukai founded the Shingon branch of Buddhism and also started Shikoku's 88 temple pilgrimage route. Zentsuji Temple, number 75 on the route, was built by Kukai himself.

KAFKA ON THE SHORE GUIDE

NAOSHIMA • 直島

Naoshima, an island in the Seto-Inland Sea, attracts art lovers from all around the world. The island itself is gorgeous and there are plenty of free art works to enjoy outdoors. Unfortunately, many feel that the museums which Naoshima is mainly known for are somewhat of a rip-off. Naoshima can be accessed in about 1 hour from Takamatsu Port.

YASHIMA • 屋島

Yashima is the site of a famous historical battle and today the mountain mainly attracts visitors for its views. A bus to the top departs hourly from Yashima Station or you can hike up if you so desire. The summit also features an aquarium and a tranquil temple, which is number 84 on Shikoku's pilgrimage route.

MARUGAME • 丸亀

Marugame hosts one of the more impressive castles of Kagawa. It's a steep incline to the top, but once you get there you can see some excellent views of the town and mountains nearby. The castles closes at 16:30 and costs a couple hundred yen to enter. The city is also home to the Genichiro-Inokuma Museum of Contemporary Art.

NOGATA, TOKYO

The significant scenes of *Kafka on the Shore* which take place in Tokyo mostly all happen in the neighborhood of Nogata. Nogata is a pretty typical residential neighborhood. Around the station you'll find a number of shops and restaurants but beyond that there's nothing but houses. The area can be reached by riding the **Seibu-Shinjuku Line** from either Takadanobaba Station or Seibu-Shinjuku (a separate, yet nearby station from regular Shinjuku). Nogata is also an easy walk from Koenji.

While we don't know exactly where Kafka lives, we do know that it's about a 15 minute walk away from where Nakata likes to hang out and talk to cats. At the beginning of Nakata's story, it's mentioned that he's speaking to the black cat Otsuka in a vacant lot in the **2-chome district**. We also learn that the other vacant lot where the cats often get captured by Johnny Walker is just down the road, meaning that this place is likely located in 2-chome as well. In Japan, neighborhoods are divided into even smaller, numbered areas referred to as *cho*'s. This is how addresses are determined as opposed to street names.

The 2-chome area of Nogata is about a 5 or 6 minute walk south from the station. On the way there you can also catch a glimpse of the library that's mentioned briefly in the novel. The area hardly features anything other than houses, but it can be fun to wander around in, imagining the early scenes of the novel.

The area around the station is also mentioned a couple of times, and this is where the mackerel fall from the sky the day after Nakata kills Johnny Walker. Just outside of the station you can also find the *koban*, or police box, where Nakata goes to confess his murder to the unconvinced young officer.

Nogata's main shopping street

Top left: *In front of the main koban*

Top right: *2-chome residential street*

Bottom left: *Vacant playground*

Bottom right: *2-chome vacant lot*

KAFKA ON THE SHORE GUIDE

© Mapbox, © OpenStreetMap

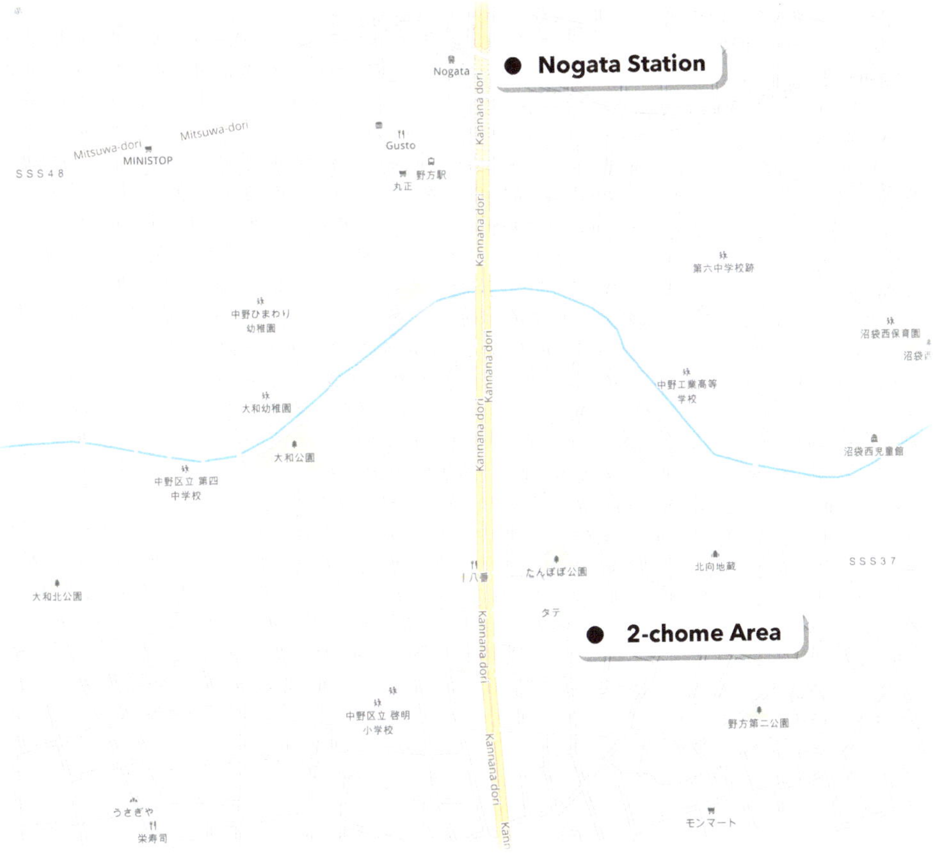

● Nogata Station

● 2-chome Area

AFTER DARK

―――

アフターダーク

"The district plays by its own rules at a time like this."[49]

SHIBU

FEATURED IN NOVEL

RECOMMENDED

The 2004 novel *After Dark* centers entirely around one single neighborhood: Shibuya. The novel is told from the perspective of a floating camera which phases in and out of different scenes, merely observing the characters and their actions over the course of a single night. We're taken into the worlds of 19-year-old Mari, young jazz musician Takahashi and love hotel manager Kaoru as they try to cope with a stressful night in Shibuya's red-light district.

After Dark may not be Murakami's most popular novel but Shibuya will always be one of Tokyo's most popular neighborhoods. And fortunately, all the major locations of the book are easy to find and entirely possible to explore during a night out. The exact Denny's and Skylark (now Gusto) restaurants that the protagonists visit are luckily a relatively easy walk from the love hotel district where Kaoru runs the fictional 'Alphaville.'

Outside of Shibuya, the scenes with Mari's older sister Eri mostly take place in their home in the southern residential district of Hiyoshi. Takahashi lives in Koenji, a neighborhood which plays a prominent role in *1Q84*, but it's only mentioned briefly and none of the scenes in *After Dark* take place there.

SHIBUYA NIGHT TOUR ITINERARY ● 渋谷

The term "Shibuya" can refer to either the area around Shibuya Station or to the entire Shibuya Ward, which encompasses neighborhoods like Harajuku, Ebisu and Sendagaya. The scenes from *After Dark* take place in the former - the central Shibuya area near the station.

The neighborhood is known as a shopping and entertainment mecca, and it's typically Shibuya where Japan's latest fashion trends are born. The area also features Tokyo's hottest nightlife and you can find many of the cities most well-known night clubs all within a short walking distance from each other.

You'd have a difficult time finding a documentary or news clip about Tokyo that *doesn't* show a clip of Shibuya's scramble crossing, the largest crosswalk in the world. Just next to it is another iconic landmark, the statue of the loyal dog Hachiko that waited daily by the station well after his owner's death. As these two popular spots are just outside the station, you can check them out first before starting this itinerary.

After some shopping and walking around the area, head uphill to the district's Dogenzaka area. You'll know you've arrived when everything around you seems to be a love hotel. Remember, trains in Tokyo stop a little past midnight and don't start again until around 5am.

① SHIBUYA SHOPPING & CULTURE

While Shibuya is famous for its nightlife, there's also plenty to do and explore before the sun goes down. Nearly anything you can think of can be purchased at department stores like **Tokyu Hands**, **Loft** or **Parco**. The Udagawacho section of Shibuya is a vinyl lover's paradise, with notable shops including **Disk Union**, **Technique** and **RECOfan**. **Tower Records Shibuya**, considered the largest music retail store in the world, is where Takahashi once ran into Eri Asai before they went to a nearby cafe for a long chat.

If you're into fashion, stopping at the iconic **109** building is a must. And Shibuya is one of Tokyo's best places for both international and Japanese cuisine, with something for just about every taste and price range. Be sure to check out **shibuyaguide.com** for more info on specific stores and restaurants.

Center-Gai is one of Tokyo's most crowded and liveliest streets. Here you can find a mix of everything: fast-food chains, shoe shops, late-night izakayas, a hookah bar and a whole lot more. The street is incredibly popular with young people.

Dogenzaka could be considered Shibuya's main street. In fact, it's even considered its own district. This is where you'll find the 109 department store and numerous night clubs and izakayas. Reaching the top of the hill, you'll soon find yourself in Maruyamacho where much of the novel takes place.

Bunkamura, which translates to "Culture Village," is a large complex which contains a concert hall, theater, cinema, museum and art gallery, run by the same firm that operates 109 and Tokyu Hands. You can see concerts or an opera at Orchard Hall or view exhibitions by artists as such as Picasso at the gallery.

② MARUYAMACHO ● 円山町

A countless number of love hotels can be found in the appropriately named 'Love Hotel Hill,' an area that overlaps parts of both the Dogenzaka and Maruyamacho districts. Love hotels, of course, are accommodations which offer short stays and which protect their customers' anonymity. *After Dark*'s Alphaville is fictional, but it's easy to picture what it looks like after a brief walk through Maruyamacho.

Love hotels aren't the only thing here, of course. You can find restaurants, nightclubs and bars very similar to the one which Kaoru and Mari visit after the incident at the hotel.

This area is considered a red-light district but it's safe to walk around in at night.

③ DENNY'S ● デニーズ

The central Shibuya area has two Denny's restaurants - one in Nanpeidai and the other in Jinnan. It's most likely that Mari and Takahashi meet in the latter, about a ten minute walk from Love Hotel Hill. Visitors from abroad may be surprised to see that Denny's in Japan specializes in steaks rather than breakfast combo meals.

📍 *1-16-3 Jinnan, Shibuya*
🕐 *24 hrs.*
📅 *Every day*

④ GUSTO (SKYLARK) ● ガスト

After Mari and Kaoru have a drink in the small Maruyamacho bar, Mari goes to a Skylark restaurant to continue reading her book. Skylark restaurants are now known as Gusto, and there are many of them around Shibuya. There are a few very close to the love hotel area, but this Gusto in Jinnan is a likely candidate because it's so close to the park that Mari later visits with Takahashi. This restaurant is also just one block down from the Denny's on Koen-dori.

☕ Chains like Denny's, Gusto, Royal Host, etc. are referred to as "family restaurants." All of these restaurants offer 'drink bars' which mean you can enjoy unlimited coffee, tea or juice for as long as you like - perfect for when you need to kill some time or like Mari, just want somewhere to sit and read for awhile.

📍 1-15-3 Jinnan, Shibuya
🕐 7:00 - 3:00
📅 Every day

⑤ KITADANI PARK ● 北谷公園

📍 1-7-5 Jinnan, Shibuya

"The park is a small one on a narrow strip of land in the middle of the city... Mercury lamps illuminate the area. Trees stretch their dark branches overhead, and below there are dense shrubberies."[50]

There aren't many small parks in central Shibuya, which leaves Kitadani Park in Jinnan as the likely candidate. Kitadani fits the description in the novel well, or at least it did at one time. The park used to have a slide and a swingset but they've since been paved over to make way for a little parking lot. The benches still remain, and it's not uncommon to see at least a couple of people hanging around at strange hours of the night.

6 SHIBUYA MUSIC & NIGHTLIFE

A DJ Bar just across from Kitadani Park

Shibuya is one of the main centers for nightlife in Tokyo and many of the city's most famous music venues can be found here. Even on a weeknight you should be able to find something going on past sunrise.

In addition to its well-known clubs, the Shibuya area has many small, intimate "DJ bars" that are typically tucked away on quiet backstreets. One such as example is Koara, (yes, that's how they spell it) which just happens to be right across from Kitadani Park. Koara is fairly representative of most DJ bars in Tokyo, i.e., it's open until morning on the weekdays and only has a 30-40 person capac-

A Dogenzaka backstreet famous for live music

ity. On good nights these small venues with their friendly and passionate patrons can be some of the funnest places to party in Tokyo. But on other nights, you may find yourself in a half-empty bar with a completely dead dancefloor. Considering how even these small venues often charge a cover to enter, exploring Japan's underground music scene often comes with some financial risk.

A popular venue for seeing live bands

Shibuya, of course, is also home to many of the country's mega clubs, most of which can be found around the Maruyamacho love hotel district or by Dogenzaka street. There's also a particular backstreet which runs in between Bunkamura and Dogenzaka that's home to many popular venues like O-East and Duo Music Exchange. There are also quite a few smaller venues in this area as well.

The turnover rate for music venues in Tokyo is high and clubs are coming and going all of the time, so always try to look up what's going on online before going out for the night. If you're just looking to have a drink, you shouldn't have to walk far before finding a bar somewhere in the area.

SHIBUYA MAPS

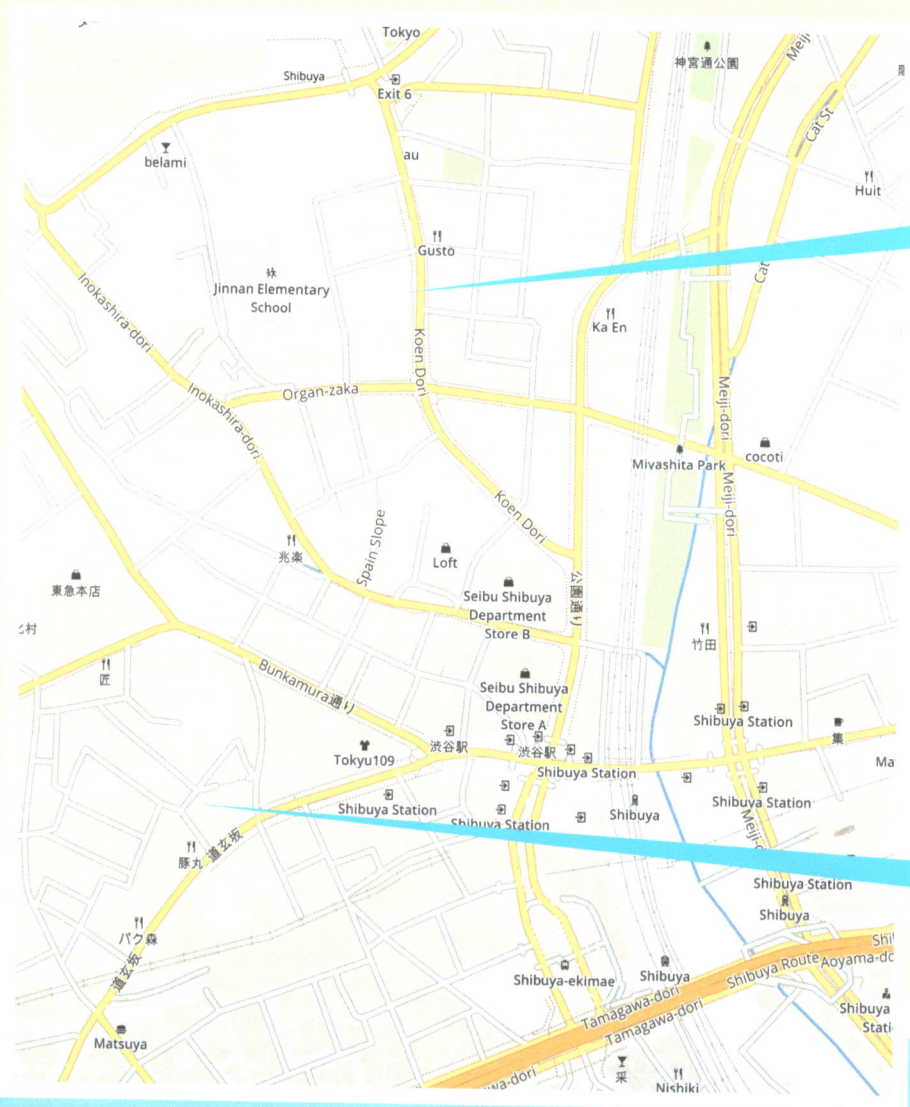

© Mapbox, © OpenStreetMap

> "Please remember: things are not what they seem."[51]

Sunset over the Metropolitan Expressway Number 3

1 Q84 is one of Haruki Murakami's most ambitious projects. It's a massive novel which spans over 3 books in its original Japanese form, and the story takes us to a myriad of locations all over Japan's Kanto region. There are scenes taking place as far west as the suburb of Ome to the far eastern town of Chikura, Chiba. Despite being such a massive book, the story jumps from location to location so often that it's harder for the reader to get a feel for any particular neighborhood or setting compared to other Murakami works. One major exception, however, would be the neighborhood of Koenji.

Tengo, one of the two main protagonists, lives in Koenji over the course of the novel and it's also where Aomame moves to near the end of the book. Though not especially evident by reading the novel, the area is actually quite lively and has been synonymous with music and creativity for decades. Some other well-known neighborhoods that come up frequently throughout the book are Shinjuku and Akasaka. And if you're looking to escape from the city for a day, taking a short trip to either Ome or Ichikawa, Chiba will surely be worth your while. Just be careful not to walk down any mysterious stairways while exploring the scenes from this best-selling novel.

TOKYO DAY TRIP ITINERARY ● 東京

The novel's scenes are so scattered throughout the Kanto region that visiting every single one of them would take at least a couple of days. However, it's possible to visit the places where the book's most significant scenes take place in one single day trip.

Let's start the day off where the novel itself begins - in the Setagaya Ward neighborhood of Sangenjaya. As Sangenjaya is located on the Den-En Toshi Line, one of the few train lines in Tokyo that does not pass through Shinjuku, you may prefer to visit these locations in reverse order depending on where you're staying. But also keep in mind that the Den-En Toshi Line and the Hanzomon Line are really one train line, which means you can access Sangenjaya directly from eastern Tokyo neighborhoods such as Otemachi or Kinshicho.

The Akasaka area is where one of the novel's most important scenes takes place. Aomame's meeting with the Sakigake Leader happens in the Hotel Okura Main Wing which was recently demolished and is currently undergoing reconstruction. Nevertheless, the South Wing is still operating and there are also some areas of interest nearby.

After a stop in Shinjuku, let's finish the day in Koenji. The Suginami Ward neighborhood is known for its trendy thrift stores and homely atmosphere but the area mostly comes alive in the evening. There are plenty of izakayas in the area and the park with the slide is a short walk from the station, so you can easily enjoy dinner and drinks before looking up at the moon(s).

FEATURED IN NOVEL

RECOMMENDED

① SANGENJAYA ● 三軒茶屋

The Metropolitan Expressway Number 3 is where the very first scene of the novel takes place, and it's revisited a couple more times over the course of the story. It is here where Aomame slips through dimensions and enters the alternate reality of 1Q84 when climbing down an emergency staircase. While not exactly like the one described in the book, if you look closely you can find such a staircase a few minute walk from Sangenjaya Station.

Sangenjaya is a residential yet lively Setagaya Ward neighborhood filled with restaurants and bars. Recently, the area has become especially popular with young creative types looking to live in a fun area that's easy accessible from Shibuya via the **Den-En Toshi** line.

② SHIBUYA ● 渋谷

Shibuya doesn't play such a major role in the novel overall, but it is where we're first introduced to Aomame's job as a hired assassin. At a nice hotel somewhere up Dogenzaka Street, Aomame uses her "ice pick" to kill a wealthy businessman that had caused a woman harm.

Later in the story, Aomame's policewoman friend Yumi is found murdered not too far away in a Maruyamacho love hotel. The Maruyamacho "Love Hotel Hill" area is the focal point of Murakami's previous novel *After Dark*. If you've not read that novel then today would be ideal to explore the Shibuya area. Check the web site **shibuyaguide.com** for tips on restaurants, sightseeing and nightlife in the area. In any case, you will need to transfer at Shibuya Station to the **Ginza Line** if you'd like to visit Hotel Okura. If not, ride the JR Yamanote Line instead if you prefer to go straight to Shinjuku.

③ HOTEL OKURA ● ホテルオークラ

Hotel Okura is one of Tokyo's most famous hotels. In the novel, this is where Aomame goes to meet and kill the Leader of Sakigake. Located right by the US Embassy, Okura is typically where foreign heads of state stay during their visits to Japan. The hotel's Main Wing was constructed in 1962 and was widely considered to be a masterpiece of modernist architecture. To the dismay of many, the main wing was demolished in 2015 and at the time of writing is still being completely rebuilt, with a reopening scheduled for 2019. The South Wing, constructed in 1973, still remains open, however.

There are some other spots in the area that may interest you, and if you'd like to explore this part of town you can take a Ginza Line train from Shibuya station and ride 6 stops to **Toranomon Station** (¥170). From there it's about a 10 minute walk south to the hotel.

The Main Wing under construction

Okura's less popular South Wing

2-10-4 Toranomon, Minato

④ AROUND AKASAKA ● 赤坂

After seeing the hotel, you may want to head over to the **Ark Hills** shopping complex which also contains **Suntory Hall**, one of the prominent venues in Tokyo for classical music. Ark Hills has plenty of shopping and dining options and would be perfect for a lunch or a coffee break, though you may want to save that for Shinjuku.

Aside from the scene in Hotel Okura, the Akasaka District is mentioned several other times throughout the novel. It's the district where Aomame often goes out at night to pick up men, either solo or with her friend Ayumi. At the end of the novel, Aomame and Tengo spend the night together in a hotel somewhere in the area.

Also nearby is Akasaka-Mitsuke station where the Little People cause the massive downpour to disrupt the Tokyo subway system. If you've read *The Wind-Up Bird Chronicle*, you can learn more about that area on p114, and it's roughly a 20 minute walk from Hotel Okura. You will need to do a fair bit of walking in any case, as the nearest station which connects directly to Shinjuku, **Kokkaigijido-Mae Station**, is about a 12 minute walk north from either Ark Hills or Okura.

Akasaka Ark Hills

 1-21-32 Akasaka, Minato

5 SHINJUKU ● 新宿

Shinjuku appears multiple times throughout the story. Outside the JR East Exit you can find the **Nakamuraya Cafe**, the place where Tengo and Fuka-Eri meet for the first time. There are actually a few cafes of this name, all located in the Nakamuraya Building. It's unclear on which floor the scenes from the novel take place, but Nakamuraya is best known for its Indian-style curry which can be ordered in the basement floor restaurant. Expect to pay more than what you would for a similar portion size elsewhere, but the quiet atmosphere and attentive service are all part of the package.

Just across the street is the **Kinokuniya** bookstore where Tengo stops before his meeting with Fuka-Eri. This bookstore is also mentioned from time to time in other Murakami novels. For foreign language books try the 7th floor.

Shinjuku Station, of course, is where Aomame returns to take her things from the coin locker after carrying out her mission at Hotel Okura, but that's near the West Exit on the opposite side. Back at the station, hop on a **JR Sobu Line** train and head west to **Koenji**.

| Nakamuraya Cafe (B2F) |

 3-26-3 Shinjuku
11:00 - 22:00
Every day

6 KOENJI ● 高円寺

Shopping on Koenji's 'Look Street'

Reading *1Q84*, it would be easy to get the impression that Koenji is a relatively dull residential neighborhood without much going on. It's even written that Tengo doesn't care much for the place and only lives there because "he just happened to find a cheap apartment."[52] In contrast to its depiction in the novel, Koenji is a lively neighborhood with a thriving local culture and nightlife, renowned for its unique atmosphere and affordable dining options.

Some common words associated with Koenji are "retro" and "vintage." In the day time Koenji is one of Tokyo's best neighborhoods for used clothes shopping. Most of these stores can be found in the area south of Koenji Station. There are also used toy shops, used record shops and other second-hand goods shops scattered throughout the area. Even the neighborhood itself maintains its own retro atmosphere, as Koenji was one of the few major Tokyo districts to avoid the massive construction boom of the late '80's bubble economy.

Koenji also has a reputation for being a hotbed of Japanese alternative youth culture, as it was the prominent neighborhood where punk culture surged in popularity in the early '80's. Today Koenji is still known for its many small music venues where one can see live experimental, avant-garde and electronic performances that probably wouldn't go over quite as well in some of Tokyo's glitzier districts.

Underneath the train tracks

The neighborhood comes alive at night. Along the railroad tracks one can find numerous izakaya-style restaurants with outdoor seating - a rarity in Japan. Whether you visit in the afternoon or at night, you'll likely realize why many consider Koenji to be one of Tokyo's best kept secrets.

The most memorable Koenji location from *1Q84* would have to be the park with the slide where Tengo first notices the two moons, and which just happens to be right outside Aomame's safe-house. This is **Koenji Chuo Park**, an easy 4 minute walk southeast from the station. The scene fits the novel's description so perfectly that it makes you wonder how many fans of the book have tried ringing the doorbell of the poor person now living in Aomame's apartment!

📍 *4-31-7 Koenjiminami, Suginami*

Don't be fooled by the names of these thrift shops - Koenji is a laid-back neighborhood you can explore at your own pace.

Tengo's apartment is described as being about 200 yards from a Marusho supermarket, facing a main road and nearby an elementary school. No Marusho's currently operate in Koenji but the location is likely one of these buildings facing Kannana Dori, just a minute walk from Suginami Dai-Yon Elementary.

THE MURAKAMI PILGRIMAGE

1Q84 TOKYO MAPS

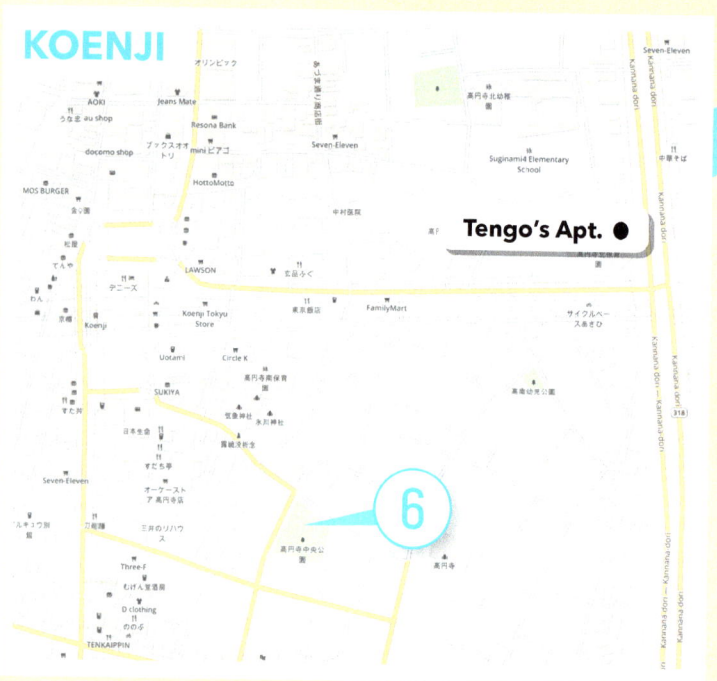

© Mapbox, © OpenStreetMap

Shinjuku
5
Shibuya
2
SHIBUYA 1-CHOME
Setagaya
Koenji
Nakano
Higashi-Nakano
Higashi-koenji
Okubo
Seibu-Shinjuku
Shinjuku
Shinjuku Gyoen National Garden
Minami-Shinjuku
Sendagaya
Shinanomachi
Yotsuya
Sophia University
Ichigaya
Hatsudai
Sangubashi
Hatagaya
Sasazuka
Daitabashi
Meidaemae
Higashi-Kitazawa
Shindaita
Shimo-Kitazawa
Ikenoue
Komaba-todaimae
Setagaya-Daita
Umegaoka
Gotokuji
Shinsen
Ikejiri-ohashi
Sangen-jaya
Daikan-yama
Aoyama Gakuin University
Aoyama Cemetery
University of the Sacred Heart
Waseda-dori
Okubo Dori Ave
Ome Kaido
Yasukuni-dori
Koshu Kaido
Inokashira-dori
Omotesando
Meiji-dori
Shinjuku Route
Shibuya Route
Central Circular Route
Meguro Route
Kannana-dori
Nakano dori
Akazutsumi-dori
Awashima-dori
Komadome-dori

AKASAKA
minister's residence
Tameike-sanno
Roppongi-dori
Sotobori-dori
Sannenzaka
Ministry of Eco Trade & Indu
Japan Post Hol
Toranomon
4
3
Akasaka Intercity
オークラ公園
Hotel Okura Tokyo Main Building
Suntory Hall
Hotel Okura Tokyo South Wing
Roppongi-itchome
Embassy of Sweden
Kamiyacho
Sakurada-dori
Iwaida Dori
Inner Circular Route
Shibuya Route
泉通り

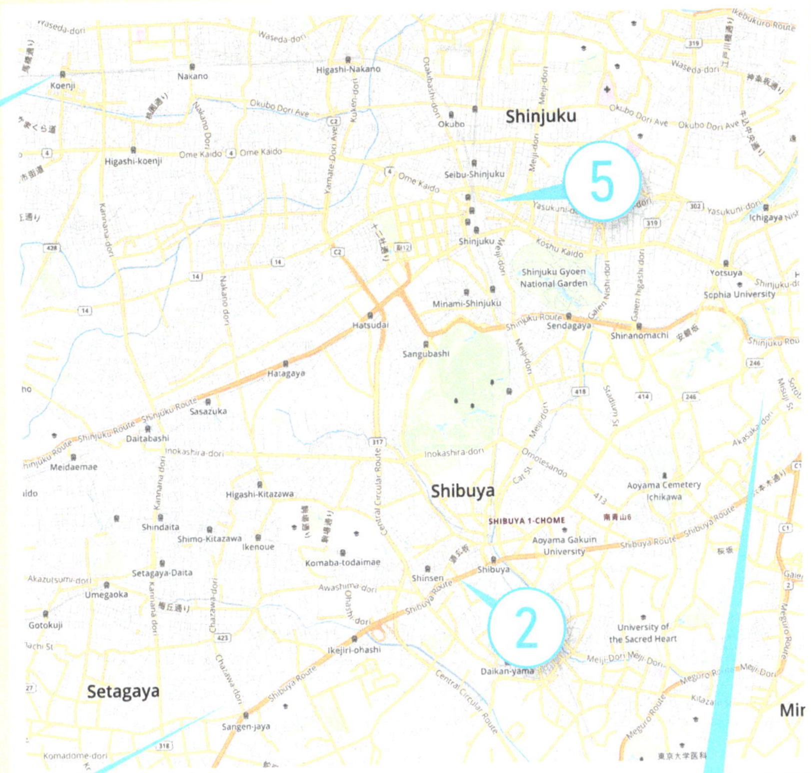

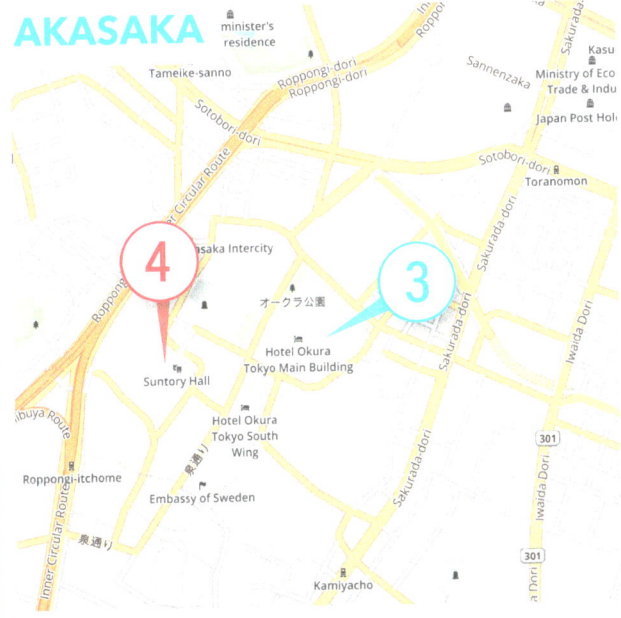

OME, TOKYO • 青梅市

After Fuka-Eri left her family and the rest of Sakigake in Yamanashi, she travelled to Ome, Tokyo to stay with Professor Ebisuno, an old friend of her father's. Fuka-Eri takes Tengo to meet the professor and they ride the train together all the way west to a station called **Futamatao**. The journey is a fairly long one, about 80 minutes west of central Tokyo. Futamatao is a pretty minor station and there's not a whole lot to do or see there, but a few stops away is **Ome Station** which provides easy access to some excellent hiking trails. If you want to do some light hiking and enjoy great views of both Ome City and the distant Tokyo skyline, a trip to Ome is well worth your visit.

From Shinjuku Station you can ride there directly in some cases on a **JR Chuo Rapid Service** train (¥800). The platform sign should say that the train is headed for Ome, which will be the last stop. If the sign instead says the last stop is Takao, you can still get to Ome but you'll need to transfer to the JR Ome Line at **Tachikawa Station**.

Once at Ome Station, the hiking trail is just a couple minutes away. Turn left outside the station, walk parallel to the tracks for a couple of minutes until you're able to make another left, walking uphill and over the tracks. Continue further uphill and you'll soon find yourself surrounded by nature. This area is perfect for beginner hikers because the slopes are not very steep and it's hard to get lost. Most of the side trails eventually lead back to the main trail and the views of the city in the distance remind you which direction you're headed.

Back at Ome Station you can ride the **JR Ome Line** further west to Futamatao and get there in about 10 minutes. Just as described in the novel, the station is small and has no staff. The station does, however, have an electronic card reader for your Suica or Pasmo card. Nearby the station is a nice little temple called Kaizen-ji. If you time things right, you could arrive in Futamatao with 20 or 30 minutes to walk around before the next train back to Tokyo. That should be enough time to hang out at the temple, enjoy the scenery and get a feel for the place. To get back to central Tokyo you'll need to transfer at Tachikawa to a Chuo Line train.

Kaizen-ji

4-962 Futamatao, Ome-shi,

Kaizen-ji Temple

ICHIKAWA, CHIBA ● 市川市

Ichikawa in Chiba Prefecture is the town where both Aomame and Tengo grew up. Ichikawa mostly appears in flashbacks, such as when Tengo recalls making the rounds with his NHK collector father in the central district of the city. In the year 19(Q)84, Ushikawa is the one to travel out to Ichikawa when digging for information on Aomame and her family. He even visits the elementary school where the two main protagonists studied.

Only 40 minutes on the JR Sobu Line from Shinjuku, this city of around half a million people makes for a surprisingly pleasant day trip. Turning right out of the central exit you can find the **I-Linktown Observatory** from which you can catch a great view of the local area and even Tokyo's skyline from 46 stories high. Best of all, it's completely free. Even the cafe at the top is much cheaper than you'd typically find at an observatory in Japan, with coffees going for ¥200. The main downside is that some of the best vantage points are completely blocked off for some reason, but it's hard to complain when the price is ¥0.

From the station area, a 30 minute walk along the Edo River (Edogawa) will take you to the scenic **Satomi Park**. Head west along the train tracks before making a right on to the main road, and shortly thereafter you'll find a walkway up to the river. You can take it easy and appreciate the view as you walk along Edogawa without any traffic to worry about. After half an hour you should see a sign for Satomi Park, the entrance being just to the right.

Once the site of an old battlefield, today you'll find a large flower garden and a fountain. The park's main attraction, however, is its vantage points of surrounding Chiba Prefecture, Tokyo and even Mt. Fuji on a clear day. If you have a free afternoon sometime then you could easily depart for Ichikawa after lunch and still make it back to central Tokyo in time for dinner.

View from the I-Linktown Observatory

CHIKURA

Throughout the novel Tengo visits the town of Chikura, also in Chiba, to see his dying father. Now a part of Minamiboso City, the coastal town is known for its large flower beds. From Koenji it's a long 3 hour train ride.

📍 3-3-9 Kounodai, Ichikawa-shi, Chiba

Satomi Park flowers

OTHER TOKYO LOCATIONS

AZABU

The posh Azabu district is the location of the Willow House, the shelter for women run by the dowager. Aomame visits Azabu several times throughout the novel but we don't know quite which part. The Azabu area is known for the Tokyo Tower and its many foreign embassies.

HIROO

Hiroo is the location of the sports club where Aomame teaches a couple of martial arts classes. Hiroo, surrounded by Azabu, Ebisu and Roppongi, is one of the many opulent Tokyo neighborhoods mentioned in the novel. But other than Arisugawa Park there's not much in the way of sightseeing.

JIYUGAOKA

Jiyugaoka is where Aomame lives before moving to the Koenji safehouse. She moved to the neighborhood after the death of her friend Tamaki. The area is popular for shopping and dining and can be accessed in about 10 minutes from Shibuya.

ROPPONGI

Aomame and Ayumi visit Roppongi, along with neighboring Akasaka, a few times throughout the novel. As depicted in the book, the area is known for its bar and nightlife scene. Another attraction is the Mori Art Museum which also offers excellent views of the Tokyo skyline.

YOYOGI

Yoyogi is the neighborhood where Tengo teaches math at the cram school. Situated in between Harajuku and Shinjuku, Yoyogi is most well-known for its NTT DoCoMo Yoyogi Building, a famous skyscraper which can be spotted from all over Tokyo.

DOLORES

TSUKURU TAZAKI

AND HIS YEARS OF

PILGRIMAGE

Colorless Tsukuru Tazaki and His Years of Pilgrimage takes us to a number of Tokyo locations which are also frequently mentioned in other works - namely Shinjuku, Aoyama, Ginza and Jiyugaoka. While the settings within Tokyo may be predictable for longtime Murakami readers, this 2013 novel provides us with a fresh perspective on some familiar areas from the eyes of protagonist Tsukuru, a man who designs train stations. The end of the novel gives us a fascinating insight on Shinjuku Station, the busiest station in the world. Even if you've already passed through Shinjuku many times, reading about the intricate details required to keep it running smoothly helps one appreciate it even more.

What sets this book apart from other Murakami novels is that it's the only one to feature scenes in the city of Nagoya, the protagonist's hometown. Throughout the book, Tsukuru recalls many events from his childhood and teenage years which take place there and he even visits the city to meet with his old friends. While his visit to Nagoya may not take up much space, Nagoya will be the overall focus of this part of the guidebook and you can find a detailed day trip itinerary on the following pages.

Colorless Tsukuru Tazaki is also one of only a few Murakami novels in which the main character takes a trip abroad. Tsukuru visits Finland where his old friend Kuro lives. Here Murakami does an excellent job of describing the feel and atmosphere of the place.

Another notable part of the book takes place in Oita Prefecture which is located on the southern island of Kyushu. The book ends, however, without us ever knowing the fate of the mysterious jazz pianist who could see other people's 'true colors.'

> **ⓘ NAGOYA**
> **Population:** *5.5 million*
> **Area:** *83,454 km²*
> **Region:** *Chubu*

NAGOYA DAY TRIP ITINERARY ● 名古屋

Colorless Tsukuru Tazaki and His Years of Pilgrimage is the first Murakami novel to have scenes in the city of Nagoya. The city is mentioned briefly in other novels but this is the first time a main character makes a visit. Nagoya is the city, of course, where protagonist Tsukuru and his four best friends grew up. In the middle of the novel, Tsukuru, now living in Tokyo, decides to return to the city of his youth to finally ask his former friends why they rejected and abandoned him 16 years prior.

Nagoya, with a population of over 2 million people, is one of Japan's largest cities, although it's not a common destination for tourists. The region is mainly known for its automobile industry and it's the home of the world's largest automaker, Toyota. But as far as tourism and sightseeing is concerned, the city has little to offer in comparison with other midsize cities like Osaka or even Sapporo.

With all that said, there are still some interesting things to do and see in Nagoya which can be accomplished in a day or so. The city happens to be conveniently located between the Kanto and Kansai regions which makes for an easy stopover.

FEATURED IN NOVEL

RECOMMENDED

ACCOMMODATION

Staying near Nagoya Castle, the central Sakae Area (near the TV tower) or somewhere close to Nagoya Station would all be convenient for seeing the main sights in a day or two. There are plenty of cheap rental apartment options in these areas, not to mention regular business hotels.

GETTING THERE

From Tokyo, a Shinkansen to Nagoya (100 min.) costs ¥11,000 while a bus from Tokyo to Nagoya goes for as little as ¥3 - 4,000 (6 hrs.). Without a JR rail pass, you could take a bus to Nagoya, spend a night in a cheap rental apartment and take another bus to Kansai, all for roughly the same price as a single shinkansen ticket from Tokyo to Kyoto.

① NAGOYA TV TOWER ● 名古屋テレビ塔

Let's start the day off at the Nagoya TV tower. Built in 1954, this TV Tower is the oldest in Japan. Like most Japanese towers, this one also has an observation deck. Disappointingly, however, the cost to observe the city from 90 meters high is ¥1,000, even more expensive than the Tokyo Tower. Furthermore, the windows are not very clear, but there is at least a caged open-air viewing area on an upper floor. If you do decide to go up, you can enjoy a great view of the long, green Hisaya Odori park.

View of Oasis 21 from the tower

View of the tower from Oasis 21

- 3-6-15, Nishiki, Naka-ku
- ¥1000
- 10:00 - 21:00
- Every day

② HISAYA ODORI PARK ● 久屋大通公園

The quieter, northern edge of the park

This is a long, rectangular park that stretches out over 2km, very reminiscent of Sapporo's Odori Park. The central area surrounding the tower is the liveliest and if you're here during the weekend it's likely you'll encounter a farmer's market, art show, live band or all of the above. The far north and south areas of the park are much quieter and more spacious. Around here you'll see people relaxing on benches and reading books.

While Hisaya Odori Park is not mentioned by name in the novel, it's most likely here that Tsukuru and Ao have their chat, probably in one of the quieter sections in the north part of the park.

Near the center of the park by the TV tower is another popular Nagoya landmark called **Oasis 21** (pictured on p195) which can be accessed for free.

③ THE LEXUS SHOWROOM

📍 2-1-1, Higashisakura, Higashi-ku

There are a number of Lexus dealerships throughout Nagoya, the hometown of Lexus and Toyota. In the novel, the showroom where Ao works is described as being "in a quiet area near Nagoya Castle."[53] This would likely be the one near **Takaoka Station**, about a 10 minute walk northeast of the TV Tower. While not incredibly close to the castle, it's still the closest at 25 minutes away on foot.

> ℹ️ Car lovers may want to visit the Toyota Automobile Museum, 45 min. outside Nagoya in Nagakute City

④ NAGOYA CASTLE ● 名古屋城

Nagoya Castle is only referred to briefly in the novel but if you're in Nagoya this is a must-visit destination. Originally built as the seat of the Owari branch of the Tokugawa shogunate, Nagoya Castle has been one of the city's most prominent symbols since the Edo period and remains so to this day. In addition to the scenic moat and lush greenery surrounding the main structure, the castle itself contains a multi-story museum with informational displays on Nagoya and the Edo period. The top floor also offers excellent views of the city.

If you'd rather skip the 30 minute walk from the Lexus dealership you can take a subway from Takaoka to **Shiyakusho Station**. The journey takes 8 minutes and costs ¥200. After taking the Sakuradori Line to Hisayaodori Station, transfer to the Meijo Line and ride one stop.

⌖ 1-1, Honmaru, Naka-ku
💰 ¥500
🕘 9:00 - 16:30
📅 Every day

After meeting at the dealership, Tsukuru and Ao then go out to meet at a Starbucks which Ao says is just after a left turn from the showroom. Even though Starbucks chains are ubiquitous throughout Japan's major cities, at the time of writing, the area around the Lexus dealership is oddly one of the few parts of Nagoya without a Starbucks nearby. As mentioned, the park Tsukuru and Ao go to chat is likely the northern section of Hisaya Odori Park, so it's also possible they walked all the way to a Starbucks around there.

5 NAGOYA STATION AREA ● 名古屋駅

ⓘ Aka's office is described as being on the 8th floor of a highrise about 5km from the showroom. Most of the tall buildings in Nagoya are located around Nagoya Station, which is also about 5km from the Takaoka area, so it's probably safe to assume that Aka's business seminar company is around here.

At some point in your visit you will most likely be making a stop at or around Nagoya Station, whether you're travelling by train or by bus. The area around the station is one of the busiest in the city and inside the station itself is a massive department store full of shops and restaurants. Unfortunately, the very top floor of the station's **JR Central Towers** requires you to eat at one of the expensive restaurants to get a glimpse of the view. There is a place nearby the station, however, known as **Midland Square**, which allows access a large area with a 360° view of the city for ¥750. The "Sky Promenade," as it's called, offers impressive views of Nagoya and the surrounding area from 46 stories up.

Midland Square

- 4-7-1, Meieki, Nakamura-ku
- ¥750
- 11:00 - 22:00
- Every day

Several minutes on foot from the station you can find the **Noritake Gardens**, a park which also contains a gallery, a museum and a cafe. The view of Nagoya's skyscrapers also isn't bad.

View of the JR Central Towers from Midland Square

AROUND TOWN

The Nagoya City Science Museum is one of Nagoya's most well-known museums and landmarks. Located inside Shirakawa Park, the museum consists of multiple floors and a large planetarium. Bear in mind that all exhibitions and planetarium presentations are in Japanese only.

Osu-Kannon is one of Nagoya's prominent Buddhist temples. Inside the temple is a statue of the goddess Kannon carved by Kobo Daishi. If you've read *Kafka on the Shore*, you can learn more about him on p146. The temple is an easy walk south from Shirakawa Park.

Atsuta Shrine is one of the three most important shrines in all of Japan. It enshrines the Sun Goddess Amaterasu, one of the major deities of Shintoism. This is also a popular place to try Nagoya's local style of noodles called *kishimen*, which can be purchased for several hundred yen a bowl. You can reach Atsuta by getting off at Jingunishi station on the Meijo Line.

COLORLESS TSUKURU TAZAKI AND HIS YEARS OF PILGRIMAGE GUIDE

NAGOYA MAP

TOKYO LOCATIONS

SHINJUKU

Shinjuku Station, the world's busiest, appears often throughout the novel and is an object of fascination for Tsukuru, who's dedicated his life to station design. At the end of the book he sits on a bench on platforms 9 and 10 and watches commuters get on and off the long distance trains. You will undoubtedly pass through Shinjuku Station multiple times throughout your stay in Tokyo and like Tsukuru, you'll likely be amazed that no riots ever break out.

AOYAMA

The fashionable Aoyama district and Omotesando Street appear several times throughout the novel. At one point Tsukuru visits a French restaurant here with Sara. Later, after buying a souvenir to take to Finland, Tsukuru sits at an Omotesando coffee shop where he spots Sara with another man. Aoyama appears frequently throughout Murakami's work, most notably in *South of the Border, West of the Sun*.

JIYUGAOKA

Jiyugaoka is where Tsukuru lives in the condo he's occupied since college, and which was transferred to his name upon his father's death. This posh Meguro-ku neighborhood is popular for shopping and dining without the crowds of central Tokyo. The station is about a 10 minute ride west from Shibuya.

EBISU

Ebisu is yet another fancy neighborhood where Tsukuru and Sara go out on a date. Just one stop from Shibuya on the Yamanote Line, Ebisu attracts an older crowd than Shibuya or Harajuku and the area is home to many well-known restaurants. It's also known for the Yebisu Garden Place, which houses both a beer and a photography museum.

GINZA

Ginza is the ritzy shopping district where Tsukuru and Sara meet at a coffee shop and where she tells him about the results of her research on his old friends from Nagoya. The district is known for its high-end shopping and eating options and famous department stores such as Wako and Mitsukoshi.

Near the end of the novel, Tsukuru travels to Finland to meet his friend Kuro. She lives in Helsinki, where Tsukuru first flies to, only to find out that Kuro's at her summer cottage in the town of Hämeenlinna. After a short time in Helsinki he sets off to the village. On the drive up to Hämeenlinna he observes lush greenery on either side of him. Sipping coffee at the town square, he notices the church and outdoor vegetable carts, both rarities in Japan. Later on he remembers his time at Helsinki Station where he sat at observed all the details of the trains and their destinations.

FINLAND

OITA

Oita Prefecture, located in the southernmost of Japan's main islands, Kyushu, is known for its scenery and hot springs. It comes up in the novel when Haida tells a strange tale about his father who was working at a mountain resort when he came across a mysterious jazz pianist. When the two were drinking, the pianist explained that he was given the ability to see people's colors, or auras, but in exchange, he only had one month to live. Many feel this is one of the most intriguing sections of the book but neither the pianist nor Oita are mentioned again.

COMBINED ITINERARY IDEAS

SPOILER ALERT: These itinerary suggestions are intended for people who have read ALL of Haruki Murakami's novels.

AKASAKA TOUR

The neighborhood of Akasaka is featured in many of Murakami's novels and appears in this guide book for the guides on *Dance, Dance, Dance*, *1Q84* and *The Wind-Up Bird Chronicle*. Akasaka is a big neighborhood and all three of these novels take place in a different part of it.

Let's begin with the area mentioned in the *1Q84* itinerary. Take the train to either **Roppongi-Itchome Station** or to **Toranomon Station**, whichever is easier for you. If you've arrived at Roppongi-Itchome, you can walk to the **Ark Hills** area mentioned on **p178**. From there you can head over to **Hotel Okura**. If you've arrived at Toranomon Station instead, simply do the reverse.

Next, head over to **Hie Shrine (p114)**, about a 15 minute walk from either location. While not mentioned in the novels, it's definitely worth a visit if you're in the area. After visiting the shrine you can walk through the Akasaka **2-chome area** where Nutmeg and Cinnamon have one of their shell companies in *The Wind-Up Bird Chronicle* **(p115)**. When finished, walk toward Akasaka-Mitsuke Station. The area contains plenty of restaurants if you're hungry and you can find a building reminiscent of where Nutmeg had her 'Akasaka Fashion Design' office.

A little bit north of the station is Akasaka Excel Hotel Tokyu and farther north is Hotel New Otani. Mei of *Dance, Dance, Dance* gets murdered in a luxury hotel and these are two potential candidates. Or, if you don't want to depress yourself too much, imagine them as one of the hotels where Aomame goes out to drink in *1Q84*.

From Akasaka-Mitsuke Station it's about a 7 minute walk to the **Akasaka Police Station**, the place where the protagonist of *Dance, Dance, Dance* gets kept for days after the death of Mei. On the way there you can check out an interesting temple called Toyokawa Inari **(p58)**. Another 15 minute walk west beyond this point is **Nogi Shrine**, a famous Tokyo landmark right next to where Yuki and her mother have a condo in *Dance, Dance, Dance*. **(p58)**

Some other Akasaka landmarks include Tokyo Midtown (next to Roppongi), Akasaka Palace (nearby Hotel New Otani) or the National Diet Building (nearby Nagatacho station). Also nearby Akasaka is Roppongi's Mori Art Museum. The museum itself is worth a look but perhaps even more impressive is the view from the roof.

SHINJUKU TOUR

Shinjuku is an area that comes up often in Murakami's work and most Tokyo train lines run through Shinjuku Station, which makes it easy to access no matter where in Tokyo you're staying. Shinjuku appears in 3 different day trip itineraries in this book: the guides for **Norwegian Wood**, **The Wind-Up Bird Chronicle** and **1Q84**. The area also comes up in many other novels and short stories. Hitting all the Shinjuku locations at once will inevitably involve a fair amount of backtracking, as Shinjuku Gyoen and the main skyscraper district are on opposite ends of the neighborhood. Shinjuku Gyoen closes fairly early, at around 4:30pm, but the same eastern part of Shinjuku is also where most of the nightlife is. Feel free to mix up the order of this combined tour as it suits you.

Let's start the day off at **Shinjuku Station** itself. The end of *Colorless Tsukuru Tazaki and His Years of Pilgrimage* contains a scene with Tsukuru sitting on the platform, admiring the complexities required to keep such a busy station running smoothly. **(p202)** As it's the world's busiest station, a walk through it is both overwhelming and fascinating, regardless of how long you've lived in Tokyo. Around the station you'll see a number of coin locker storage places which come up in both *Hard-Boiled Wonderland* **(p66)** and *1Q84*. **(p179)**

Coming out the **JR West Exit** you'll find the area where Toru likely sits and people watches in *The Wind-Up Bird Chronicle*, although no seating area remains. If you're into electronics or cameras, this part of Shinjuku is home to Tokyo's most prominent Yodobashi Camera store. The west side of the station is also where you can find many of Shinjuku's well-known skyscrapers, such as Tocho and the Mode Gakuen Cocoon Tower. **(p119)**

Now you'll need to do some backtracking. Head over to the station and walk around it to the east side, which is easier said than done. Nearby the **East Exit** is where you'll find the **Nakamuraya Cafe** mentioned in *1Q84* **(p179)**. Just across the street is the **Kinokuniya** bookstore which comes up in *1Q84*, *Sputnik Sweetheart* and even some of Murakami's nonfiction. This general area is also one of the best places in Tokyo for shopping and it's where you'll find the Isetan Department Store. Keep heading east until you get to **Shinjuku Gyoen** and enjoy the park until closing time. **(p116)** Once you're finished with Gyoen, head back closer to the station where you can find the jazz bar **Dug** which Watanabe and Midori often visit together in *Norwegian Wood*. **(p85)** Close by is the Robot Restaurant, a wildly popular tourist destination that you'll want to make reservations for online in advance.

After dark, head to the nearby Kabukicho district, one of Tokyo's most well-known nightlife spots. It doesn't appear much in Murakami's fiction except for the short story *Super-Frog Saves Tokyo*. The protagonist would often collect debts for the bank in the district, which is somewhat notorious for having many gang-related businesses. Fortunately, the area has cleaned up in recent decades and is much safer than it used to be. A popular drinking spot in the area for foreigners and locals alike is Golden Gai, where many small and sometimes eccentrically decorated bars are situated right next to each other. Be aware that each bar charges a table cover.

COMBINED ITINERARY IDEAS

WESTERN TOKYO TOUR

Tokyo's western suburbs, often collectively referred to as the "Tama District" come up a lot in Murakami's fiction. As mentioned on **p128**, nearly all of these stations can be accessed by the **JR Chuo Line**. The main book to feature this region is *Sputnik Sweetheart* but the western suburbs also play a role in *Pinball, 1973* and *1Q84*.

If you get an early start then it should be possible to visit all of these Chuo Line destinations in a day. Much depends, however, on how much time you'd like to spend hiking. If you really want enjoy the mountains then you may want to visit Ome first before gradually making your way back eastward toward central Tokyo. Either way, you probably wouldn't have time for a stop in Kichijoji if you add in all the other destinations. Kichijoji is the closest neighborhood to central Tokyo so you could save that for another time, such as the day tour for *Norwegian Wood*.

Let's start off at **Higashi-Koganei Station**. This is the location of the **International Christian University** and the **golf course** mentioned in *Pinball, 1973* and *A Wild Sheep Chase*. (**p23**) This is the most inconvenient stop on this itinerary, as the golf course is 20 minutes or so one-way on foot from the station. You may want to skip the college campus altogether as there's not a whole lot to see and it's also easy to get lost in. After visiting **Nogawa Park**, the current incarnation of the old golf course, walk or take a taxi back to the station. Board a Chuo-Line train and head just two stops west for Kokubunji.

Kokubunji does not play a major role in the novels but it is where Naoko from *Norwegian Wood* lives before she leaves Tokyo. (**p132**) It's also where the author himself lived and ran the first incarnation of his jazz bar Peter Cat. He also wrote a short story about living in the middle of three railroad tracks close to Nishi-Kokubunji station. The main sightseeing spots of Kokubunji would be the **Tonogayato Garden** and **Sugatami Pond**. From here on follow the rest of the itinerary in the *Sputnik Sweetheart* guide which will take you to **Kunitachi** and then **Tachikawa**. (**p133**)

From Tachikawa station you can access **Ome** and **Futamatao** stations. Futamatao is where Fuka-Eri lives with Professor Ebisuno in *1Q84*, but Ome Station provides access to some great hiking trails. (**p184**) The town of Ome itself is also worth a walk around thanks to all the old Showa Era artwork displayed throughout the city. Whether you want to stop in Ome or Futamatao first is up to you, but you'll want to ride the **JR Ome Line** to get to either station.

By the time you make it to the area it will likely be late afternoon. As described on p184, the hiking trails are easily accessible from Ome Station and since the trails are not difficult, you can relax and enjoy the scenery even if you don't have much time before sunset. Or visit these places in reverse and catch the sunset from the golf course as the narrator of *Pinball, 1973* often does in that novel.

THE "USUAL COURSE" EXTENDED

In *Dance, Dance, Dance*, the protagonist has a usual walking route which you can read more about on **p56**. While his route doesn't play a huge role in that novel, it happens to bring us through three neighborhoods which are the focus of other itineraries in this guide book. By following this course you'll walk through Sendagaya, the focus of *Hard-Boiled Wonderland and The End of The World*, Aoyama, the focus of *South of the Border, West of the Sun* and Shibuya, where *After Dark* takes place. If you really want to see everything mentioned in each individual guide then you may want to schedule more than one day for this. But if you start early and are up for a late night out in Shibuya, you could potentially fit everything into one day.

You can start and finish in Shibuya if you like, but starting off in **Harajuku**, one stop away on the JR Yamanote Line, would save you some time. Harajuku is one of Tokyo's most popular neighborhoods but scarcely appears in Murakami's work. Regardless, it's definitely worth a visit during your time in Tokyo. The times it is mentioned, the protagonist of *Dance, Dance, Dance* visits **Takeshita Street** and Sumire of *Sputnik Sweetheart* also works in the area. Harajuku is where you'll find **Yoyogi Park** and **Meiji Shrine**, two of Tokyo's top sightseeing spots.

Continue on the "Usual Course" route until you find yourself in **Sendagaya (p64)**. This is the shortest of all the itineraries in the guide book and most of the destinations are close by each other, with the exception of Aoyama-Itchome station which you may want to save for another day.

From there head onto the **Aoyama** neighborhood. Keep in mind that you're now coming from the reverse direction of the itinerary outlined on **p96**. Start by visiting the **Aoyama Cemetery**, then check out some of the art museums and architecture in the area. Eventually turn on to Aoyama Boulevard and walk toward **Shibuya**. Aoyama would be a good place to stop for lunch or dinner and if you stick around there are plenty of opportunities for live music.

You'll want to walk down **Miyamasuzaka Street (p97)** and make your way to the central Shibuya area. You can find the itinerary for the scenes from *After Dark* on **p197**. Shibuya is the ideal place for experiencing Tokyo's nightlife, but understand that the trains stop running a little after midnight. Most night owls simply stay out until the trains start running again at around 5:00 the next morning.

JR YAMANOTE LINE TOUR

If you have a JR rail pass, it can be fun to ride 360 degrees around the Yamanote Line and get off at each station that's mentioned in this guide book. You can start anywhere you like but let's say we're starting in Shinjuku and riding clockwise. **Shinjuku** appears on pages **66, 85 119, 179** and **202**. Next, get off at **Otsuka (p88)**, followed by **Komagome (p83)**. Ride to **Ueno** and spend some time in the park (**p90**). You might also want to get off at Tokyo Station which is mentioned in several books (**p216**). From there make a brief stop in **Shinagawa (p124)**, followed by **Ebisu (p203)** a good place to get some dinner and drinks. At the end of the route you'll end up in **Shibuya (pp. 54, 97, 177)**, **Harajuku (p55)** and **Yoyogi (p189)** which are all right next to one another.

LOCATION REFERENCE GUIDE

This following pages provide information on virtually every location ever named in Haruki Murakami's fiction, short stories included (at least those which have been translated into English). The information is divided into three sections: Japan (excluding Tokyo), Tokyo and Locations Around The World. Be aware that this section contains **major spoilers for all books**.

JAPAN LOCATIONS (EXCLUDING TOKYO)

This section is ordered alphabetically by Japanese prefecture.

AICHI

A populous coastal prefecture in Japan's Chubu region.

Hamamatsu: The city where Shiro from *Colorless Tsukuru Tazaki and His Years of Pilgrimage* moved to from Nagoya to teach piano. This is also where she was found strangled to death.

Nagoya: Japan's 4th largest city known for its automobile industry.
- Tsukuru, the protagonist of *Colorless Tsukuru Tazaki and His Years of Pilgrimage* is from here and visits over the course of the novel to meet his old friends. **(p194)**
- In *Kafka on the Shore* the character Hoshino is from here.
- Nagasawa from *Norwegian Wood* is from here and it's where his father runs a big hospital.
- Mizuki from *A Shinagawa Monkey* (*Blind Willow, Sleeping Woman*)[42] also originally comes from Nagoya.
- Hajime once received a mysterious postcard from Nagoya in *South of the Border, West of the Sun*.

Toyohashi: A small city neighboring Nagoya where Izumi, Hajime's ex-girlfriend, moved to from their hometown *(South of the Border, West of the Sun)*.

AKITA

The northern Honshu prefecture where Haida from *Colorless Tsukuru Tazaki and His Years of Pilgrimage* is from. His father teaches at a public university there.

AOMORI

- Honshu's northernmost prefecture. In *A Wild Sheep Chase*, a letter arrives here from the Rat with a return address belonging to an unnamed city about an hour away from the capital. The protagonist mentions having visited the prefecture several times before.
- In *Norwegian Wood*, Midori takes a trip to Aomori alone to make a travel brochure of the area.

CHIBA

- Ichikawa, Chiba is the town where Aomame and Tengo grew up in *1Q84*. Ushikawa even visits over the course of the story **(p186)**. In addition, he visits Tsudanuma to speak with one of Aomame's former elementary school teachers. Also in *1Q84*, Tengo visits the town of Chikura multiple times to see his ailing father. **(p187)**
- In *Kafka on the Shore*, Sakura tells Kafka on the bus that she's from Ichikawa.
- In *The Wind-Up Bird Chronicle*, Toru recalls traveling to a small town in Chiba with his girlfriend at the time so that she could get an abortion. Later in the book, Ushikawa tells Toru that he's the son of a tatami maker from Funabashi, a city in the northwestern part of the prefecture.
- K of *Sputnik Sweetheart* grew up in the town of Tsudanuma, also in the northwest of the prefecture. Tsudanuma is currently part of a city called Narashino, where Murakami himself lived for a time after closing his bar Peter Cat.

FUKUSHIMA

Fukushima is a prefecture in Japan's northeastern Tohoku region. Today it's most known for its ongoing nuclear crisis which started after the Tohoku earthquake of 2011.
- In *The Wind-Up Bird Chronicle*, Fukushima is the hometown of a woman from Toru's work (whom he almost slept with but didn't). She explains a frightening childhood memory of almost getting stuck in a culvert.
- Fukushima is also the hometown of Midori's late mother in *Norwegian Wood*. She also has an aunt there and ran away from home a couple times to visit her. Her father came to pick her up and it's the train rides from Fukushima to Ueno Station that he remembers so fondly before his death.

LOCATION REFERENCE GUIDE

GIFU

Gifu is a rural mountainous prefecture which neighbors Aichi.
- In *Kafka on the Shore*, Hoshino recalls growing up in Gifu and experiencing leeches falling down from trees while walking in the forest. He also later recalls an ex-girlfriend which worked in a bar in Gifu City.
- In *Colorless Tsukuru Tazaki and His Years of Pilgrimage*, Gifu is where Tsukuru's father was born. Kuro's Finnish husband also lived there for a time learning how to make Japanese pottery.

HIROSHIMA

Hiroshima is the southern Honshu prefecture perhaps best known for being one of two cities to be struck with an atomic bomb at the end of World War II.
- In *Kafka on the Shore*, it's where Nakata's elementary school teacher was originally from and the city's University Hospital is where Oshima goes for regular health checkups.
- Lieutenant Mamiya from *The Wind-Up Bird Chronicle* is also from Hiroshima and before retiring, taught social studies at a public high school there.

HOKKAIDO

Japan's largest prefecture and the northernmost of its 4 main islands.

Abashiri: A small town on Hokkaido's northern coast. In *Kafka on the Shore*, Sakura mentions running away to the northern town of Abashiri when she was 16.

Asahikawa: Hokkaido's second-largest city, located in the central part of the island.
- In *A Wild Sheep Chase*, the protagonist and his girlfriend transfer here on their way to Junitaki-cho **(p50)**.
- Yumiyoshi, the receptionist of the Dolphin Hotel in *Dance, Dance, Dance*, was raised here and her parents ran a well known inn in the city.
- In *The Wind-Up Bird Chronicle*, Asahikawa is the hometown of Mr. Honda. This is where he started a printing business before moving to Tokyo.
- At the end of *Norwegian Wood*, Reiko stops in Tokyo before moving to Asahikawa. She plans to teach music there at a school run by a friend of hers. Watanabe also mentions having been to the city before.
- In *New York Mining Disaster* (*Blind Willow, Sleeping Woman*), the narrator's friend recalls seeing a cat and a dog at a zoo in Hokkaido (likely Asahikawa Zoo). You can in fact see dogs and cats there along with the usual exotic animals.

Bifuka: A small town of several thousand people located in the northern part of Hokkaido. Many believe it to be the real-life inspiration for *A Wild Sheep Chase*'s Junitaki-cho, the town where the picture of the special sheep was taken by the Rat. Bifuka contains many waterfalls and a pasture very similar to the scene described in the novel **(pp. 40 - 49)**.

Hakodate: A city of around 280,000 in the southern part of Hokkaido.
- It's where the protagonist of *Dance, Dance, Dance* visits for work before heading on to Sapporo.
- Tamaru from *1Q84* was sent to an orphanage here during his childhood.

Kushiro: The short story *UFO in Kushiro* (*After The Quake*)[3] takes place here. After his wife disappears, the protagonist does his coworker a favor by taking a "small package" to the isolated east coast town.

Nakatonbetsu: In *Drive My Car* (*Men Without Women*)[54], this small town is where Kafuku's driver Misaki is from.

Nayoro: A northern city in Hokkaido close to Bifuka **(p41)**. In *A Wild Sheep Chase*, the sheep caretaker mentions how most of the lumber from Junitaki (Bifuka) is now taken to places like Nayoro and Asahikawa.

Sapporo: Hokkaido's largest city and capital.
- In *A Wild Sheep Chase*, Sapporo is where the protagonist and his girlfriend first arrive to search for the mysterious sheep and where they stay at the Dolphin Hotel. **(pp. 28 - 39)**
- In *Dance, Dance, Dance*, the same protagonist returns to the city twice over the course of the novel. He stays at the Dolphin Hotel again, although this time it's been completely rebuilt.
- In the prequel, *Pinball 1973*, the same narrator talks about taking a company trip to Hokkaido.
- In *The Wind-Up Bird Chronicle*, Toru recalls visiting Hokkaido on a business trip. He stepped into a bar where the musician held up a flame up to his hand at the end of his performance. He later has a chance (and violent) encounter with this same musician in Tokyo. Also in the same novel, Toru recalls having a friend named Onoda who was transferred to the Sapporo branch of his company.

Shiokari Pass: In northern Hokkaido, the original settlers of Junitaki-cho pass here before settling the town, as described in *A Wild Sheep Chase*. Shiokari Pass also happens to be the name of a famous novel and movie in Japan.

Yubari: A coal mining town in central Hokkaido. In *1Q84*, Aomame reads an article of a mining accident that supposedly happened a few years prior, although she personally has no recollection of the event.

HYOGO

A prefecture in the Kansai region where Haruki Murakami himself is from.
Murakami's first two novels, **Hear The Wind Sing** and **Pinball, 1973**, take place in an unnamed town in Hyogo simply referred to as "the town." However, some of the locations mentioned in this fictional town can be found in the city of Ashiya **(p15)**. In the sequel, **A Wild Sheep Chase**, the same protagonist returns to the town to visit J's Bar and an old girlfriend of the Rat's **(p61)**.

Ashiya: A wealthy city nearby Kobe with a population of around 100,000.
- The narrator of the short story **Yesterday** (Men Without Women)[55] is from here and points out that despite the city's reputation, his family was not especially wealthy.
- Real-life Ashiya contains the park with the monkey cage and the library from **Hear The Wind Sing** (pp. 15 - 16).

Kobe: The capital of Hyogo Prefecture, home to around 1.5 million people.
- In **Norwegian Wood**, Kobe is the hometown of Watanabe, Naoko and their late friend Kizuki **(p89)**.
- In the story **A Folklore For My Generation** (Blind Willow, Sleeping Woman), the narrator was raised in Kobe.
- In **Kafka on the Shore**, Nakata and Hoshino drive to Kobe and stop there for breakfast before moving on to Shikoku.
- In the short story **Blind Willow, Sleeping Woman**, the narrator's uncle runs a printing company in Kobe.
- A bar very similar to J's Bar from 'the Rat trilogy' called Half Time can be found in Kobe today. This is where the bar scenes of the "Hear The Wind Sing" film were shot **(p18)**. On the subject of films, the Kyoto scenes of the film "Norwegian Wood" were not shot in Kyoto but were actually filmed in the mountains of Hyogo.
- Every story in the short-story collection **After The Quake** is connected somehow to the devastating Kobe earthquake which occurred in 1995 **(p17)**. In many of the stories, however, the city is only mentioned in passing and most characters have no real connection to the region. A couple of exceptions are the story **Landscape With Flatiron**, in which the character Mr. Miyaki is from the Higashi-Nada part of Kobe, and the story **Thailand**, in which Satsuki mentions a man living in Kobe that she secretly hopes was harmed in the earthquake.

Nishinomiya: A city located near Ashiya that's home to about half a million people.
- In **1Q84**, a man Aomame meets in a bar is from Nishinomiya and he talks about the sailboat he has there.
- In the short story **Honey Pie** (After The Quake) the main character Junpei is originally from Nishinomiya.

IBARAKI

A coastal prefecture located a few hours north of Tokyo.
- The short story **Landscape With Flatiron** (After The Quake) takes place here.
- Tengo of **1Q84** graduated from Ibaraki's Tsukuba University.
- In **Dance, Dance, Dance**, Gotanda tells the protagonist that he could not have killed Mei because he drove to Mito, Ibaraki with his manager the same night she was murdered.

ISHIKAWA

A rural prefecture facing the Sea of Japan.
- In **South of the Border, West of the Sun**, Hajime and Shimamoto travel to a river in Ishikawa which is where she disposes of the ashes of her dead baby **(p105)**.
- In **Sputnik Sweetheart**, the narrator K reminisces about his experience with an older women he had while travelling in Ishikawa's capital of Kanazawa.
- Kanazawa is also mentioned in the short story **A Shinagawa Monkey** (Blind Willow, Sleeping Woman). The parents of Yuko, the pretty girl who lent Mizuki her nametag before killing herself, ran an inn in Kanazawa.

KAGAWA

A Shikoku prefecture famous for its udon noodles. It's Japan's smallest prefecture by area.
- Most of **Kafka on the Shore** takes place here. Kafka, as well as Nakata and Hoshino, base themselves at some point in Kagawa's capital Takamatsu (**pp. 140 - 149**). While unnamed in the novel, the location of the Komura Public Library is likely in Takamatsu's neighboring city of Sakaide (**pp. 150 - 157**).
- In **The Wind-Up Bird Chronicle**, Toru receives a letter from his missing wife which seems to be addressed from Takamatsu. However, the couple have no connection to Takamatsu and the address is smudged, leaving Toru unsure of the letter's true origin. Later in the book, it's written that Mr. Miyawaki who vacated the house with the well ended up strangling his daughter with a belt at an inn in Takamatsu. Afterward, he and his wife hanged themselves.
- In the short story **Kino** (Men Without Women)[56], Kino leaves Tokyo and goes to Takamatsu via express bus. He stays for 3 days at a business hotel near Takamatsu Station.

LOCATION REFERENCE GUIDE

KANAGAWA

Japan's second-most populous prefecture, located right next to Tokyo.

Chigasaki: A coastal city of about a quarter million people.
- Sumire of **Sputnik Sweetheart** was born and raised here.
- In the short story **Man-Eating Cats** (*Blind Willow, Sleeping Woman*), the narrator's wife took their children with her to her parent's place in Chigasaki. *Man-Eating Cats* shares many similarities with *Sputnik Sweetheart*.

Fujisawa: A city on the Shonan coast which encompasses the island of Enoshima.
- In **Dance, Dance, Dance**, the narrator and Yuki stop by the beach in Enoshima on their way to her father's house **(p60)**.
- In **Kafka on the Shore**, Nakata looks out at the sea from Kobe and recalls that he had not seen it since visiting Enoshima as an elementary school student.
- Enoshima is where May Kasahara from **The Wind-Up Bird Chronicle** got into a motorcycle accident with her boyfriend.
- In **1Q84**, Aomame's deceased friend Tamaki often took a yacht out to Enoshima with her husband.
- Shimamoto of **South of the Border, West of the Sun** tells Hajime that her family had moved to Fujisawa when she was young.

Hakone: A mountain town known for its hot springs and views of Mount Fuji.
- Yuki and her mother from **Dance, Dance, Dance** live here and the narrator visits at one point in the story. This is also where Dick North gets hit by a car **(p60)**.
- In **South of the Border, West of the Sun**, Hajime and his family have a cottage in Hakone. This is also where Hajime sees Shimamoto for the last time **(p105)**.
- Kafuku of the short story **Drive My Car** (*Men Without Women*) would drive with his wife to places like Hakone.
- Reiko from **Norwegian Wood** mentions spending a couple nights in Hakone shortly after her wedding.

Odawara: A western Kanagawa city known for Odawara Castle.
- At one point in **Dance, Dance, Dance**, the narrator and Yuki drive to Odawara to see a movie. They end up seeing Gotanda's "Unrequited Love."
- In **The Wind-Up Bird Chronicle**, Toru's uncle brings him fish-paste cakes from Odawara when he visits his home in Setagaya.

Ofuna: The town where the zoo veterinarian (Nutmeg's father) from **The Wind-Up Bird Chronicle** was born.

Yamato: Ushikawa from **1Q84** mentions living in the Chuorinkan part of Yamato for a time.

Yokohama: The second-most populated city in Japan.
- In **Dance, Dance, Dance**, the narrator drives Gotanda to Yokohama and drops him off at the New Grand Hotel **(p60)**.
- In **Kafka on the Shore**, a salesman named Togeguchi gives Nakata a ride to a rest stop on his way to Yokohama.
- In the story **Sleep** (*The Elephant Vanishes*)[57], the narrator drives to a parking lot in Yokohama at the end of the story.
- The narrator of **Family Affair** (*The Elephant Vanishes*) takes his date to Yokohama.
- In **A Slow Boat to China** (*The Elephant Vanishes*), a Chinese girl with whom the narrator used to work tells him her father ran an import business in Yokohama.
- In **The Wind-Up Bird Chronicle**, the family of Nutmeg's mother ran an import-export business in Yokohama.
- Mizuki of the story **A Shinagawa Monkey** (*Blind Willow, Sleeping Woman*) went to boarding school in Yokohama.
- Mari of **After Dark** lives in the Yokohama neighborhood of Hiyoshi. She also mentions going to a Chinese school somewhere in Yokohama.

KOCHI

The largest prefecture of Shikoku. In **Kafka on the Shore**, Kafka stays in a cabin in the woods of an unnamed part of Kochi prefecture **(p147)**.

KYOTO

The ancient capital of Japan which is famous for its historical temples, shrines and gardens.
- In **Norwegian Wood**, the mountains of Kyoto Prefecture is the location of the Ami Hostel where Naoko and Reiko stay. Watanabe takes a bullet train to Kyoto Station and then gets to the mountains by bus **(p89)**.
- In **South of the Border, West of the Sun**, the cousin of Izumi, Hajime's girlfriend at the time, lived in Kyoto near the old Imperial Palace. Hajime would visit Kyoto periodically to sleep with his girlfriend's cousin but eventually got caught.
- Satsuki of **Thailand** (*After The Quake*) is from Kyoto and lived there until she was eighteen.
- Yumiyoshi from **Dance, Dance, Dance** mentions checking a phone book wherever she goes to see if anyone has the same family name as her. She remarks that there's one other Yumiyoshi in Kyoto.

KUMAMOTO

A prefecture on the western coast of Kyushu.
- In **Kino** (*Men Without Women*), the character Kino stays in a business hotel in Kumamoto, near the main station. He hardly leaves the hotel room but at one point sends a postcard of Kumamoto Castle to his aunt.
- Mei from **Dance, Dance, Dance** was born in Kumamoto and her father is a powerful public servant there.

MIYAGI

The Tohoku prefecture where the city of Sendai is located.
- In the short story **Where I'm Likely to Find It** (*Blind Willow, Sleeping Woman*), the man who disappears from his apartment building mysteriously reappears in Sendai Station, Miyagi Prefecture.
- The Sheep Professor from **A Wild Sheep Chase** was born in Sendai in 1905.

NAGANO

A mountainous prefecture a couple hours west of Tokyo.
- Nakata from **Kafka on the Shore** lived with relatives in Nagano for a time in his mother's hometown.
- In **1Q84**, Tengo's mother was strangled to death in Nagano Prefecture at a hot springs resort.
- In **The Seventh Man** (*Blind Willow, Sleeping Woman*), the narrator moved to a village near Komoro, Nagano Prefecture after the traumatic experience of seeing his friend get swallowed up by a large wave.
- Takatsuki from the story **Honey Pie** (*After The Quake*) comes from Nagano Prefecture.
- The narrator of **Hard-Boiled Wonderland and The End of The World** mentions getting his sofa, the one that got toppled over, from a friend who quit his career and moved to Nagano.
- In **The Wind-Up Bird Chronicle**, Toru and Kumiko took a trip to Karuizawa, Nagano shortly after her abortion.
- Near the end of **Colorless Tsukuru Tazaki and His Years of Pilgrimage**, Tsukuru sits at the platform of Shinjuku station, tempted to suddenly board a long-distance train to Matsumoto, Nagano. However, he doesn't do it and returns home.

NAGASAKI

A Kyushu prefecture that was one of Japan's only cities to open up to foreign trade during the period of isolation.
- In **The Wind-Up Bird Chronicle**, Nutmeg Akasaka recalls arriving by boat from China to Sasebo, Nagasaki when she was a little girl.
- Watanabe's friend Ito in **Norwegian Wood** comes from Nagasaki.
- In **Tony Takitani** (*Blind Willow, Sleeping Woman*), Tony's father Shozaburo took a boat to Shanghai from Nagasaki.

NARA

The very first capital of Japan, located in the Kansai region near Osaka and Kyoto.
- Midori from **Norwegian Wood** travels to Nara with her boyfriend before they split up.
- In **Hear The Wind Sing**, the Rat mentions visiting the Emperor's tomb in Nara on a date with a girl.

NIIGATA

A mountainous prefecture popular for skiing and music festivals.
- The family of Kumiko in **The Wind-Up Bird Chronicle** comes from Niigata. She lived there as a child and later in the book, her brother Noboru Wataya takes over his uncle's position as Niigata's representative to the Lower House.
- Tsukuru of **Colorless Tsukuru Tazaki and His Years of Pilgrimage** was seeing a woman that had another boyfriend in Sanjo City, Niigata.
- In the beginning of the **The Silence** (*The Elephant Vanishes*), the narrator mentions that he was waiting for a plane to depart for Niigata that got delayed by heavy snow.
- In the story **The Mirror** (*Blind Willow, Sleeping Woman*), the narrator recalls working as a night watchman at a junior high school in rural Niigata.

OKAYAMA

A prefecture in the Chugoku region known for its peaches.
- In **Kafka on the Shore**, Kafka mentions passing through Kurashiki, Okayama, on the night bus to Kagawa. At the end of the book he rides to Okayama Station from where he rides a bullet train to Tokyo.
- Kino of the short-story **Kino** (*Men Without Women*) works for a sports apparel company based in Okayama.

LOCATION REFERENCE GUIDE

OKINAWA

A tropical island prefecture that was formerly part of the Ryukyu Kingdom.
- In **Honey Pie** (*After The Quake*), Takatsuki has to take a last-minute business trip to Okinawa, leaving his wife, daughter and friend to visit Ueno Zoo without him.
- The dowager from **1Q84** keeps a special butterfly that can only get nourishment from a special flower only found in Okinawa - a very troublesome and expensive butterfly to keep.

OITA

A prefecture in Kyushu known for its hot springs and mountains.
- In **Colorless Tsukuru Tazaki and His Years of Pilgrimage**, Oita is where Haida's father worked at a resort and during this time he met the mysterious jazz pianist who could see people's auras **(p205)**.
- In the short-story **Birthday Girl** (*Blind Willow, Sleeping Woman*), the main character is originally from Oita.

OSAKA

The largest city of Japan's Kansai region, known for its cuisine and its colorful dialect.
- In the story **Lederhosen** (*The Elephant Vanishes*), the storyteller's mother goes to stay with her sister in Osaka upon returning to Japan from Germany. She does so without a word to her husband in Tokyo.
- In **Norwegian Wood**, Watanabe transfers at Osaka to return to Tokyo after his month of traveling following Naoko's death. Naoko had also been taken to an Osaka hospital shortly before her suicide.
- In **Kafka on the Shore**, some other visitors present during a tour the Komura Memorial Library are a couple from Osaka.
- The mother of Yoshiya from **All God's Children Can Dance** (*After The Quake*) goes to stay at her church's Osaka facility when volunteering to help the victims of the Kobe earthquake.
- In **Honey Pie** (*After The Quake*), the father of Junpei owned a jewelry store in Osaka along with one in Kobe.
- Kitaru from **Yesterday** (*Men Without Women*) is known for speaking with an Osaka accent despite not being from there. Eventually he goes to attend a cooking school there.

SAITAMA

A prefecture just north of Tokyo from which many thousands commute every day to work in the capital.
- Ushikawa in **1Q84** is from Urawa, Saitama, despite being from Chiba in *The Wind-Up Bird Chronicle*.
- In **Landscape With Flatiron** (*After The Quake*), Junko is originally from Tokorozawa, Saitama.

A TALE OF TWO USHIKAWAS

Those who've read both *The Wind-Up Bird Chronicle* and *1Q84* know that the two novels contain one character in common - the repugnant yet oddly compelling Ushikawa. Both novels take place in the year 1984 so it's only natural to assume that this is the same Ushikawa in both books. However, when examining the character's background in each novel there are some glaring inconsistencies. In *The Wind-Up Bird Chronicle*, it's written that Ushikawa's father was a tatami maker in Funabashi, Chiba. In *1Q84*, on the other hand, it's explicitly stated that "Ushikawa had no ties to Chiba Prefecture"[58] and that he's from Urawa, Saitama. Did Murakami mean to hint that the universes of these two novels are similar yet slightly different alternate realities? Or perhaps it was simply a mistake. Regardless, Ushikawa will forever remain one of Murakami's most memorable characters.

SHIGA

A rural prefecture to the north of Kyoto that's home to Japan's largest lake. In **Colorless Tsukuru Tazaki and His Years of Pilgrimage**, Tsukuru's four close friends took a trip to Lake Biwa in Shiga prefecture. Tsukuru couldn't come because he was already living in Tokyo.

SHIZUOKA

A scenic prefecture known for the Izu Peninsula.
- In the story **Family Affair** (*The Elephant Vanishes*), the narrator's father runs a number of gas stations in Shizuoka.
- In **Kafka on the Shore**, Fujigawa, Shizuoka is where the leeches fall from the sky at the Tomei Highway rest stop.

Izu: A scenic peninsula known for its hot springs resorts.
- In **Kino** (*Men Without Women*), Kino's aunt lives at a resort condo in Izu.
- In **The Wind-Up Bird Chronicle**, May tells Toru that her family left for their summer house in Izu.
- Reiko of **Norwegian Wood** went to rest at her grandmother's place in Izu after one of her mental breakdowns.
- Kafuku of **Drive My Car** (*Men Without Women*) liked to go for drives in Izu with his wife before she passed away.

TOKUSHIMA

A Shikoku Prefecture known for the Awa Odori festival. In **Kafka on the Shore**, Hoshino and Nakata stay for a couple days in Tokushima after crossing the bridge from Kobe. This is where Nakata enters one of his very long and deep sleeps for the first time **(p145)**.

YAMAGATA

A rural, mountainous prefecture in the Tohoku region.
- In **After Dark**, Kaoru mentions building a house for her parents in Yamagata with the money she made from her pro-wrestling career.
- In **UFO in Kushiro** (*After The Quake*), Komura's wife is from Yamagata and she leaves him to return there shortly after the Kobe earthquake.
- In **A Shinagawa Monkey** (*Blind Willow, Sleeping Woman*), Mizuki's husband's family is from Yamagata. His father is a doctor with a clinic in Sakata.

YAMAGUCHI

The southernmost prefecture of Honshu island. In **The Wind-Up Bird Chronicle**, Lieutenant Mamiya recalls finding it easy to talk to Sergeant Hamano who was from Yamaguchi, close to his own hometown of Hiroshima.

YAMANASHI

A mountainous prefecture just west of Tokyo.
- In **1Q84**, Yamanashi is the base of the Sakigake cult as well as its previous incarnations. They first moved to a depopulated village and worked the fields. In 1981, there was a shootout near Yamanashi's Lake Motosu. In 1984 (or 1Q84), their headquarters are still located somewhere in Yamanashi. Fuka-eri was raised in Yamanashi but left to live with Professor Ebisuno in Ome, Tokyo **(p184)**.
- Nakata of **Kafka on the Shore** was sent to Yamanashi as a young boy during the war. This is where he blacked out and entered a long coma **(p147)**. Hoshino had also been stationed at one point at a military base in Yamanashi.
- Stormtrooper of **Norwegian Wood** is from somewhere in the mountains of Yamanashi.
- In **South of the Border, West of the Sun**, Hajime recalls meeting his wife in Yamanashi's Yatsugatake mountain range.
- Takahashi of **After Dark** recalls ending up in the Yamanashi mountains one time after falling asleep on the Chuo Line.

LOCATION REFERENCE GUIDE

TOKYO LOCATIONS

This section is ordered alphabetically by Tokyo municipality. Anything ending in *ku* is one of Tokyo's central 23 wards. Anything ending in *shi* or *machi* is a suburb to the west of the 23 wards.

Please note that a number of famous Tokyo neighborhoods overlap more than one ward. Aoyama is located in both Minato and Shibuya wards but most of the locations mentioned in the novels fall in Minato. Sendagaya covers both Shibuya and Shinjuku Wards but the locations mentioned mostly fall in Shinjuku. Hiroo spreads out over both Minato and Shibuya Wards and most places mentioned are in Shibuya. Komagome covers both Bunkyo and Toshima Wards.

For those unsure of where Tokyo's more famous neighborhoods can be found, Akasaka is in Minato-ku, Ginza is in Chuo-ku, Harajuku is in Shibuya-ku, Kichijoji is in Musashino-shi, Roppongi is in Minato-ku and Ueno is in Taito-ku.

BUNKYO-KU

A ward that's home to many book publishers as well as the famous Tokyo Dome.
- In *Norwegian Wood*, Midori moves from Otsuka to Myogadani in Bunkyo-ku. Wakeijuku, the dorm where Watanabe lives in the beginning of the novel is also located in Bunkyo **(p87)**. During Watanabe and Naoko's initial long walk, they end up in the Komagome neighborhood which is part of both Bunkyo and Toshima Wards **(p83)**. A number of these Bunkyo locations are also mentioned in the short story *Firefly* (*Blind Willow, Sleeping Woman*) which was a precursor to Norwegian Wood.
- Lieutenant Mamiya from *The Wind Up Bird Chronicle* stays in Hongo 2-chome, Bunkyo Ward when visiting Tokyo after Mr. Honda's death
- In *1Q84*, Ushikawa lives in a two-bedroom condo in Kohinata, Bunkyo-ku.
- In the short story *A Slow Boat to China* (*The Elephant Vanishes*), the narrator works in a publisher's warehouse in Bunkyo Ward.
- In *Yesterday* (*Men Without Women*), Kitaru mentions going to a haunted house in Bunkyo Ward with his girlfriend.

Tokyo University: Japan's most prestigious university which many Murakami characters have attended.
- Nagasawa attends Tokyo University in *Norwegian Wood* **(p81)**.
- In *A Folklore For My Generation* (*Blind Willow, Sleeping Woman*), the narrators's friend enrolled in the law department of Tokyo University.
- In *A Family Affair* (*The Elephant Vanishes*), the narrator meets a girl at a bar who's studying commercial design there.
- Kumiko's father in *The Wind-Up Bird Chronicle* graduated from Tokyo University with honors.
- One of the cats that Nakata speaks with in *Kafka on the Shore* mentions a friend being used in an experiment there.
- In *Sputnik Sweetheart*, K mentions that his sister graduated from Tokyo University law school.
- The Sheep Professor from *A Wild Sheep Chase* studied agriculture there when it was known as Tokyo Imperial University.

CHIYODA-KU

One of Tokyo's main business districts. This large ward contains some of the city's most significant neighborhoods and sightseeing attractions.

Akihabara: The world-famous neighborhood for all things anime, electronics and video games. Komura of *UFO in Kushiro* (*After The Quake*) is a salesman here.

Hibiya Park: One of eastern Tokyo's largest and most well-known parks.
- At the end of *Hear The Wind Sing*, the narrator mentions going to the park to feed pigeons with his wife **(p22)**.
- In *Hard-Boiled Wonderland and The End of The World*, this is where the protagonist and his librarian girlfriend have their final date **(p72)**.

Iidabashi: A prominent central business district.
- In *Norwegian Wood*, Watanabe and Naoko pass through Iidabashi during their first long walk together **(pp 75 - 77)**.
- In the short story *A Window* (*The Elephant Vanishes*), the narrator works for a company in Iidabashi called "The Pen Society."

Imperial Palace: In *Hard-Boiled Wonderland and The End of The World*, the INKlings have an underground lairs established somewhere near the Imperial Palace.

Jinbocho: (Also referred to as 'Kanda') An area famous for its numerous second-hand bookstores.
- Watanabe was on his way here when meeting Naoko by chance on the train, but they eventually walk through the neighborhood on foot together **(p79)**.
- In *Sputnik Sweetheart*, K and Sumire spend time together browsing books in the neighborhood.

Continued on next page

CHIYODA-KU (CONT'D.)

Kanda: The name Kanda may refer to the business district around JR Kanda station or a larger area which also encompasses Jinbocho and some of Akihabara. In *A Wild Sheep Chase*, the narrator's girlfriend works at publishing house in Kanda three days a week.

Kasumigaseki: A district where many government offices are located.
- In *All God's Children Can Dance* (*After The Quake*), Yoshiya spots the man with the missing earlobe, who just might be his father, at Kasumigaseki Station.
- Takahashi of *After Dark* observed trials at the Tokyo District Court in Kasumigaseki which left a lasting impression on him.

Kitanomaru Park: A large park located near Kudanshita which is home to many museums.
- In *Norwegian Wood*, Watanabe and Naoko walk past the moat outside of the park **(p78)**.
- In *Kafka on the Shore*, Kafka's father's work got displayed at the Tokyo National Modern Art Museum which is located inside the park.

Kojimachi: Another business district where many major company headquarters are located. In *1Q84*, Ushikawa's front company New Japan Foundation for the Advancement of Scholarship and the Arts is located here.

Ochanomizu: A district most synonymous with musical instrument shops.
- In *Norwegian Wood*, Watanabe and Naoko walk through here and Ochanomizu is also the location of the hospital where Midori's father stays **(p79)**.
- In *A Shinagawa Monkey* (*Blind Willow, Sleeping Woman*), Mr. Sakurada, who helped capture the monkey, was captain of the karate team of Meiji University in Ochanomizu.

Sophia University: A Jesuit university located in the Chiyoda section of Yotsuya (a district mostly located in Shinjuku).
- Dick North of *Dance, Dance, Dance* attended Sophia University and studied Japanese poetry there.
- Kitaru's girlfriend in *Yesterday* (*Men Without Women*) attends Sophia.

Tokyo Station: The station with the most trains running through it daily in all of Japan.
- In *Colorless Tsukuru Tazaki and His Years of Pilgrimage*, Tsukuru sits on the Tokyo Station platform for over an hour, watching the trains embark and disembark.
- In *Norwegian Wood*, Watanabe goes to meet Reiko at Tokyo Station when she arrives in the city.
- Tengo of *1Q84* takes a Chuo Line train from Koenji to Tokyo Station and from there decides to go all the way to Chikura in Chiba to see his father.
- In *Kafka on the Shore*, Nakata attempts to make it as far as Tokyo Station but ends up overwhelmed in Shinjuku.

CHUO-KU

Ginza: One of Tokyo's most well-known shopping and entertainment districts.
- In *The Wind-Up Bird Chronicle*, Toru and May go to Ginza to conduct their survey of balding men **(p113)**. Both Toru's uncle and Kojiro Miyawaki of the Miyawaki residence used to run restaurants in Ginza.
- In *Hard-Boiled Wonderland and The End of The World*, the protagonist goes shopping in Ginza at the end of the book **(p72)**.
- In *Colorless Tsukuru Tazaki and His Years of Pilgrimage*, Tsukuru and Sara meet in a Ginza coffee shop and this is where she tells him what she discovered from her research on his old friends **(p203)**.
- Kafuku of *Drive My Car* (*Men Without Women*) often performs in Ginza and the district is also where he goes drinking with Takatsuki, the actor he believes had an affair with his late wife.
- In *Dance, Dance, Dance*, the protagonist's old business partner mentions how he often takes clients out to fancy Ginza clubs.
- Midori from *Norwegian Wood* mentions going to meet her sister in Ginza before handing Watanabe a note.
- In *The Fall of The Roman Empire . . .* (*The Elephant Vanishes*) the narrator mentions running into an old friend at a Ginza bookstore.
- In *Tony Takitani* (*Blind Willow, Sleeping Woman*), Tony goes to see his father perform at a Ginza nightclub for the first time since his childhood.

Nihonbashi: A business district known for its bridge. In *Norwegian Wood*, Watanabe and Midori visit a Takashimaya department store in Nhonbashi and eat at a restaurant situated in the basement.

Shinbashi: A Chuo-ku business district just next to Ginza. May Kasahara's toupee company in *The Wind-Up Bird Chronicle* is located here. Toru and May stop in Shinbashi before and after conducting their baldness survey in Ginza.

EDOGAWA-KU

An eastern Tokyo ward named after the Edo river. In *Kino* (*Men Without Women*), the protagonist lives in Kasai, Edogawa with his wife but he sells their condo after catching her in bed with his friend.

LOCATION REFERENCE GUIDE

HACHIOJI-SHI
One of the most prominent of the western Tokyo suburbs, also home to Mount Takao.
- Fuka-Eri of **1Q84** first arrived in Takao after leaving Sakigake's compound in Yamanashi. At Takao Station she called Professor Ebisuno with whom she would start to live.
- After catching the monkey in **A Shinagawa Monkey** (*Blind Willow, Sleeping Woman*), the captors consider releasing the monkey at Mount Takao.

ITABASHI-KU
A northern Tokyo residential ward. In **1Q84**, Aomame reads an article about an NHK subscription fee collector who stabs a college student that refused to pay somewhere in Itabashi.

KITA-KU
A northern ward of Tokyo. In **Drive My Car** (*Men Without Women*), Kafuku's driver Misaki lives in Akabane, Kita-ku.

KOGANEI-SHI
A western Tokyo city with a population of about 120,000.
- Koganei is the location of the International Christian University mentioned at the beginning of **A Wild Sheep Chase** when the narrator recalls an ex-girlfriend from his college years. Therefore, we can assume that this area around where the same protagonist lives during the events of **Pinball, 1973 (pp 22, 23)**. However, the golf course just next to the campus is technically in Mitaka-shi and not in Koganei.
- In **Colorless Tsukuru Tazaki and His Years of Pilgrimage**, the jazz pianist at the inn in Oita Prefecture wrote his address as being in Koganei City.

KOKUBUNJI-SHI
A Western Tokyo city where the author himself ran his first jazz bar.
- In **Norwegian Wood**, Naoko lives in Kokubunji before moving to the mental hospital in Kyoto.
- In an untranslated short story, the narrator recalls living on a piece of land in Kokubunji surrounded by train tracks on all three sides. This area can be found nearby Nishi-Kokubunji station **(p132)**.

KOTO-KU
A ward bordering Chiba Prefecture that's home to half a million people.
- In **1Q84**, Ushikawa's grandfather's cousin, the one relative who happened to look like him, ran a metal shop in Koto Ward before the war.
- At one point in **Drive My Car** (*Men Without Women*), Kafuku and Misaki are driving close to Shinohashi in Koto-ku.

KUNITACHI-SHI
A quiet western city known for being home to many universities.
- Kunitachi is where K lives in **Sputnik Sweetheart**. Sumire even uses the local Kunitachi area code, 0425, as the combination for her suitcase **(p133)**.
- In **1Q84**, it's written that Fuka-Eri grips Tengo's hand up until their train reaches Kunitachi station.

MEGURO-KU
A wealthy central Tokyo ward best-known for the Meguro River.
- In **The Wind Up Bird-Chronicle**, the clairvoyant Mr. Honda lives somewhere in Meguro.
- In the short-story **Family Affair** (*The Elephant Vanishes*), the narrator's sister's future in-laws live in a large house in a wealthy part of Meguro.
- Tsukuru of **Colorless Tsukuru Tazaki and His Years of Pilgrimage** lives in a condo in Jiyugaoka, Meguro that his father bought for him **(p203)**.
- Aomame of **1Q84** also lives in a Jiyugaoka apartment until she moves to the safe house in Koenji **(p189)**.

MINATO-KU

Akasaka: A central business and entertainment district that's a prominent location in much of Murakami's fiction.
- In *The Wind-Up Bird Chronicle*, Nutmeg and Cinnamon Akasaka (nicknamed after the area) have a couple of companies here, including Akasaka Research in the 2-chome district and Akasaka Fashion Design, likely somewhere near Akasaka-Mitsuke station **(p115)**.
- In *A Wild Sheep Chase*, the narrator's girlfriend works for an Akasaka-based escort service.
- The sequel *Dance, Dance, Dance* features many scenes in Akasaka. The district is the headquarters of the company involved in the development of the new Dolphin Hotel in Sapporo. Yuki and her mother have a small condo in Akasaka close to Nogi Shrine, a part of Akasaka which is also referred to as Nogizaka. The prostitute Mei was murdered in an Akasaka luxury hotel and the protagonist was taken into the Akasaka Police Station for a few days for an interrogation **(p58, 59)**.
- In *1Q84*, Aomame frequently visits hotels, bars and restaurants around the Akasaka area. When she goes on her mission to kill the Sakigake Leader, she visits him at Hotel Okura which is located in the general Akasaka area but technically part of Toranomon. At the end of the book, Aomame and Tengo spend a night together in an Akasaka hotel **(pp. 178, 179)**.
- Sumire and Miu of *Sputnik Sweetheart* meet for the first time at an Akasaka hotel. The neighborhood is also where Miu's company has its main office **(p135)**.
- In *South of the Border, West of the Sun*, Hajime's father-in-law takes him to an Akasaka eel restaurant for a long talk.
- In *Hanalei Bay* (*Blind Willow, Sleeping Woman*), the father of one of the young surfers runs a Western pastry shop somewhere in Akasaka.
- In *Yesterday* (*Men Without Women*) the narrator attends a wine-tasting party at an Akasaka hotel.
- The narrator of the short story *Barn Burning* (*The Elephant Vanishes*) runs into the guy who likes to burn barns nearby Nogizaka station.

Aoyama: A fashionable district known for art, fashion and architecture. It spreads out over both Minato and Shibuya-ku.
- Most of *South of the Border, West of the Sun* takes place here. Some of the locations mentioned include Kinokuniya supermarket, Aoyama Cemetery and Omotesando Street **(pp. 96 - 107)**.
- Tsukuru of *Colorless Tsukuru Tazaki and His Years of Pilgrimage* goes to Aoyama to buy souvenirs for Kuro in Finland. He and Sara also visit a French restaurant in the area **(p202)**.
- The protagonist of *Dance, Dance, Dance* frequently visit's Aoyama's Kinokuniya Supermarket throughout the novel. Part of his usual walking course goes through Aoyama and past the Nezu Museum **(pp. 56, 57)**.
- In *Hard-Boiled Wonderland and The End of The World*, the protagonist and the girl in pink emerge from the underground INKling lair at one of the platforms of Aoyama-Itchome Station **(p65)**.
- Miu and Sumire go to a fancy Aoyama restaurant in *Sputnik Sweetheart*. Miu herself also has her own apartment in the area.
- The short story *Kino* (*Men Without Women*) mostly takes place here. Kino takes over his aunt's bar behind the Nezu Museum and even sees a snake outside.
- Kafuku and Takatsuki of *Drive My Car* (*Men Without Women*) go drinking at a small bar behind the Nezu Museum. Could this perhaps be where Kino worked?
- The narrator of *A Wild Sheep Chase* and his girlfriend meet in person for the first time at a French restaurant in Aoyama after the protagonist becomes infatuated with the photograph of her ears.
- In *1Q84*, Sakigake owns some properties in Aoyama.
- In *The Wind-Up Bird Chronicle*, Nutmeg takes Toru clothes shopping at a fancy store in Aoyama. Nutmeg also lived in the neighborhood when she was married.
- Tony's wife in *Tony Takitani* (*Blind Willow, Sleeping Woman*) often bought expensive clothes in Aoyama and this is also where Tony's studio is.
- In *A Slow Boat to China* (*The Elephant Vanishes*), the narrator gets spotted by an old classmate at a cafe on Aoyama Boulevard.

Azabu: A wealthy neighborhood known for its many embassies and Tokyo Tower.
- Gotanda from *Dance, Dance, Dance* lives in Azabu and the protagonist visits any number of times throughout the novel. His apartment features a view of Tokyo Tower **(p55)**.
- In *1Q84*, the dowager runs the Willow House, a safe house for women, somewhere in Azabu **(p188)**.
- Azabu is where Toru's uncle lives in *The Wind-Up Bird Chronicle*.
- At one point in *Norwegian Wood*, Watanabe, Nagasawa and Hatsumi eat dinner together at a French restaurant in Azabu.
- Dr. Tokai from *Independent Organ* (*Men Without Women*)[54] lives in an apartment in Azabu.

Hiroo: A fashionable district which is situated in both Minato and Shibuya wards. In *Drive My Car* (*Men Without Women*), Kafuku tells Misaki to drive him to Arisugawa Park.

Odaiba: An artificial island off the coast of Tokyo popular for shopping and entertainment.
- At the end of *Hard-Boiled Wonderland and The End of The World*, the protagonist drives his car out here and "falls asleep" as Bob Dylan plays on the stereo. Earlier in the novel, five Calcutec bodies are discovered floating in Tokyo Bay, of which Odaiba is a part.
- Tokyo Bay is also where Gotanda kills himself at the end of *Dance, Dance, Dance*.

LOCATION REFERENCE GUIDE

MINATO-KU (CONT'D.)

Roppongi: One of Tokyo's most prominent nightlife and entertainment districts.
- Aomame visits the district a number of times in *1Q84* to meet men, often with her friend Ayumi **(p189)**.
- The narrator and Gotanda of *Dance, Dance, Dance* visit a fashionable steak house in Roppongi.
- The short story **Birthday Girl** (*Blind Willow, Sleeping Woman*) takes place at an Italian restaurant in Roppongi. The mysterious owner lives on one of the building's upper floors with a view of Tokyo Tower.
- In **Hanalei Bay** (*Blind Willow, Sleeping Woman*) Sachi opened up a piano bar in Roppongi where she would play every night. She later runs into one of the surfer boys near a Roppongi Starbucks.
- The narrator of the story **New York Mining Disaster** (*Blind Willow, Sleeping Woman*) attends a New Years party at a Roppongi bar.
- In **Kino** (*Men Without Women*) the protagonist had spent time working at a bar in Roppongi during college.
- Dr. Tokai's clinic in **Independent Organ** (*Men Without Women*) is located in Roppongi.

Shirokanedai: An upper-class residential district near Meguro. The narrator's friend in **A Folklore For My Generation** (*Blind Willow, Sleeping Woman*) used to live here.

MITAKA-SHI

A residential suburb perhaps best known for being home to the Ghibli Museum.
- In **Pinball, 1973**, the golf course that the protagonist often visits with the twins is located in Mitaka City. Today it's a public area called Nogawa Park **(pp. 22, 23)**.
- In the sequel, **A Wild Sheep Chase**, the narrator reminisces about an ex-girlfriend who would stop by his apartment outside Mitaka **(p22)**.

MUSASHINO-SHI

A fashionable Tokyo suburb just to the west of the 23 wards. In **Kafka on the Shore**, Kafka's father has a studio and office somewhere in Musashino City.

Kichijoji: A neighborhood considered to be one of Tokyo's most desirable places to live. It's home to Inokashira Park.
- Sumire of **Sputnik Sweetheart** lives in Kichijoji before moving to Yoyogi-Uehara. She and K often hang out in Inokashira Park in the novel and she sometimes calls him from the park's public payphone **(pp. 130, 131)**.
- In **Norwegian Wood**, Watanabe moves to Kichijoji after leaving his dorm. He has an entire small house to himself and he and Reiko have a special ceremony for Naoko there at the end of the book **(p85)**.

NAKANO-KU

A large ward just to the west of Shinjuku.
- In **Kafka on the Shore**, both Kafka and Nakata are from Nogata, Nakano. At the beginning of the novel, Nakata is searching for a missing cat in the 2-chome area. He is then taken to Kafka's house and ends up killing his father in a house somewhere about 15 minutes away on foot. The young police officer to whom Nakata confesses the murder works in the koban just outside the station **(pp. 160, 161)**.
- In **Fall of The Roman Empire...** (*The Elephant Vanishes*), the narrator's girlfriend lives in Nakano.

NERIMA-KU

A western residential ward. Shirakawa, the antagonist of **After Dark**, lives in Tetsugakudo, Nerima Ward.

OKUTAMA-MACHI

A mountainous village in western Tokyo that's home to Mt. Okutama. In **Sputnik Sweetheart**, K takes his elementary school students climbing there, although the field trip doesn't go very smoothly.

OME-SHI

A mountainous city about an hour west of central Tokyo. In *1Q84*, Professor Ebisuno and Fuka-Eri live in an area called Futamatao which is part of Ome-City. This is where the Air Chrysalis story was written **(pp. 184, 185)**.

OSHIMA ISLAND

A small island administered by Tokyo but actually a 6 hour ferry ride away from the city. In **All God's Children Can Dance** (*After The Quake*), Yoshiya's mother had planned to kill herself by jumping off the ferry to Oshima.

OTA-KU

A southern Tokyo ward that's home to Haneda airport.
- In the short story **Yesterday** (*Men Without Women*), Kitaru lives in the fancy Denenchofu part of Ota Ward but claims his house is shabby.
- In **Man-Eating Cats** (*Blind Willow, Sleeping Woman*), the narrator was living in Unoki, Ota-ku with his wife and son before their split.
- Haneda Airport is mentioned occasionally throughout Murakami's work, such as when Hajime and Shimamoto use it to fly to Ishikawa in **South of the Border, West of the Sun**. The narrator of **Dance, Dance, Dance** also flies there from Sapporo with Yuki.

SETAGAYA-KU

A large commercial and residential ward that makes frequent appearances throughout Murakami's work.
- In **The Wind-Up Bird Chronicle**, Toru and Kumiko, as well as May Kasahara, live in Setagaya near an unnamed Odakyu Line station. Some likely possibilities are Umegaoka, Gotokuji or Kyodo (**p120**).
- The protagonist of **Hard-Boiled Wonderland and The End of The World** also lives in an unnamed part of Setagaya Ward (**p70**).
- At the beginning of **1Q84**, Aomame walks down an expressway emergency staircase in Sangenjaya, This is supposedly where she enters the alternate reality of 1Q84 (**p177**). Aomame's friend Tamaki lived in Okusawa, Setagaya Ward.
- In **Dance, Dance, Dance**, Dick North's estranged family lives in Gotokuji, Setagaya. The protagonist briefly visits the house after Dick's death.
- Miu of **Sputnik Sweetheart** lives somewhere in Setagaya with her husband when she's not staying at her apartment in Aoyama.
- In **Tony Takitani** (*Blind Willow, Sleeping Woman*), Tony lives in a large house in a rich part of Setagaya.
- In the story **A Window** (*The Elephant Vanishes*), the narrator goes to the house of one his Pen Masters pen pals somewhere along the Odakyu line.
- The narrator of **The Last Lawn of The Afternoon** (*The Elephant Vanishes*) works for a Kyodo, Setagaya-based lawn mowing service but carries out his last job just over the border in Kanagawa Prefecture.
- The narrator's date in **Family Affair** (*The Elephant Vanishes*) lives somewhere in Setagaya.
- The woman whom the piano tuner gets to know in **Chance Traveller** (*Blind Willow, Sleeping Woman*) is from a well-off Setagaya family.

SHIBUYA-KU

One of Tokyo's busiest and most popular wards, home to prominent neighborhoods such as Shibuya and Harajuku.
Ebisu: An upscale neighborhood one stop away from Shibuya on the Yamanote Line.
- Tsukuru and Sara of **Colorless Tsukuru Tazaki and His Years of Pilgrimage** meet at a bar in Ebisu for cocktails (**p203**).
- In **Norwegian Wood**, Nagasawa's girlfriend Hatsumi lives in Ebisu. At one point she helps seal Watanabe's wound in her apartment.
- Kafuku of **Drive My Car** (*Men Without Women*) lives in an apartment in Ebisu.

Harajuku: One of Tokyo's most famous neighborhoods for youth culture and fashion.
- In **Dance, Dance, Dance**, the protagonist often walks to Harajuku as part of his usual walking route. At another point in the novel he visits Takeshita Street and eats some tempura (**pp. 55 - 57**).
- In **Sputnik Sweetheart**, Miu's office where Sumire works is located in the Jingumae section of Harajuku (**p134**).
- The short story **On Seeing the 100% Perfect Girl One Beautiful April Morning** takes place entirely in Harajuku, when a boy and a girl pass each other on a narrow street.
- In **Man-Eating Cats** (*Blind Willow, Sleeping Woman*) the couple visit a Denny's in Harajuku in the early morning.

Hiroo: A upper-class neighborhood that's popular with expats. Parts of it also cover Minato-Ward.
- In **1Q84**, Aomame teaches martial arts at a fancy Hiroo sports club (**p188**).
- Tsukuru and Sara of **Colorless Tsukuru Tazaki and His Years of Pilgrimage** go on a date in a small bistro in Hiroo.
- At the end of **Sputnik Sweetheart**, the protagonist spots Miu in her Jaguar at an intersection near the Meidi-Ya store.
- In **Drive My Car** (*Men Without Women*), Kafuku goes shopping in Hiroo's Meidi-Ya store.
- Cinnamon Akasaka of **The Wind-Up Bird Chronicle** lives in Hiroo.

Sendagaya: A fashionable district that spreads out over both Shinjuku and Shibuya wards, known for being home to many sports facilities. In **Hard-Boiled Wonderland and The End of The World**, the narrator mentions the Hope-Ken ramen restaurant located in the Shibuya-ku part of Sendagaya (**p66**).

SHIBUYA-KU (CONT'D.)

Shibuya: The central Shibuya area is home to the scramble crossing and the 109 building. It's comprised of districts such as Dogenzaka, Maruyamacho, Udagawacho and Jinnan.
- The majority of **After Dark** takes place in central Shibuya, namely the Maruyamacho and Jinnan districts. Many significant events take place around "Love Hotel Hill" **(pp. 166 - 173)**.
- The protagonist of **Dance, Dance, Dance** lives in Shibuya, somewhere near the expressway. Throughout the novel he visits local movie theaters, Tokyu Hands and Shakey's Pizza **(p54)**.
- At the beginning of **1Q84**, Aomame goes to kill one of the dowager's targets in a Shibuya business hotel **(p177)**. Aomame's friend Ayumi gets murdered in a Maruyamacho love hotel. In Japan there is a famous true story of a female TEPCO employee who secretly prostituted herself at night, only to end up murdered in Maruyamacho.
- Hajime of **South of the Border, West of the Sun** spots Shimamoto in Shibuya and follows her up Miyamasuzaka Street and into Aoyama. Much of Aoyama is located in Shibuya Ward in addition to Minato **(p97)**.
- In **Pinball, 1973**, the protagonist's office is in Nanpeidai, Shibuya and he and his coworker pass out fliers near the station on slow days **(p22)**.
- In **Norwegian Wood**, Watanabe and Nagasawa often go out drinking in Shibuya to pick up girls. Watanabe also visits Shibuya one time with Hatsumi, Nagasawa's girlfriend.
- Tsukuru and Sara walk together to Shibuya at one point in **Colorless Tsukuru Tazaki and His Years of Pilgrimage**.
- The couple of **Man-Eating Cats** (Blind Willow, Sleeping Woman) goes out drinking all night in Shibuya before heading to Harajuku.

Yoyogi: A bustling district right in between Shinjuku and Harajuku.
- Yoyogi is where Tengo teaches math at his cram school in **1Q84 (p189)**.
- In **South of the Border, West of the Sun**, Hajime's father-in-law's company used to be in Yoyogi.

Yoyogi-Hachiman: A trendy Shibuya residential district.
- At the end of **Dance, Dance, Dance**, the protagonist takes Yuki to Yoyogi-Hachiman station so she can board the Odakyu Line.
- Aomame of **1Q84** lived in a company dorm in Yoyogi-Hachiman while working for a sports drink company.

Yoyogi-Uehara: An upscale residential district nearby Yoyogi Park. Sumire of **Sputnik Sweetheart** moves here from Kichijoji **(p135)**.

SHINAGAWA-KU

A southern Tokyo ward that's home to a number of international businesses.
- In **The Wind-Up Bird Chronicle**, Toru goes to meet Malta Kano in Shinagawa at the Pacific Hotel, now known as the Keikyu Ex Inn Shinagawa **(p124)**.
- Takahashi and Mari of **After Dark** first met at a pool in Shinagawa a couple years before they meet at a Denny's.
- Mizuki of **A Shinagawa Monkey** (Blind Willow, Sleeping Woman) lives in the ward and goes for counseling sessions which are free to local residents.
- In **Where I'm Likely to Find It** (Blind Willow, Sleeping Woman), the apartment from which the man disappears is located in Shinagawa Ward.
- In **A Folklore For My Generation** (Blind Willow, Sleeping Woman), the narrator's friend recalls meeting his ex-girlfriend at her apartment in Shinagawa.

SHINJUKU-KU

One of Tokyo's main districts and home to the world's busiest station. Shinjuku is also home to many of Tokyo's famous skyscrapers **(p119)** and the popular nightlife district Kabukicho.

Sendagaya: A fashionable district that spreads out over both Shinjuku and Shibuya wards, known for being home to many sports facilities.
- In **Hard-Boiled Wonderland and The End of The World**, a number of Sendagaya locations are mentioned, such as Meiji Jingu Stadium and Gaien Park **(pp. 64 - 71)**.
- In **Dance, Dance, Dance**, the narrator walks by Meiji Jingu Stadium as part of his usual walking route **(p56)**. He also sometimes visits the Sendagaya Pool.

Shinanomachi: Fuka-Eri of **1Q84** stays in an apartment in Shinanomachi when she's not staying in Futamatao. Shinanomachi happens to be heavily affiliated with the Japanese religious group Soka Gakkai. Could Murakami have possibly been hinting at parallels between this group and Sakigake?

Continued on next page

SHINJUKU-KU (CONT'D.)

Shinjuku: The bustling area around Shinjuku Station.
- In **Norwegian Wood**, Watanabe works in a Shinjuku record shop and often goes out drinking with Midori in the neighborhood at places like Dug **(p84)**.
- Toru from **The Wind-Up Bird Chronicle** watches the faces of passerbys outside the station before going to people watch near a large skyscraper. He also mentions going on one of his early dates with Kumiko to Shinjuku Gyoen **(pp. 116, 117)**.
- In **1Q84**, Tengo meets Fuka-Eri for the first time at Nakamuraya Cafe near the station's East Exit. He also mentions visiting the nearby Kinokuniya bookstore. Aomame returns to Shinjuku Station after her meeting with Sakigake's leader to pick up her luggage from a coin locker **(p179)**.
- At the end of **Colorless Tsukuru Tazaki and His Years of Pilgrimage**, Tsukuru sits for awhile on a platform bench, observing the people and the incoming trains **(p202)**.
- The game center that the narrator recalls going to in **Pinball, 1973** was located somewhere in Shinjuku **(p24)**.
- In **Hard-Boiled Wonderland And The End of The World**, the narrator leaves his Nike bag with the unicorn skull in a locker at Shinjuku station **(p66)**.
- In the story **Super-Frog Saves Tokyo** (*After The Quake*) Katagiri, who works for the Shinjuku branch of Tokyo Security Trust Bank, often went to Kabukicho to collect debts. The battle between Super-Frog and Worm was set to take place in the boiler room of the bank, nearby the Shinjuku Ward office. Katagiri later gets attacked outside nearby.
- K of **Sputnik Sweetheart** mentions going to Kinokuniya in Shinjuku to pick up a few books before seeing a Luc Besson movie.
- In **A Wild Sheep Chase**, the narrator goes for a drink at a high-rise hotel near Shinjuku Station's West Exit.
- Nakata of **Kafka on the Shore** takes a bus to Shinjuku from where he's able to find a ride to the nearest rest stop.
- In **Hear The Wind Sing**, the narrator recalls meeting a girl at Shinjuku station on a night when there were violent demonstrations all over the area.
- In **South of the Border, West of the Sun**, Shimamoto mentions always looking to be blown away by jazz performances in Shinjuku.
- In **A Slow Boat to China** (*The Elephant Vanishes*), the narrator says goodbye to his Chinese coworker after their date in Shinjuku before realizing he put her on the wrong train.
- In **Firefly** (*Blind Willow, Sleeping Woman*), the narrator mentions buying a birthday cake in Shinjuku.

Waseda University: One of Japan's top private universities, located in Shinjuku Ward.
- Watanabe in **Norwegian Wood** likely attends Waseda although it is not named in the novel **(p86)**. Murakami himself attended the university and the student dorm described in the novel, Wakeijuku, is a close walk from there.
- The narrator of **Yesterday** (*Men Without Women*) was a sophomore at Waseda when he met Kitaru.
- Junpei of **Honey Pie** (*Blind Willow, Sleeping Woman*) attended Waseda and enrolled in the literature department without telling his parents.

Yotsuya: A central Tokyo business district located mostly within Shinjuku Ward but also in parts of Chiyoda.
- In **Norwegian Wood**, Watanabe and Naoko start their long walk through Tokyo in Yotsuya after a chance meeting on the train **(pp. 75 - 77)**.
- The short story **Firefly** (*Blind Willow, Sleeping Woman*), on which **Norwegian Wood** was based, also mentions the same long walk as in the novel.
- Tengo and Komatsu meet in a Yotsuya bar in **1Q84** and Tengo also rides to Yotsuya when searching for Ushikawa's company.
- In **South of the Border, West of the Sun**, Hajime's father-in-law works in a seven-story building in Yotsuya.
- At one point in **The Wind-Up Bird Chronicle**, Toru mentions walking to Yotsuya Station.
- In **Hard-Boiled Wonderland and The End of The World**, the man from Tokyo Gas hired to enter the protagonist's apartment has a daughter attending high school in Yotsuya.

SUGINAMI-KU

A residential ward in western Tokyo popular with young creative types.

Asagaya: A lively neighborhood on the JR Chuo Line.
- Toru of **The Wind-Up Bird Chronicle** was living in Asagaya at the time he first met Kumiko.
- In **All God's Children Can Dance** (*After The Quake*), Yoshiya and his mother live together in Asagaya.

Koenji: A popular Chuo-Line neighborhood known for its music, culture and nightlife.
- Tengo lives in Koenji throughout the events of **1Q84**. Near the end of the book, Aomame moves to Koenji as well. The park with the slide mentioned in the novel is Koenji Chuo Park **(pp. 180, 181)**.
- Toru and Kumiko of **The Wind-Up Bird Chronicle** lived together in Koenji before moving to Setagaya.
- Takahashi of **After Dark** lives in Koenji.

LOCATION REFERENCE GUIDE

TACHIKAWA-SHI

A large suburb in western Tokyo on the JR Chuo Line.
- In *1Q84*, Fuka-Eri and Tengo transfer at Tachikawa station to get to Futamatao where Professor Ebisuno lives **(p184)**.
- At the end of *Sputnik Sweetheart*, K is called to Tachikawa after his student (and son of his girlfriend) gets caught shoplifting in a supermarket **(p84)**.
- In *After Dark*, Takahashi tells Mari about a trial he witnessed in Tachikawa.

TAITO-KU

A northeastern Tokyo Ward that's home to Ueno.

Ueno: A popular neighborhood famous for Ueno Park and its many museums.
- *Norwegian Wood* ends with Watanabe calling Midori from Ueno station after dropping Reiko off. Earlier in the novel, Midori mentions her long talks with her father on the train rides from Fukushima to Ueno **(pp. 90, 91)**.
- In *The Wind-Up Bird Chronicle*, Toru recalls his first date with Kumiko at Ueno Zoo where they looked at the jellyfish in the aquarium together **(p124)**.
- In *Honey Pie* (*After The Quake*), Junpei, Sayoko and Sala go to Ueno Zoo together and look at the bears.

TOSHIMA-KU

A bustling ward in northern Tokyo. In *Where I'm Likely to Find It* (*Blind Willow, Sleeping Woman*), the man who disappears is the son of a Buddhist priest that headed a temple in Toshima-ku.

Ikebukuro: Home to one of the busiest stations on the JR Yamanote Line. In *Kafka on the Shore*, Kafka recalls taking the train to Ikebukuro to see "The Sound of Music."

Komagome: A neighborhood on the Yamanote Line known for the Rikugien Gardens.
- In *Norwegian Wood*, Naoko and Watanabe end their very long walking journey in Komagome **(p83)**.
- In *A Slow Boat to China* (*The Elephant Vanishes*), the Chinese girl lives in an apartment with her brother in Komagome.

Mejiro: A prestigious residential district in northwestern Tokyo.
- The narrator and the Spanish instructor of *Pinball, 1973* drive through Mejiro on their way to the pinball warehouse **(p24)**.
- The narrator of *Hear The Wind Sing* recalls meeting the second girl he slept with in Shinjuku before they walked together all the way to Mejiro.
- In *A Slow Boat to China* (*The Elephant Vanishes*), the narrator lives in a dorm in Mejiro.

Otsuka: Midori of *Norwegian Wood* lives in Otsuka and Watanabe often visits her via the tram line **(p88)**.

Sugamo: In *A Wild Sheep Chase*, The Boss spent some time in Sugamo Prison after the war. Allied forces would keep suspected war criminals there.

LOCATIONS AROUND THE WORLD

Though a large majority of Murakami's fiction takes place within Japan, a number of other countries are mentioned and sometimes even visited by major characters.

AFGHANISTAN

In **Dance, Dance, Dance**, Yuki's father Hiraku Makimura mentions having travelled to Afghanistan.

ALGERIA

In the short story **Barn Burning** (*The Elephant Vanishes*), the narrator's friend went on a trip to Algeria where she met the man who likes to burn barns.

AUSTRALIA

In **Kafka on the Shore**, a similar event to the one where the entire class of schoolchildren passed out in a Yamanashi forest is mentioned as having happened once in Adelaide, Australia.

BRAZIL

Hajime of **South of the Border, West of the Sun** meets an old friend at his bar who had worked for two years in Brazil. He even met an old classmate in São Paulo by chance.

CHINA

The story **A Slow Boat to China** (*The Elephant Vanishes*) is all about people of Chinese descent living in Japan and the narrator's own dreams of China, although no character actually visits China over the course of the story.

Manchuria: The northeastern region of China where the Japanese established the puppet state of Manchukuo from 1931 until the end of World War II.
- In **The Wind-Up Bird Chronicle**, Lieutenant of Mamiya was first sent to Hsin-Ching, the capital of Machukuo, where he was assigned to make maps.
- It was in Manchuria that the Sheep Professor from **A Wild Sheep Chase** encountered the sheep with the star on its back. The Boss, the next person to establish a relationship with this sheep, had gone to Manchuria and got involved with the Kanto Army and was also rumored to deal drugs there.

Shanghai:
- In **Hear The Wind Sing**, the narrator mentions that one of his uncles died in Shanghai.
- In **Tony Takitani** (*Blind Willow, Sleeping Woman*), Shozaburo Takitani went to Shanghai and often played trombone in the city's nightclubs.

Beijing: At the end of **After Dark**, Mari tells Takahashi that she's headed for Beijing as an exchange student.

CZECH REPUBLIC

The short story **Samsa in Love** (*Men Without Women*)[59] takes place in Prague, Czech Republic.

ENGLAND

- In **Kafka on the Shore**, a similar event to the one where the entire class of schoolchildren passed out in a Yamanashi forest is mentioned as having happened once in Devonshire, England.
- Malta Kano of **The Wind-Up Bird Chronicle** once used her psychic powers to help find a missing girl in England.

LOCATION REFERENCE GUIDE

FINLAND

- Kuro, Tsukuru's old friend in **Colorless Tsukuru Tazaki and His Years of Pilgrimage**, lives in Finland and Tsukuru goes to visit her. She normally lives in Helsinki but stays in a cottage in the village of Hämeenlinna in the summer **(p204)**.
- At the end of the **Hard-Boiled Wonderland and The End of The World**, the girl in pink's grandfather goes to Finland because he likes the quiet.

FRANCE

- Miu and Sumire travel to France together in **Sputnik Sweetheart** and K even receives a letter from there. Miu also previously used to live in Paris.
- The dowager from **1Q84** lived in Paris when she was a young girl.
- In **Tony Takitani** (Blind Willow, Sleeping Woman), Tony and his wife spent their honeymoon in Europe and his wife bought an exorbitant amount of clothes in Paris and Milan.
- In **Honey Pie** (After The Quake), Sayoko and Takatsuki spent their honeymoon in France.

GERMANY

- In the short story **Lederhosen** (The Elephant Vanishes), the woman whom the story is about visits Hamburg alone and her experience buying lederhosen causes her to rethink her entire marriage.
- **Norwegian Wood** begins with an older Watanabe reminiscing about Naoko while in the Hamburg airport. Later in the book, Reiko mentions planning to study piano in Germany and Nagasawa sends Watanabe a letter from Bonn.

GREECE

- A large chunk of **Sputnik Sweetheart** takes place in Greece on an unnamed little island near Rhodes. After Sumire suddenly disappears, K visits the island to meet with Miu in hopes of tracking her down **(p204)**.
- The short-story **Man-Eating Cats** (Blind Woman, Sleeping Willow), the precursor to **Sputnik Sweetheart**, also takes place on an unnamed island near Turkey.

HONG KONG

Kaoru from **After Dark** mentions having some professional wrestling matches in Hong Kong and Taiwan.

INDIA

In **Kafka on the Shore**, Sakura stays in the apartment of her friend who'd gone to travel around India for awhile.

INDONESIA

In **Sputnik Sweetheart**, K's girlfriend returns well-tanned from a family vacation in Bali.

ITALY

- In the story **A Folklore For My Generation** (Blind Willow, Sleeping Woman), then narrator runs into an old schoolmate in the town of Lucca. He was travelling solo throughout the country while his friend was there on business.
- Sumire and Miu from **Sputnik Sweetheart** visit Milan, Florence, Venice and Rome during their business trip together.
- In **Tony Takitani** (Blind Willow, Sleeping Woman), Tony and his wife spent their honeymoon in Europe and his wife bought an exorbitant amount of clothes in Milan and Paris.

KOREA

- Miu of **Sputnik Sweetheart** is an ethnic Korean born in Japan. She recalls visiting a small mountainous Korean town where a statue of her father was erected as thanks for him building a number of public buildings there.
- The Sheep Professor of **A Wild Sheep Chase** researched rice cultivation in Korea.

LEBANON

The narrator's friend in the story **Barn Burning** (The Elephant Vanishes) sends him a telegram from Beirut with her flight number on it, hoping he will come pick her up.

MALTA

Malta Kano of **The Wind-Up Bird Chronicle** adopted her name from the island country. She claims that there is water in a certain spot of the island with special healing powers.

MONGOLIA

- In **The Wind-Up Bird Chronicle**, Mongolia is where Lieutenant Mamiya witnessed a man get skinned alive before he himself got thrown into a well.
- The Sheep Professor of **A Wild Sheep Chase** helped develop a framework for ovine productivity in Mongolia.

NEPAL

In **Dance, Dance, Dance**, Yuki's mother goes to Kathmandu for a photography project.

PHILIPPINES

Nakata's schoolteacher, whose interview is documented at the beginning of **Kafka on the Shore**, mentions her husband getting killed outside Manila by American shells.

RUSSIA

In **Hard-Boiled Wonderland and The End of The World**, the librarian reads about a unicorn skull being found by the Russian front in 1917.

Sakhalin: An island north of Hokkaido that was once the center of a territorial dispute between Japan and Russia.
- In **1Q84**, Tamaru was born on the island of Sakhalin. Tengo also reads about the Gilyaks to Fuka-Eri, a group that inhabited parts of Sakhalin.
- In **A Wild Sheep Chase**, the narrator wonders if the Rat had gone as far north as Sakhalin but knows it'd be impossible to send a special delivery to Tokyo from there.

Siberia:
- Lieutenant Mamiya of **The Wind-Up Bird Chronicle** was taken to a Siberian internment camp during the war where he happened to meet Boris the Manskinner.
- The 'West of The Sun' part of **South of the Border, West of the Sun** refers to the illness *hysteria siberiana*. As Shimamoto explains to Hajime, this is when Siberian farmers suddenly break down, stop working and journey westward to find the land which lies west of the setting sun.
- Yuki's father Hiraku Makimura in **Dance, Dance, Dance** mentions going to Siberia and that it was a "horrible place."
- A man the narrator of **A Wild Sheep Chase** speaks to on the street mentions fending off rats in a Siberian camp.
- In **Kafka on the Shore**, the forests around the Kochi cabin where Kafka stays were once used to prepare soldiers for battle in Siberia.

SINGAPORE

- The story **Crabs** (Blind Willow, Sleeping Woman) takes places entirely in Singapore. The couple visits a local seafood restaurant throughout their vacation and they eat crab every day until the man ends up vomiting large amounts of crab meat.
- Sara of **Colorless Tsukuru Tazaki and His Years of Pilgrimage** goes on a business trip to Singapore, which she describes as "fascinating."
- Hajime's father in **South of the Border, West of the Sun** was sent to fight in Singapore during the war.

SPAIN

In **Honey Pie** (After The Quake), Junpei was doing work for an airline magazine in Barcelona when he saw the news of the Great Hanshin Earthquake on TV.

SWITZERLAND

The hair of Miu from **Sputnik Sweetheart** turned white in Switzerland after an incident. In a small town near the French border she rode a ferris wheel and saw her own self with the man named Ferdinando through her apartment window.

LOCATION REFERENCE GUIDE

TAIWAN
Kaoru from *After Dark* mentions having some professional wrestling matches in Taiwan and Hong Kong.

THAILAND
The short story *Thailand* (*After The Quake*), as the name suggests, takes place in Bangkok, Thailand.

TUNISIA
The man who likes to burn barns in *Barn Burning* (*The Elephant Vanishes*) is interested in water supplies in Tunis.

UNITED STATES

California:
- In the short story *Family Affair* (*The Elephant Vanishes*), the narrator's sister met her fiancé on a group tour to San Francisco.
- In *A Wild Sheep Chase*, The Boss's personal secretary graduated from Stanford.

Colorado: In *Yesterday* (*Men Without Women*), Kitaru goes to Denver to work as a sushi chef.

Connecticut: Noboru Wataya of *The Wind-Up Bird Chronicle* did two years of graduate study at Yale.

Hawaii:
- In *Dance, Dance, Dance*, the protagonist and Yuki take a long trip to Hawaii on her parents' dime. Some of the locations mentioned include Waikiki, Makaha and Honolulu **(p61)**.
- The story *Hanalei Bay* (*Blind Willow, Sleeping Woman*) mostly takes place by the Kauai Island bay. Sachi's son died while surfing there and she repeatedly visits the Hanalei area to commemorate his death.
- Malta Kano from *The Wind-Up Bird Chronicle* had lived on Kauai for two years as part of a commune.

Illinois: Sachi from *Hanalei Bay* (*Blind Willow, Sleeping Woman*) attended a cooking school in Chicago.

Maryland: Satsuki from the story *Thailand* (*After The Quake*) had worked in a hospital in Baltimore.

Massachusetts: Murakami himself narrates the short story *Chance Traveller* (*Blind Woman, Sleeping Willow*) and recalls seeing live jazz in a Cambridge venue near where he lived at the time.

Michigan: Satsuki of *Thailand* (*After The Quake*) worked at a hospital in Detroit for around ten years.

New Mexico: In *Norwegian Wood*, an adult Watanabe recalls interviewing a painter in Santa Fe and watching the sunset, only to be suddenly reminded of Nagasawa's girlfriend Hatsumi.

New York:
- In *Hear The Wind Sing*, the narrator mentions the author Hartfield jumping off the roof of the Empire State Building.
- Kafka's father in *Kafka on the Shore* once put on an exhibition at New York's Museum of Modern Art.

Ohio:
- Derek Hartfield (fictional), the narrator's favorite author in *Hear The Wind Sing*, was from a small town in Ohio. The narrator mentions riding a bus from New York to the town to see Hartfield's grave.
- In the story *Hunting Knife* (*Blind Willow, Sleeping Woman*), the man in the wheelchair mentions that his father runs a tile company in Cleveland.

Utah: In *Hunting Knife* (*Blind Willow, Sleeping Woman*) a woman tells the narrator that she used to live in Salt Lake City but that she wouldn't recommend it.

Washington: In *Yesterday* (*Men Without Women*), Kitaru was a sushi chef in Seattle before moving to Denver.

URUGUAY
In *Norwegian Wood*, Midori says her father had gone off to Uruguay, although he's really in the hospital the whole time.

VIETNAM
Dick North from *Dance, Dance, Dance* lost his arm in the Vietnam War.

Notes and References

1. Haruki Murakami, *Hear The Wind Sing* of *Wind / Pinball; Two Novels By Haruki Murakami*, trans., Ted Goossen (London: Harvill Secker, 2015), Ebook edition, Chapter 28.
2. Ibid., Chapter 27.
3. Haruki Murakami, *After The Quake: Stories*, trans., Jay Rubin (New York: Vintage Books, 2007)
4. Haruki Murakami, *Pinball, 1973*, trans., Alfred Birnbaum (Tokyo: Kodansha, 1985), 57.
5. Ibid., 51
6. Haruki Murakami, *A Wild Sheep Chase*, trans., Alfred Birnbaum (New York: Vintage Books, 2002), 229.
7. Ibid., 200
8. Ibid., 192
9. Ibid., 192
10. Ibid., 251
11. Ibid., 251
12. Ibid., 278
13. Ibid., 278
14. Ibid., 304
15. Ibid., 245
16. Haruki Murakami, *Dance, Dance, Dance*, trans., Alfred Birnbaum (New York: Vintage Books, 1995), 152.
17. Haruki Murakami, *A Wild Sheep Chase*, 103.
18. Haruki Murakami, *Dance, Dance, Dance* [Japanese Edition], (Tokyo: Kodansha, 1988)
19. Haruki Murakami, *Hard-Boiled Wonderland and The End of The World*, trans., Alfred Birnbaum (New York: Vintage Books, 2010), Kindle edition, Chapter 31.
20. Ibid., Chapter 29.
21. Akutagawa, Ryūnosuke, *Kappa*, trans., Geoffrey Bownas (London: Peter Owen, 2009)
22. Jorge Luis Borges, Margarita Guerrero, *The Book of Imaginary Beings*, trans. Andrew Hurley (New York: Penguin, 2006)
23. Haruki Murakami, *Hard-Boiled Wonderland and The End of The World*, Chapter 29
24. Ibid., Chapter 24.
25. Haruki Murakami, *Norwegian Wood*, trans., Jay Rubin (London: Harvill Press, 2000), 24,25.
26. Ibid., 22
27. Haruki Murakami, *Norwegian Wood* [Japanese Edition], (Tokyo: Kodansha, 2004)
28. Haruki Murakami, *Norwegian Wood*, 28
29. Ibid., 202
30. Ibid., 350
31. Haruki Murakami, *South of the Border, West of the Sun*, trans., Philip Gabriel (New York: Vintage Books, 2000), 118.
32. Ibid., 69
33. Haruki Murakami, *The Wind-Up Bird Chronicle*, trans., Jay Rubin (New York: Vintage Books, 1998), 225.
34. Ibid., 114.
35. Ibid., 329
36. Ibid., 110
37. Ibid., 329
38. Ibid., 114
39. Haruki Murakami, *Sputnik Sweetheart*, trans., Philip Gabriel (New York: Vintage Books, 2002), 221.
40. Ibid, 30
41. Wikipedia. "チーズ・ケーキのような形をした僕の貧乏." Accessed November 30, 2016. https://ja.wikipedia.org/wiki/チーズ・ケーキのような形をした僕の貧乏
42. Haruki Murakami, *Blind Willow, Sleeping Woman*, trans., Jay Rubin, Philip Gabriel (New York: Vintage Books, 2007).
43. Haruki Murakami, *Kafka on the Shore*, trans., Philip Gabriel (New York: Alfred A. Knopf, 2005), 317
44. Ibid., 326
45. Ibid., 31
46. Ibid., 213
47. Haruki Murakami. "讃岐・超ディープうどん紀行." In 辺境・近境. (Tokyo: Shinchosha, 1998).
48. Ueda Akinari. "Shiramine." In *Tales of Moonlight and Rain*, trans., Anthony H. Chambers (New York: Colombia University Press, 2007).
49. Haruki Murakami, *After Dark*, trans., Jay Rubin (London: Harvill Secker, 2007), 4
50. Ibid., 117
51. Haruki Murakami, *1Q84*, trans., Jay Rubin, Philip Gabriel (New York: Alfred A. Knopf, 2011), Kindle edition, Book 1: Chapter 1.
52. Ibid., Book 2: Chapter 20.
53. Haruki Murakami, *Colorless Tsukuru Tazaki and His Years of Pilgrimage*, trans., Philip Gabriel (New York: Alfred A. Knopf, 2014), Kindle edition, Chapter 10.
54. Haruki Murakami, *Hombres sin mujeres* [Spanish Edition] trans., Gabriel Álvarez Martínez (Barcelona: Tusquets Editores S.A., 2015)
55. Haruki Murakami. "Yesterday." *The New Yorker*. June 9, 2014. http://www.newyorker.com/magazine/2014/06/09/yesterday-3.
56. Haruki Murakami. "Kino." *The New Yorker*. Feb. 23rd, 2015. http://www.newyorker.com/magazine/2015/02/23/kino
57. Haruki Murakami, *The Elephant Vanishes*, trans., Alfred Birnbaum, Jay Rubin (New York: Vintage Books, 1994).
58. Haruki Murakami, *1Q84*. Book 3: Chapter 7
59. Haruki Murakami. "Samsa In Love." *The New Yorker*. Oct. 28th, 2013. http://www.newyorker.com/magazine/2013/10/28/samsa-in-love

About The Author

Ken Lawrence is a writer, photographer and designer who's lived in Japan for over a decade. He loves literature and jazz.

Also by The Author:

START YOUR LIFE IN JAPAN:
A GUIDE TO JOBS, VISAS AND LIVING OUT YOUR DREAM IN THE LAND OF THE RISING SUN

Dream of Living in Japan?
It's time to turn that dream into a reality!

Start Your Life in Japan contains everything you need to know in order to move to Japan and earn a living. You'll learn how to come as a student, how to find a job from either abroad or from within Japan, and the steps required to rent an apartment. The book also contains interview tips and a resume sample, a detailed list of different visa categories and comprehensive information on work opportunities outside of the ESL industry. In addition, you'll learn about some fundamental concepts of Japanese culture and some of the best ways to go about picking up the language.

Available on Amazon and at select bookstores.

Sailingstone Press LLC
978-0692696972

www.ingramcontent.com/pod-product-compliance
Lightning Source LLC
Chambersburg PA
CBHW042058290426
44113CB00001B/6

© 2017 Holmes, Investments and Holdings, LLC.
All Rights Reserved
No part of this publication may be reproduced, stored in a retrieval system, or transmitted, in any form or by any means, electronic, mechanical, photocopying, recording, or otherwise, without the written permission of the author.
This book is a work of fiction. Places, events, and situations in this book are purely fictional and any resemblance to actual persons, living or dead, is coincidental.
Printed in the United States of America

ISBN: 978-0-9992369-9-4

JOHNNY SKIP 2

The Amazing Adventures of Johnny Skip 2 in Australia

By Quentin Holmes

We can use my little device; I call it The Amazing, Instant-Travel-Skip 2. It's fifty percent magic and fifty percent science. But altogether, it's one hundred percent cool!

Collecting little things is what I love to do. Do you like collecting little things too?

I have little bitty books, baskets and bags. I collect mini-toy pugs and multi-colored mugs.

Although my best friend is little and rounder, he's an eager brown beagle whose first name is Grounder.

Our travel gear is ready, so we're off on another journey. There's no time to waste. Come on now, let's hurry! Will you travel with us? We could really use your help. Australia is amazing; come see it for yourself!

The Amazing, Instant-Travel-Skip 2 buzzes when you press the button 'begin.' It pauses for a moment and pulls us all in. Off we go quickly and travel so swiftly.

The Amazing, Instant-Travel-Skip 2 is quite fantastic and fast, it makes all of our trips a tremendous blast; and in a blink we land in a field with tall rocks and pale grass.

Welcome to Australia, the place where they say G'day! To fit in with the locals, we've got to speak their way. It never means we're leaving; it's just like saying 'hey!' Now say it like a true Aussie, instead of hello we say... G'day!